FOLLOW ME

*[What I said was "Get the hell off the beach! God damn it, get
up and get moving—Follow me!"* . . . *as correctly stated in our
division's unofficial history. The Army's official history,* **Return to
the Philippines,** *omits "God damn it" but keeps "Get the hell off
the beach." Just a little genteel censorship.]* (Chaps. 50, 57)
*This poster is from the "U.S. Army in Action" series—one for each
war—memorializing the Pacific part of World War II, as this is the
spot where Gen. Douglas MacArthur would soon land in his famous
"return" to the Philippines. The caption records this, and adds,
"The regimental commander, Colonel Aubrey S. Newman, arrived
on the beach and, taking in the situation at a glance, shouted to his
men, 'Get up and get moving: Follow me!'"*

FOLLOW ME

The Human Element in Leadership

Maj. Gen. Aubrey S. Newman (Ret.)

PRESIDIO

Copyright © Presidio Press 1981

Published by Presidio Press, 31 Pamaron Way, Novato, CA 94947

Text of this book represents a selection of the author's columns, "The Forward
Edge." Return of copyright from the original publishers of these articles is grate-
fully acknowledged. All were published by ARMY Magazine — including several that
appeared in its predecessor, *The Infantry Journal.*

Library of Congress Cataloging in Publication Data

Newman, Aubrey S., 1903—
    Follow me, the human element in leadership.

    "Selection of the author's columns, 'The Forward
Edge,' reprinted from Army magazine"—Verso t.p.
        1. Leadership—Addresses, essays, lectures.
2. United States. Army—Military life—Addresses,
essays, lectures. 3. Newman, Aubrey S., 1903—
I. Army (U.S.) II. Title.
UB210.N48   355.3'3041   81-14363
ISBN 0-89141-124-0   AACR2
ISBN 0-89141-136-4 (pbk.)

Jacket design by Jill Losson
Printed in the United States of America

To the fine soldiers of our Army
during the times recalled here,
especially to the senior
noncommissioned officers who
extended a helping hand in my early
years — and to NCOs of all grades who
provided the pervasive, irreplaceable
inner strength to every unit in which it
was my privilege to serve.

CONTENTS

Preface

Monday morning quarterbacks can tell you how it should have been done on Saturday, with sage hindsight for your future guidance. So this book is Monday morning quarterbacking, except my views do not come from the grandstand seats or the TV set — because I was in the ball game.

In military service we are concerned primarily with handling men, money, and materials — the same basic elements that must be managed in civilian life. This book deals throughout with the first of these basics, the management of men in command and leadership; thus it involves a continuing study of the human element in military life.

Since human nature is the same in or out of uniform, the principles for organizing and controlling people are the same. Therefore I believe the lessons I learned about people management will be of interest not only to military men today (and to all who have ever been in uniform), but also to civilians in their dealings with others.

Aubrey S. ("Red") Newman
Major General, U.S. Army
Retired

PART I
COMMAND PRESENCE

1
Looking Backward to
See Ahead

AFTER WORLD WAR II, when I was in Heidelberg, Germany, the story went the rounds that Secretary of State John Foster Dulles had traveled to Europe by plane, along with several congressmen. The secretary, a very large man, rose from his seat and stood in the aisle — then leaned over to pick up something from his seat.

One of the congressmen, seated directly across the aisle, looked upward at the secretary's towering posterior and said to another congressman:

"Now this is the view of the State Department that I am accustomed to."

The view you get of anything depends on where you sit, and your mental approach. Famous generals have written books about their lives and the deeds that made them famous. This book is by a not-so-famous general about the human element in military service.

Sun Tzu, an ancient Chinese general and one of the earliest military theorists (about 400–320 B.C.), summarizes in his *Art of War* a most perceptive idea:

> The musical notes are only five in number but their melodies are so numerous that one can not hear them all.
>
> The primary colors are only five in number but their combinations are so infinite that one can not visualize them all.
>
> The flavors are only five in number but their blends are so various that one can not taste them all.

> In battle there are only the normal and extraordinary
> forces, but their combinations are limitless; none can
> comprehend them all.

This same proliferative thought applies to the vital intangibles in command and leadership. No one can know how all the personality facets and human angles are best integrated into countless situations. To understand this fascinating subject we must examine many small but significant sidelights and happenings within our own ken, along with knowledge gained from others. Thus we will look at soldiers of all ranks during the years I served with them, and some known to me via the ubiquitous grapevine.

Like the time that a colonel was walking his dog on one of the Army's posts. As he passed a major general's house, the general invited the colonel in for a drink, saying, "Bring your dog in too."

In the house the colonel found another guest, a lieutenant general. As the colonel took a sip from his drink, his dog lifted a leg and wet the trouser leg of the host major general. In the resulting embarrassed silence the colonel said, "I'm very sorry, but Bowzer has never done that before. Maybe all these stars around make him nervous."

Whereupon Bowzer waddled over, lifted a leg, and gave the lieutenant general's trouser leg a couple of squirts too. Before the mortified colonel could think of what to say the lieutenant general said:

"Colonel, your pooch needs instruction in military courtesy because he treats me just like he does major generals. Tie him outside, and we'll have one for the road when you get back."

That was a special situation, which was met with easy courtesy by the lieutenant general. It illustrates the fact that an element of human understanding and consideration for others is an all-pervading factor in military life.

Then there was the private in my first company command whose appearance belied his amorous nature. A small, wizened little man, almost completely illiterate, he was nevertheless much loved by all who knew him, for he was loyal and friendly and always did his modest best.

In fact his friendliness with play-for-pay ladies led to contracting their occupational hazard, gonorrhea. In due course the hospital cured him—but he got it again, and yet again. After he was discharged from the hospital the third time, his company commander (my predecessor) started to deliver a lecture on the desirability of continence . . . or better sanitary measures.

"Listen, Romeo," his captain began, "I'm getting damn tired of you getting VD."

"Yes sir, Captain," was the feeling reply, "I am too!"

From top to bottom of the Army, people act like people, as they always have — each in his own way. We hear so much about modernizing the Army with new weapons and techniques that we rather expect to see new model soldiers. An old sergeant put it this way:

"First we had the old Army, then we had the New Army . . . and now we got This Here Thing today."

But if you asked him why he did not get out of it, he would wonder why you didn't understand that every soldier has a right to gripe. He was married to the Army, loved her, and knew very well she would change in appearance with the passing years. But he also knew her heart would remain the same disciplined, human, demanding heart it had always been.

We have looked here at only a tiny fraction of the countless facets, angles, nuances, ideas, and thoughts about command and leadership that occur in military service. So it is well to remember the words of Sun Tzu that "none can comprehend them all." Some added comments are:

- Command and leadership are two quite different functions, yet they are inextricably interrelated — each supplementing and strengthening the other. I think of them as Siamese twins, each essential to the life of the other, joined at the head and heart — with the head symbolizing command and the heart denoting leadership.
- There is not nor can there ever be a finite summary of all you need to know about the human element in military life. However, by noting significant little things as we gain experience, by observing other commanders (good and bad); and by reading and study with a sense of awareness, we can develop an *understanding*. Only with this understanding, based on innumerable small things, can we meet unexpected command and leadership situations (large and small) with confidence and good judgment.

- Each of the chapters that follow discusses a separate intangible of military human relations. Taken as a whole they record the comprehensive and vital role of human nature in military service. Perhaps I may even have captured a glimpse of the shining bond that joins the hearts of the brave in war, and cements the esprit of good soldiers in peace.

2
West Point's Tradition of Prankish Humor

I HAVE OFTEN wondered how many potentially outstanding Army officers decided not to seek an appointment to the U.S. Military Academy at West Point because news stories pictured it as a grim, bleak, unfeeling, and harshly disciplined place. It *is* disciplined, but not bleak, grim, or unfeeling. In fact there was more imaginative humor there than any place I have ever been—although it did not seem that way at first.

On the morning of 1 July 1921, I left the train at Garrison, New York, boarded the Hudson River ferry, and walked up front for my first glimpse of the massive gray stone buildings of the academy. As the ferry crossed the river the buildings loomed larger and more fortresslike. This was a storied place of giants, of men tried in the flame of battle and found great in the pages of history. I could only resolve, with uncertainty in my heart, to do my best.

After the ferry docked, I walked up the steep, winding road, under a stone arch and stopped in silent awe. Spread before me was "The Plain," scene of West Point's famous parades. To the left, near Old Barracks, uniformed figures clustered around a table. Under the trees near the barracks were statues of men out of the past. In this aura of history I walked to the table and signed my name under the eyes of immaculately uniformed officers.

A sign on the table read: "Leave all money, cards, and gambling devices here." After surrendering my money and declaring my lack of other items, one officer said in a clipped tone, "Report to that sally port for room assignment." He pointed to Old Barracks.

"Double time!" he added sharply. That was the pace from then on for new plebes. But I had not gone far when a sudden thought caused me to wheel about in nervous haste and doubletime back. Before the officers could say anything, I halted and fished two pennies out of my watch pocket. Without a word I placed them on the table and took off again at the double.

The humor of this did not occur to me then. Nor did it occur to me as I departed on the double that those officers would have a good chuckle at seeing that scared redheaded kid drop his two pennies and run. Only later would I realize that all was not serious there. Here are several illustrative examples out of the past that show humorous intangibles were there long before my day:

Scuttlebutt has it that more than 140-odd years ago a cadet (who later became world famous) was having trouble with his academic work. One night after supper he worked himself into a wild-eyed frenzy, telling his roommates about his deadly hatred for a professor who had given him a hard time that day.

"I'm going to get that so-and-so!" he muttered over and over. "I am going to get that so-and-so!"

Finally, almost frothing at the mouth, he rushed out into the night. Several hours later he returned, carrying something heavy and roundish in a bloodstained sack.

"There!" he said, glaring at his alarmed and puzzled roommates as he plopped the bloody sack on the floor where it landed with a sodden, sullen thump. "I said I was going to get that so-and-so. This is his head!"

After the curiosity of his roommates overcame their horror at what might be in the sack, they discovered it contained a dead turkey.

The story has the ring of truth—the cadet failed to graduate but became an internationally renowned writer: one of Edgar Allen Poe's many achievements was the invention of the detective-story genre when he wrote the ghastly tale, *The Murders in the Rue Morgue*.

The next footnote to West Point's past was recounted to me by one of Gen. Dwight D. Eisenhower's classmates. Late one night a cadet mounted a ladder and removed the hands from the clock in the center of the barracks quadrangle. He then substituted hands he had made from hardwood, and nobody knew the difference for several days.

Then at reveille one morning everybody was surprised to discover there was no way to tell time by the area clock. It had no hands.

The plot thickened when the mystery was reported to the superintendent. While he and his staff were trying to figure out where to get another pair of hands, the postman arrived with a special-delivery package for the superintendent. It had been mailed the day before in New York City and contained the original hands of the area clock.

That little exercise took thought, planning, and careful timing — like one that occurred during summer camp my last year at the academy. It was engineered by two of my classmates who were first class bucks (that is, they had no cadet military rating). I was an interested witness through the corner crack in my pyramidal tent.

There was a cordon of plebe sentries around the summer-camp tent area near Trophy Point, each plebe walking post in full dress uniform with bayonet fixed. The first class bucks noticed that the plebe near Thaddeus Kosciusko's monument was far removed from the guardhouse. They also observed that when he was at one end of his post and facing the guardhouse to make the prescribed calls for help, his back would be to his post.

After lunch one day they buckled on web belts, with bayonets attached as though for drill. Watching the way the plebe walked, they timed their approach and began to argue in loud voices. The quarrel grew acrimonious and the first class buck with the deep bass voice drew his bayonet and shouted, "I'll fix you!"

He then lunged at an angle to give the plebe the best illusion of reality as the bayonet passed over the shoulder of the other first class buck. The latter let out a strangled gurgle and swiped his left hand (full of tomato catsup he had brought back from the mess hall in a saltcellar) upward to his throat as he fell.

The plebe looked in white-faced horror at the body lying on its back with the red stain across throat and face. But training was strong in him, so he came down to port arms, faced toward the guardhouse to more or less scream, "Corporal of the Guard — Post Number 5! Turn out the guard — Post Number 5!"

Then he turned around again. But the body was gone, having departed the instant the sentry turned toward the guardhouse.

The plebe had a lot of talking to do as various people congregated on the scene. Then there was a real flap when the cadet officer of the day found "blood" (catsup) in the gravel. He launched a search for the "body," stirred up the Army tactical officer on duty—and a good time was had by all until the drama petered out when no *corpus delicti* was found.

Of course, pranks between cadets at West Point and midshipmen at Annapolis, as preludes to the annual Army-Navy football game, have been publicized. But the widest curve the Navy pitched us, in my opinion, has not seen the light of print.

It happened in the early 1950s. The first public indication of anything wrong came one morning when military police detoured traffic away from the Washington monument at West Point while the fire department screened it off.

The monument is a heroic size bronze of General George Washington riding a horse, which is mounted on a large and high granite base. Just what all the commotion and secrecy was about around the statue finally leaked out. A little cleanup job was in progress. Somebody had noticed that the two masculine appendages on General Washington's charger had been painted blue and gold—the Navy colors.

Jokes and verbal humor have always been a part of the austere life at West Point, adding the light touch needed among men in uniform everywhere. Here are three comments:

- No matter where you go in military life, humor seems to hold a broader place than in civilian life. The road to the top in the Army can begin in enlisted ranks, in college ROTC, at West Point, or from the reserve forces. But if you cannot see the fun in life, you will be handicapped. Nowhere is this more true than at the place some choose to call "Hell on the Hudson." But it is really not that way unless you make it so for yourself.
- A military career is a fine and rewarding way of life. Do not be deterred by twisted stories from those who have failed to measure up, or by distorted reports about what a grim, bleak, and harshly disciplined existence you will lead at West Point, or elsewhere in uniform. Of course military service is not just a series of shenanigans, jokes, and funny stories, but the leaven of humor and the bonds of a special friendship pervade service in uniform.
- It must be remembered, however, that neither humor

nor friendship—in uniform or out—can change the fundamental fact of life stated by William Penn when he said, "No pain, no palm; no thorns, no throne; no gall, no glory; no cross, no crown."

3

The Big Decision

EVERY YOUNG SOLDIER faces the same big decision I did more than fifty years ago: whether or not to make the Army a career. The hardships, complexities, and difficulties of military service today exceed anything in my early days, yet my decision came at a time of trial in my life too.

After graduating from West Point in 1925, I reported for duty with the 29th Infantry at Fort Benning, Georgia. It was the custom there for newly joined officers to call on the regimental commander without delay. So with three classmates, and chaperoned by an older lieutenant named Bill, we went calling. The regimental commander, his wife, and several lovely daughters received us graciously on a glassed-in porch.

After a pleasant but correctly brief call, Bill gave the sign to withdraw.

In shaking hands with my commanding officer I bowed. As my head went forward, a basic law of physics moved my fanny rearward —against a large potted plant on a pedestal, butting it over. A thunderous crash of broken pottery was followed by astonished silence, then a confused babel of voices.

Bill started to pick things up, but realized this looked like a confession of guilt, so he blurted, "It wasn't me . . . I didn't do it!" At this point I came out of my trance and escaped from the house.

On my first day in the Army I had become famous.

My first tour as officer of the guard began with routine guard mount and sentry-posting, under the same procedures we had used at West Point. But there was one difference: the sixty-odd inmates were guarded with loaded shotguns.

A wartime frame building provided office space for the guard, and arms racks and sleeping rooms for men on relief from post. I sat down in the Officer-of-the-Guard chair, leaned back, and nonchalantly hoisted my booted and spurred feet to the top of the desk.

Later a sentry stopped in the doorway and turned, working the slide of his pump shotgun to eject the shells before putting his gun in the arms rack. Something went wrong, for buckshot blasted a section of the eave off the roof six feet from my chair.

After a violent struggle I got my spurs unhooked from the desk top, my feet on the floor, my voice back, and briskly told the sergeant of the guard to unload the gun.

The sergeant worked the slide — and blew a hole in the roof over my head. As I collected my wits to decide what to tell who to do next, a runner arrived on the double from the provost marshal's office across the street.

"Lieutenant," the runner said, saluting and grinning, "the provost marshal says if you're having target practice over here, please let him know — because shooting makes him nervous."

Those were the first two shots I saw fired in the Army.

Several days later our regimental adjutant stopped me outside of regimental headquarters. He was a senior captain — and senior captains then rated about where junior lieutenant colonels do now.

"Mistuh Newman," he said, "the commanding general desires organized cheering by soldiers at our football games. You are therefore detailed as cheerleader . . . and the CG expects plenty of well-organized noise when our Fort Benning team plays its first game in Doughboy Stadium this Saturday."

During the past two weeks I'd not only been kicked around, but had also bit like a champion sucker when kidded by some of the experts in the bachelor quarters. Since I did not consider myself the cheerleading type, it looked like my leg was getting yanked again. So I decided not to bite.

"Sir," I answered with what I hoped was a knowing smile, "I'm more accustomed to receiving cheers than to leading them."

After a brief and stony silence the captain pointed out to me that the proper position of attention for a junior when talking to a senior was with heels together. He further explained things that could happen to those who questioned an official order from higher authority, and clarified my position in the Army's rank structure. Finally, he left no doubt in my mind that what I may have been accustomed to in the past had no relation to the fact that I was now a cheerleader, or — he smiled pleasantly — "You can call yourself Officer in Charge of Cheering, if that helps any."

So I dreamed up a few cheers, had them mimeographed, and organized cheering practice at calisthenics formations in the mornings.

For our first game we had a nice sunshiny day, our team licked the opposition, and the novelty of hearing themselves yell in unison produced some respectable spectator sound effects.

The following Monday morning I was summoned to the office of Maj. Gen. Briant H. Wells, commandant of the Infantry School at the time. That fine gentleman and distinguished soldier complimented me on the results of my cheerleading — even saying he had no doubt my ability to inspire enthusiasm in peacetime would carry over into leadership on the battlefield. My cheerleading career, having thus jumped from the depths to the heights, left me either drunk with success or stunned from shock, for I ran into the edge of the door trying to get out of his office.

It didn't take long for my future leadership potential to be further evaluated. The next Saturday it drizzled. We knew the Notre Dame reserves were going to give our team its lumps. Besides, the novelty of cheering had worn off for our soldiers. So the first yell I essayed to lead kind of petered out toward the end. On the second try it again petered out, then tailed off to one soldier, sitting about eight rows up, yelling with great gusto as I led him through to the bitter end — while the rest sat grinning.

I sat down, my leadership badly wilted. Waiting until the home team made a good play, I gave it one more try, first calling for a vote of confidence.

"How many," I asked, facing the enlisted stands above, my back to the officers' seats below, "are going to yell if I lead a Skyrocket for the team? Hold up your hands."

No hands, but the grins got wider. They had me, so I decided to go down shooting. "Well," I announced, pitching my voice to reach as many of the grins as possible, but away from the officers' seats behind me, "as far as I'm concerned, you can go to hell!"

This brought one last flare of cheers — unorganized.

The commanding general didn't send for me to retract his optimistic view of my future battle leadership potential. By tacit consent he and I let the matter drop. But my martial spirit was sorely bruised, and I thought about getting out of the Army and into some other profession. It is at such temporary "low points" in your career that many men have decided to leave. And regretted it later.

Of course, this hardly scratches the surface of my shavetail tribulations — some of them searing to the soul — but there was another side too. I liked military life, especially serving with American soldiers, and greatly admired some of the outstanding officers.

No career is more fascinating than that of the professional soldier. Being a good officer is not a trade. It is an art. Before the end of my tour at Benning any lingering doubts about leaving the Army had gone. I was proud to serve with the fine soldiers I had come to know, to like, and to respect.

This was the life I wanted.

Now, with our Army spread around the world, thousands of officers and men face this same decision. They also face many discouragements and difficulties that bear little relation to my struggle for a place in the sun as a shavetail. But the satisfactions and pride in achievement when overcoming the multiplicity of challenges in our modern Army are greater too.

Each man in uniform must, of course, make his own decision. You might take into your considerations, however, this intelligence report from the front lines in retirement: if proof of the military pudding is in the eating, the Army is indeed a satisfying and rewarding life, for among the hundreds of retired Army men I know, never yet have I heard one who had made it a full career say he regretted his decision.

4

Billygoating Is Like Russian Roulette

THERE'S NO MISTAKE more unintelligent than a needless "personality conflict" when two men butt heads like a couple of billygoats. Strong characters often lock horns in forthright disagreements — which is the best way to settle controversial issues — as long as logic, reason, proper authority and the best interests of the service decide the matter. It's when things descend to a personal conflict that the billygoat syndrome takes over.

At my first post I witnessed the first such conflict within my experience, between two soldiers in my platoon. We'll call them PFC Pizaro, a Latin type, and PFC Horny, whose pale tense face was spotted with freckles.

Our company street was a double line of pyramidal tents on wood floors, heated with the inverted cones of sheet-metal Sibley stoves. Bunks ranged around the sides, with the stove in the center on a sandbox. Primitive housing, yet it could be friendly group living around the hot stove if there were no personality conflicts.

I soon learned that PFC Horny, about 145 pounds, was known as the champion of all weights in our company. PFC Pizaro was about the same size, but on the quiet side. They had been tentmates, but prior to my arrival trouble arose between them. So they were housed several tents apart.

When the climactic personality explosion came, it happened like this. PFC Pizaro went to see a friend in Horny's tent, and there were sounds of violent altercation there. Then Pizaro popped out of the tent and headed for his own on the double, loudly pursued by Horny. There the champion of all weights—respecting a man's home as his castle—stamped around outside, exhorting Pizaro to "come out and settle it now."

Which Pizaro promptly did—bayonet in hand. The champion of all weights instantly became our company's fastest human, with Pizaro in silent pursuit. Others intervened, and the two panting men soon faced platoon sergeant Fugate. What he said to them as reported to me is lost to memory, except for his personal promise to Pizaro of what he, Fugate, would do with that bayonet if ever there was a next time.

This incident makes a fundamental point about billygoating personality conflicts. The habitually belligerent Horny, as will always happen eventually, found himself butting heads with the wrong man.

From varying viewpoints I saw many personality conflicts, from the level of men in ranks to four-star generals. Often chance circumstances seduced fine soldiers into these senseless conflicts, and sometimes brilliant careers were needlessly marred. Unfortunately, my own service was not free of such lapses. Consider this one where I used my skull more than my brain.

In my second year as a company commander, we got a new battalion commander. Between me and the major it was apparently mutual dislike at first sight. The first collision came on the rifle range. My idea was that every point scored must first be fired with the rifle. The major was more flexible, feeling no harm was done by a little pencil work if some poor fellow needed a few extra points to qualify.

Anyway, when I checked the scorecard of a weak shooter, he had higher marks on one course than could have resulted from the firing I watched him do. The scorer then admitted the battalion commander was the Good Samaritan, having issued some informal "no harm" instructions. So I ordered that scorecard destroyed, and the course fired over.

When the soldier failed to qualify, the major discovered my action and descended on me. He first announced that Company G was not my private property, but was also part of his battalion, and then asked, "Why did you throw out that card?"

My reply was, "Because, sir, I sign my name to certify our scorecards."

That kited scorecard could not be certified, but I didn't use good judgment in correcting the record. It would have been better to assume the scorer misunderstood the major's instructions, and for that reason to order the course fired over. Then I could have reported this to the major. He would have given me his flat, unblinking stare and let it go. But to publicly countermand his order, invoking the principle of integrity, invited an unfortunate personality conflict with billygoat overtones.

The battalion mess incident that followed didn't help. As we prepared for maneuvers, a memorandum from battalion designated Company G (my company) to run the consolidated battalion mess. This would be the third consecutive year we catered the field mess, so I went to see the major.

Rather grumpily, he reassigned the chore to Company F. They begged off because of a new mess sergeant, so Company E was given the job—and they managed to get it transferred to Company H. The CO of Company H was the senior captain in our battalion, so he was not happy to find himself mess officer.

The next day the major greeted me on the drill field with "You and your so-and-so mess!" He completed the circle by handing the mess soirée back to my company.

Apparently, by the curious inverse reasoning that often afflicts personality conflicts, he was holding me responsible for his own vacillation. Too surprised to comment, my eyes locked with his flat stare briefly and he turned away.

Back in my office I penciled a memorandum to battalion requesting that a mess sergeant and extra cooks from other companies be attached to ours to operate the maneuver mess. When that went out to be typed Big Jim Redding, the first sergeant, came in my office, pencil draft in hand and smiling a little uncertainly.

"Captain," he said, "the company understands about the mess. If you don't mind me saying so, it's time for you to give a little. Leave it to us, and I'll get help if we need it."

He was right, for the major would have viewed that memo as an invitation to butt heads some more about the mess. Although Big Jim headed that one off, I found new ways to founder deeper into a witless personality clash.

Other incidents would be hard to describe, often invoking intangible factors—such as the tone of voice, which is one of the best ways to be wrong when you are right. The simple fact was that the major and I typified the basic situation on which most personality conflicts rest: a couple of fatheads who act less intelligently than two billygoats, because billygoats have a biological reason for butting heads.

The major apparently was reluctant to let regiment know about our billygoating because he thought I was our regimental commander's fair-haired boy. This may have been true for a while, maybe because my company won the annual overall efficiency competition. But what the major didn't know was that I was then engaged in a head-butting contest with our regimental commander, too, over operation of the post bachelor officers' quarters, where I lived.

Before they compared notes and fixed my buggy, I went on the voluntary foreign service roster and got away in time. There's a special providence that takes care of fools and billygoats — sometimes. But don't count on it, for you may end up with your horns tied in a bow, which happened to me years later.

As soldiers grow older and reach higher rank, the horned-head/ cloven-hoof complex seems to grow while taking on a more refined form. Results can be equally damaging. I saw two senior officers relieved of their commands when they persisted in bucking decisions of their superiors by making themselves difficult to deal with.

There is a basic difference between a strong personality and a billygoat complex. Once that is understood, it's a matter of judgment to recognize the line of demarkation where legitimate dissent ends and head-butting begins.

You may think I'm selling all billygoating short, but that's not true. Every good soldier needs a skull-banging capacity available on call. Otherwise, a few habitual billygoats would butt the rest of us around at will. Vital points to keep in mind when you start feeling goaty are:

- Be sure you know why you're going to test skulls, and whether or not the goal is worth the possible lumps.
- Billygoating is like Russian roulette: if you keep it up you're sure to lose sooner or later, and it may be sooner.
- Big Jim Redding put his finger on a critical consideration when he said, "Captain, it's time for you to give a little."

5

Combine Empathy with a Sense of Humor

IN 1925 THE company street of Company A, 29th Infantry, was a 100-foot-wide strip of hard-packed Georgia earth between two rows of wood-floored pyramidal tents. On both sides, about six feet from the tents, wood strips were buried in the ground to outline sidewalks. At intervals along the tent side of the walks were low, square trash boxes. This set the stage for one of the most valuable lessons I learned during my first year in the Army.

On this morning, the company formed for drill in the company street and marched in column of squads toward the drill field. Opposite the head of the column, Capt. John S. Moore, with saber at the carry, turned to walk backward down the sidewalk as he counted cadence — and caught his heel against a wooden sidewalk strip. When he staggered backward his legs tangled in the dangling scabbard and he ended up sitting down in one of the trash boxes — saber still at the carry. Of course we kept right on marching at attention.

"Company!" came the sharp command from Captain Moore, still seated in his trash box, "*Halt!*"

Then, after a brief pause, "Rest . . . and *laugh,* damn it!"

The company did laugh — but *with* their captain, not *at* him. Had Captain Moore followed any other course, his loss of dignity would have been the point of the incident; instead, his sense of humor and quick-witted reaction made him the hero of misfortune. For the first time, I realized there was more to a sense of humor for soldiers than just laughing at something funny.

The exercise of command often requires disciplinary measures. On occasion, however, the best interests of the military service require reasonable tolerance and human understanding; and, in special cases, an element of humor may help keep things in perspective.

Consider the soldier in Company G, 26th Infantry, whose difficult-to-pronounce name was anglicized by his buddies for everyday use as "Pinky." He was about forty years old, and in my two years in command he had no disciplinary record. Further, he was an excellent soldier, a rifle expert, with an engaging personality that made him a favorite with the company.

But Pinky had a weakness: for several days after payday he would show up for drill with a patient, suffering look, and fine red veins in the whites of his eyes. So I knew the little man with the hammer was busy inside Pinky's skull. But Pinky was always there, always ready to carry more than his share of the load.

One payday morning, however, he was absent from the pay table. So I held his pay envelope until after lunch, when Pinky showed up to claim it. As he stood in front of my desk, I looked him over: his uniform was a trifle rumpled and he had slurred his words a trifle when reporting. Clearly, Pinky had launched his payday operation ahead of schedule.

What interested me most, however, was that the hair above his ears was mussed, standing up in a comical, frizzled effect around the bald area on top of his head. The first sergeant just happened to drift up to my office door to look in with a faint smile at the corners of his mouth. Neither the topkick nor the dozen or so men in the hallway should have let Pinky come in looking like that, so they were having a little fun with me and Pinky, waiting for him to come in and for me to chew him out.

"Why were you absent from pay call this morning?" I asked Pinky, meanwhile trying to decide what to do about the situation.

"Sir-r," Pinky replied with the overly military tone an extra drink sometimes induces, "I furget it was payday."

After a brief pause to digest that, I looked at the topkick in the doorway and said, "Sergeant Redding, give Private First Class Pinky a three-day pass. When a man comes in here with one I've never heard before, he always gets a three-day pass."

The first sergeant looked a little stunned, but not Pinky. He grabbed the pay envelope I extended to him and took off.

Later, when I left my office to go home, "Attention!" was called in the hall a little sharper than usual. Also, the eight or ten men around the bulletin board seemed to stand a bit more stiffly erect than usual, but they looked at me with conspiratorial grins showing, too. When circumstances are right — and there's mutual trust and respect among those concerned — everybody gains from a little shared humor.

But humor can be a chancy business, too, sometimes boomeranging against you. Like the time I was chief of staff to a general who took himself seriously but also fancied himself as a wit. Since I had known him from way back, on two or three occasions I responded in a light vein to his rather heavy-handed humor — and got sat on for my pains.

Naturally, after that I put my funnybone in cold storage around him. It was a surprise, years later on a visit to the Pentagon, when I looked at my efficiency reports to find the entry by that general under *Remarks:* "This officer could do with a little more sense of humor."

Oh, well, you can't win 'em all. But what had happened? Maxim Number 6 in the book *700 Chinese Proverbs* expresses it this way: "Never joke in the presence of a prince."

That's a valid idea in military life, too; thus your sense of humor around your boss should be monitored because it is apt to take the center of the stage away from him. It is an intangible but real threat to his command presence. That doesn't mean you should be a wooden Indian; merely that it is wise to temper your sense of humor enough to keep it from challenging his position as the head clown. Also, when your boss says something he thinks is funny, that makes it official. So at least smile a little (which I guess I didn't do with enough conviction).

Humor enters life in uniform in countless ways, from legitimate change-of-pace remarks to sour-note, satirical wisecracks, from unit costume parties to individual practical jokes — which can be real booby traps sometimes. One gimmick widely used to enliven military life with a smile is to inject funny stories into lectures and speeches. Senior officers often do this but they, like everybody else, can be caught in a backlash from their own jokes.

At the Armed Forces Staff College on one occasion a high-ranking VIP from the Pentagon opened his lecture with the latest racy story going the rounds in Washington. He got a prolonged belly laugh out of proportion to the merit of his yarn. This disconcerted him because he had no way of knowing he was the third speaker in a row from the Pentagon who opened his talk with that same story.

In life and in love, as in war and in apple-polishing, there is no detailed book of instructions on how to use humor with the proper finesse in all situations. But here are a few comments that may be helpful:

- Thomas Fuller, an English divine (1608–61), offers these guidelines: "It is good to make a jest, but not to make a trade of jesting." And, "Take heed of jesting; many have been ruined by it. It is hard to jest, and not sometimes leer too, which often sinks deeper than we intended or expected."

- An American, Thomas W. Higginson (1823–1911), said, "There is no defense against adverse fortune which is, on the whole, so effectual as an habitual sense of humor."

- But it is the old master, William Shakespeare himself, who gives us the pointer every military man should understand: "A jest's prosperity lies in the ear of him that hears it, never in the tongue of him that makes it." In other words, mix empathy with your humor: consider how the jest you have in mind will affect others before you utter it.

- Humor is an effective but tricky technique in command and leadership, beneficial when used wisely and with skill, but it can backfire into a dangerous booby trap if overworked or crudely employed.

6

Pets Have a Place in the Army

TACITUS, THE ROMAN historian, once said, "Liberties and masters are not easily combined." The idea can be applied to an Army-wide practice that often produces this classic conflict of interest which may be stated this way: The liberty to have pets and the responsibilities of commanders are sometimes difficult to reconcile. Like, for example, a happily roving dog at a guard-of-honor formation—especially if during ruffles and flourishes he sniffs the visiting dignitary's legs as though they were twin fire plugs.

At my first post we had a company dog, a plebian hound type: back and sides black, merging into a light tan underbelly, and tan shadings about face and ears. He didn't belong to anybody; he just owned our company in general. But when I approached to get acquainted he sidled silently away, tail drooping, and the men grinned at my puzzled discomfiture.

It soon became clear that he avoided all officers. So I went to the man whom I had quickly learned to admire, respect, trust, and go to for enlightenment on things I didn't understand—our first sergeant.

"Lieutenant," he said, "it's your leggins." (At that time all officers wore either leather leggins or knee-length boots.)

When my cerebral processes still lagged he smiled and added, "Suppose the men find an old pair of leather leggins, and pass them around in off-duty hours; then every time that little hound comes near the man wearing leggins, he gets kicked. Would that explain it?"

The first sergeant also told me about Oscar, a mascot his company had in Panama. Oscar was a very large and long snake, captured in the jungle.

Oscar spent much of his time on the dayroom pool table, lying neatly against the cushions around the edges. Apparently the green cloth-covered slate made a cool, comfortable snake mattress.

When a newcomer arrived in the company it was customary to invite him for a game of pool, at which there were always kibitzers, because usually results were interesting. More than one man had taken a screen door with him on his way elsewhere after meeting Oscar face to face.

One day there was an unexpected development in the form of a husky young recruit. As he chalked his cue and approached the table, Oscar raised his head for a better look at the new arrival.

Things happened fast. The husky recruit swapped ends with the pool cue and, with a swing like Babe Ruth and an aim like Ty Cobb, scored a bull's-eye on Oscar's noggin. Oscar promptly pitched a fit all over the dayroom as screen doors took another licking — this time from the kibitzers. By sundown even the tip of Oscar's tail had given up the ghost, so the company was minus a mascot but plus a recruit marked "handle with care."

Sometimes a mascot causes quakes in high places. That's what Moi did at Schofield Barracks where I was a military police lieutenant. Moi was quite a dog. He loved everybody, and was known all over as "that dirty little MP dog." Apparently his ancestry was scrambled, for he resembled a bird dog in body configuration and liver and white markings, except that he traveled close to the ground on stubby legs as though there was a basset hound in his lineage.

Across the road from our quadrangle the commanding general's house fronted on the post parade. This impressive, austere soldier had no children so he and his wife set more than usual store by a highly pedigreed canine female. As you've guessed by this time, the highly pedigreed lady somehow managed to escape chaperonage at a critical time in her life — and Moi did not miss the opportunity. Since there were several witnesses, "that dirty little MP dog" was positively identified.

There was unhappiness in the CG's house over what the resulting pups might look like, and the titillating news spread over the post — and the high level owners' unhappiness became more acute on learning kennel club rules would prevent the prospective mother from having pedigreed offspring after her morganatic liaison—for, apparently, the disgrace lingers on.

In war, with troops spread around the world, pets are more varied —from white parrots in New Guinea to giant lizards in Australia, and all sorts of animals. The most publicized one known to me was a small monkey named Eleanor, owned by the chief clerk in our chief of staff's office.

One morning while a brigadier general was shaving—with his removable teeth nearby—the monkey happened along and picked them up. With a muffled roar the BG gave chase and treed Eleanor, who finally flung the teeth down at him.

This not only brought a grin to weary GIs in our jungle fighting area—the combat grapevine distributed news down to the foxholes —but to uncounted thousands of Americans at home who read about it in a human-interest dispatch from the war front.

The most memorable unit mascot in my experience was a mountain lion from the Rocky Mountain area sent to a sergeant in the 511th Airborne Infantry soon after I assumed command. He started out a roly-poly little fellow not much larger than a good-sized pup, but soon he was bigger than most dogs—looking even larger when approaching you in his gangly lope.

The whole regiment got a kick out of him—especially on those occasions when a stranger entered our area who did not know we had a pet lion running loose. As regimental commander, I didn't get into the act until plans were afoot to get our mountain kitty jump-qualified. But I put the kibosh on that one, having a vivid mental picture of what could happen if our lion found himself in the door of the airplane and decided he didn't want to jump—thus maybe ending up astride the pilot's neck.

Of course you could write a book about specially trained horses and mules in the Old Army. Or even about the lovable nuisance my wife and I called Kitty, who'll be in her twenty-second year by the time this gets into print—every one of those years brightened for us by her presence.

Of course there are problems with pets, sometimes amplified by a few petulant people. But pets and apartment buildings don't go together. Further, some pets have inborn characteristics that get their owners into disfavor—like the penchant of dogs to bark and make devastating forays across neighbors' lawns. Or cats who catch birds when you have a bird-watcher CG — especially if he's as cantankerous as one we once had.

Perhaps the most irritating responsibility of many I endured as a lieutenant was as commander of a dog-catching detail — of several MPs armed with pup-tent ropes, charged with capturing any dogs running loose who might otherwise steal the spotlight at Hawaiian Division reviews. Each fido thought it was a game, gamboling just out of reach, while my red-faced and frustrated MPs, goaded by delighted comments from the crowd, kept doggedly after the loose pooches.

But it would be a sad post if any CG were so misguided as to issue a no-pets order. Further, that would be violating a basic principle of command. Proper action is to hold the owners responsible when their furry friends become an unreasonable nuisance.

It's hard to measure the place and value of pets in the Army, those privately owned as well as unit mascots. They bring a smile to the heart which, in indefinable ways, is a unifying and relaxing influence.

Perhaps it is said best in words chiseled on a small gray granite stone monument at Fort Benning — prominently placed for student officers over the years to see. It was erected in memory of a much-loved mutt who brightened life for Infantry School students in the 1920s. They called him Calculator — some said because he could calculate where officer classes would assemble in the field, and be there. Others said it was because, being a bit lame in one foot, he "picked up three and carried one." The inscription on his monument reads:

CALCULATOR
born ?
Died 29 Aug. 1923
He made better
dogs of us all.

7

Forge of Experience: The Foreign Service

EACH YEAR UNCOUNTED thousands of Americans in uniform go on their first foreign service tour. What happens to young soldiers at this fascinating and dangerous time of their lives — especially in Vietnam and other places where the cold war blows hot — is far more hazardous than a hitch in the Philippines was nearly fifty years ago. But a brief glance backward to my first foreign service there uncovers some things worth remembering.

I sailed from Brooklyn via Panama, San Francisco, and Honolulu to Manila. By the time we reached the Philippines I was feeling a long way from home as the U.S. Army Transport *U. S. Grant* moved into the great harbor and dropped anchor. Ashore, the sky reflected the glow of lights from Manila — storied Pearl of the Orient — where you could shout "Boy!" and a white-coated waiter would hurry in with a tray of bottles and glasses. Here "a man could raise a thirst!" — and legally, too, for we had left Prohibition behind us in the USA.

I leaned on the ship's rail in the darkness, the moonlight accentuating my aloneness. Soon a motorboat neared our anchored ship and a loud hail indicated the hailers were in an alcoholically cheerful mood.

"Red Newman . . . Zero Wilson . . . Let down a rope!"

Out of the darkness near the ship's bridge a dark shadow moved quickly, and the voice of the rough and tough old colonel, the transport commander, ordered, "Don't let them board. Do *not* let them *aboard!*"

There followed a crash and a thump as the colonel tripped over a deck chair and fell heavily on the deck. The boat circled the ship, and the hail was repeated, "Red Newman . . . Zero Wilson . . . Let down a rope!"

Disengaging himself from the deck chair, the colonel struggled to his feet. His voice was a little softer and more cunning as he directed, "All right, it is OK. Let them come aboard."

Anyway, with the old colonel patrolling the ship's rail like a fenced bulldog, no rope appeared. Discouraged, the motorboat turned shoreward, its hail continuing but growing fainter.

Now the glow from Manila's lights and the yellow haze of the tropical moon had lost their aloofness and become inviting. Friends were here, halfway around the world, as they would be everywhere I went in the Army. Our military forces cover the face of the earth; wherever you go you meet friends.

But it's also true that on foreign service — especially a first tour — there is the undefinable lure of strange places, and new adventures beckon. The overall effect is heightened when scotch highballs cost only ten cents and you are handed the bottle to pour your own drink. At such times friends are sometimes as apt to facilitate getting you into trouble as keeping you out of it.

For example, I have a distinct recollection of two young second lieutenants, in a rented old Model T Ford, rocketing along Manila's streets late one evening. The driver not only had to contend with a mixture of automobiles and pony-drawn two-wheeled carts; there was also the unfamiliar traffic regulation of driving on the left of the road. Because of this last fact they repeated loudly and in unison: "Left . . . left! Pass 'em on the right!"

Two budding military careers might well have ended violently that night — or been marred by disciplinary action. No observer could have guessed then that both would not only survive but would become general officers — a victory for fortuitous chance over retarded judgment.

In spite of heat, bugs, and temptations of the tropics, however, military commanders kept their eyes and our energies focused during duty hours on the primary mission: readiness to meet any military emergency. This record could, of course, go into technical intricacies of daily training and maneuvers — including manning the defenses of Corregidor. But you can imagine what the military training was like, so it will be more enlightening to examine a little footnote to history.

The story really begins in 1921, for a vivid memory of my West Point days was the first time I saw the superintendent, Brig. Gen. Douglas MacArthur. The Supe, a slender, magnificently casual figure in crushed cap and perfectly tailored uniform, was striding purposefully along the walk near French Monument, the glory of his blazing World War battle record gleaming from bright ribbons on his chest.

Later, when I was on the 1928 U.S. Olympic Team en route to Amsterdam, sitting at the captain's table in the great dining room of the S.S. *President Roosevelt,* the president of the American Olympic Committee also sat there: Maj. Gen. Douglas MacArthur. He was as impressive then as he had been at West Point, sitting quietly without chitchat and giving the impression of constantly thinking.

Now, in 1930, he was commanding general of the Philippine Department when telegraphic orders came for me to catch the next ship home in order to attend the Troop Officers Equitation Course at the Cavalry School.

The night before the transport sailed I visited the bar in the Manila Hotel to get in a suitable frame of mind for the evening. Then I lighted a Corona-Corona and walked out to the dine-and-dance pavilion.

This was a large porch, with a wooden dance floor in the center and tables around the sides on a concrete surface. The wood floor ended in a sharp 45-degree drop of about an inch and a half. I began to circle the edge of the dance floor—in white linen suit with cigar going good—looking the situation over.

Suddenly my ankle turned on the slanted edge of the wood floor and I fell sideways on top of the nearest ringside table, twisting around to land with both hands flat on the tabletop, and sort of bent over, cigar still clenched in my teeth, pointing directly at the only occupant of the table: General MacArthur.

This little tableau was frozen for a moment while my brain digested the fact that General MacArthur was not more than two feet away from the end of my cigar.

It would not be correct to say the general looked at me; rather, he looked through me, as though I were not there. Perhaps this gave me the idea it would be better if I were not. Anyway, I struggled to my feet and removed myself and the Corona-Corona from the general's field of view.

Out to the bar — and the Manila Hotel bar seems a good place to conclude this report from Manila.

Of course there was no way for either of us to imagine that night — after our eyeball-to-eyeball confrontation over the end of my cigar — that nearly fifteen years later, on the first day of my return to the Philippines, we would meet face to face again. On that future day — 20 October 1944 — I would report to him as regimental commander on the battle-torn stretch of Leyte beach where General MacArthur made good his famous promise, "I shall return!"

As I search through musty memories of years long gone, there are lessons to be learned which did not occur to me then. They are as applicable today as yesterday:

- A military career cannot be fashioned in battle or on drill fields alone, but must meet the standards expected of soldiers wherever they go — and this has never been more important than on foreign service today.
- Death and battle wounds are plain and clear dangers to soldiers in Vietnam, or anywhere else the cold war blows hot. Not so clear, but quite as real, are insidious threats to military careers from booby traps hidden in bottles, skirts, black markets, and other quicksands of foreign service.
- The Army is a small world, but its people have large memories. The longer you stay in it the more you will run into friends wherever you go. It's also equally true that as the years pass you will serve with a growing number of superiors who remember you from Back When — and what kind of soldier you were then.
- Every young officer should therefore realize that among those with whom he serves over the years will be an appreciable number who will, later, bear witness for or against his career in some manner: by making out his efficiency reports, by influencing his duty assignments in various ways — even sitting on promotion boards. Thus it's not only the written record that influences your career. Your personal and professional

reputation lives in hundreds of memories, and cannot fail to help or hinder you in some measure.

- Hence, this final double conclusion: while younger officers should guard against attacks of retarded judgment, older officers should view such occasional lapses in perspective, remembering their own salad days, when they too were green in judgment. Given time and adequate guidance, junior officers are forged into mature professional soldiers in the only way possible: by experience.

8
Army Officer, Gentleman, and . . . ?

SOME YEARS AGO an outstanding four-star general was playing golf south of the Mason-Dixon line with three wealthy civilians. One of the civilians had an unusually large and heavy golf bag carried by a small, elderly caddy who was having considerable difficulty keeping up with the fast-walking foursome.

The general observed this for several holes and tried unsuccessfully to slow things down by lagging behind himself. He then looked pointedly at the overburdened caddy and said, "Can you southern gentlemen slow down enough for an old man to keep up?"

I knew that general not only as a wonderful officer, but also as a fine gentleman. The above does not show his technical military knowledge and ability, but it does illustrate one of the many and varied facets of a gentleman: awareness of and consideration for others. Without this single gentlemanly quality any officer—whose primary reason for being is to command and lead men—would be seriously flawed in his qualifications.

"Officer and gentleman" seem to go together naturally, like "pork and beans," yet in both cases they are separate entities. But the fused attributes of the separate parts complement each other to produce a more complex, more specialized and valuable combination than either of the separate elements.

Our manuals, schools and training concentrate on military skills and knowledge required as an officer. So it seems in order to consider the "gentleman" angle, as was suggested to me in a letter from Col. Douglas B. MacMullen.

Sometimes we hear it said, "No gentleman would do (say) that." Like, "No gentleman will kiss and tell." This seems to infer it is okay to kiss if you don't tell, but my best judgment tells me not to explore that implied angle.

Dr. Henry Gibbons defined a kiss as, "The anatomical juxtaposition of two orbicularis oris muscles in a state of contraction," which is an overly narrow concept of the meaning in the above maxim. Anyway, in the practical implementation of the "never tell" angle to the "officer and gentleman" idea we have — among other unwritten guidelines — this basic rule: no lady's name should be mentioned in a bachelor officers' (or gentlemen's) mess.

One day some fifty years ago, I was a second lieutenant of the 31st Infantry in Manila on a drill field adjacent to the old "Walled City." It was a hot and sultry morning, so when "Recall" sounded my first stop was for a cool glass of San Miguel beer at a small bar inside the walls.

While the man drew my beer, I read this message lettered on the flyspecked mirror behind the bar, written by a finger dipped in some white stuff:

> Here's to lying, swearing, stealing, and drinking:
> When you lie, lie for a beautiful woman;
> When you swear, swear by your country;
> When you steal, steal away from bad company;
> And when you drink, drink with me.

The anonymous composer was laying out his guidelines on how to be a gentleman. It is inherent in the last line that, "When you drink, drink like a gentleman."

Some say these and comparable characteristics are just surface fripperies for an officer, of no real value, and that military competence is the only thing that counts. But that idea, like most oversimplifications, rests on a fallacy. No matter how great an officer's technical qualifications, his overall competence is reduced if he lacks the personal qualities of a gentleman. Nowhere is this more obvious than at company level, where I spent fifteen years of my service.

This was made clear on my first post. I remember one first lieutenant in particular who failed to measure up as an officer because ungentlemanly flaws developed in his character. It was a time when Prohibition was in full, noxious flower, and he did not "carry his liquor like a gentleman."

The grapevine reported that his lack of alcoholic control affected his judgment in gambling with cards and his discretion in romantic endeavors. Thus, it should not have been too surprising when a check for his mess bill bounced — and of that I have personal knowledge, because I was mess officer in the bachelor mess.

Since I was required to report any failure to pay bills by the tenth of the month, this put me on the spot; a rubber check pays no bills. So I took the check to him and he said, "Just add it to my bill this month and I'll give you a check for that."

When this check bounced too, I had no choice but to report to regiment that he was two months behind on his mess bill. "Don't worry about it, Mistuh Newman," the adjutant said quietly. "We will include that bill in the settlement of his financial affairs when he leaves the Army. He is resigning from the military service."

This officer did not fail in his military duties; in fact, I believe he would have been a fine combat soldier and that he had many qualities required for senior rank. But an officer must meet the required standards in peacetime — which includes his personal life — or he will not be around to enter battle as an officer.

It is important to note, however, that there is some conflict between the qualities expected in an officer and those of a gentleman in civilian life, especially one who can be described as "always a perfect gentleman." A good officer must have iron in his soul when needed, which means that he must be hard-nosed when the situation calls for it — but, as a gentleman, no more hard-nosed than the situation makes necessary.

One of the best ways to study fundamental factors in command and leadership is to read military history, and one of the most fascinating angles that history reveals about its dominant military personalities is how well or how ill the "officer and gentleman" tag fits them. Two cases in point are Robert E. Lee and Benedict Arnold.

Gen. Robert E. Lee is internationally renowned as a great military leader. He was also one of the finest gentlemen ever to wear a military uniform. In fact, many consider his only weakness to be that he was too much of a gentleman at times, thus failing to demand with enough force that several of his headstrong generals carry out his orders promptly and without equivocation.

It is not so well known that Benedict Arnold ranks at the top among battle leaders in American history, a fact obscured by his having become a traitor. Similarly, it is also often overlooked that he fell short of being a gentleman in his business deals and in his relations with some of his contemporaries. It even seems clear that it was these ungentlemanly characteristics that led to his selling out to the British for money (and rank).

So it begins to look like the words "officer and gentleman" are properly paired; but there are other angles to consider too.

To begin with, I do not like the implication that being a gentleman is exclusive to the commissioned ranks. Some of the finest gentlemen known to me in this world, and whom I hope to meet in the next, are soldiers with whom I have served. On the other hand, a few officers I have known in this world, and whom I hope not to meet in the next, fell something short of being gentlemen.

One day when I was a barefoot pre-teenager who liked to roam in the woods, I found a small snake trying to swallow a large frog. A close inspection showed the snake had a good grip on the frog between the frog's hind legs. But there was no chance whatever that he could engorge the frog, for he had come to grips with something too big for him to swallow.

This is what happened to me in tackling this subject of "officer and gentleman," for it is too complex for my analytical ability to swallow, digest and come up with a finite answer. But the first requirement is that you have "the instincts of a gentleman." Three comments are:

- In my view it is redundant to pair "officer" with "gentleman," because the connotation of the word "officer" should be inclusive. For example, you do not say "hamburger meat."
- Actually, the supplementary use of the word "gentleman" is an anachronism handed down to us from England, where it had a class-distinction meaning: you had to be a "gentleman" before you could become an officer.

The weakness in that system was demonstrated at Balaklava in the Crimea, when the famous and disastrous "Charge of the Light Brigade" was masterminded by two "gentlemen" in the sense then used — in fact, both were British aristocrats. That did not make them competent commanders in combat, although one of them proved himself a man.

- There are times to be a tough officer and times to be a well-mannered and considerate gentleman — not just with your seniors and at cocktail soirées and other social affairs, but in your everyday dealings with all under you, down to the newest recruit. When you combine these qualities in the right proportions with military competence, you will stand a good chance of being classified as a leader.

9
Adjutants and Aides

AS A LIEUTENANT in the Hawaiian Division military police at Schofield Barracks over forty years ago, I was military police officer of the day when the desk sergeant reported, "Lieutenant, there is a car with three *ladies* in it touring around the barracks area on the post. Looks like they might be trying to drum up a little business."

This was a delicate situation because, if they were wrongly arrested for "soliciting," that could result in trouble. So I said, "OK, sergeant. Send out two MPs in the Ford as a traffic patrol. If the car violates any traffic regulations, bring them to me. And while they are in here, check their car."

Sure enough, the car ran a stop sign. When the personable-appearing young ladies were escorted into my office I rose and invited them to be seated in chairs facing my desk: a tall bold blonde, a medium-size brown hair, and a small brunette with snapping dark eyes. Then, in my best judicial manner, I explained about traffic regulations on the post, saying that we obeyed our rules and expected visitors to do the same. I mentioned the menace of reckless driving to little children of our military families and expounded on the evils of running stop signs. And, all the while, tried to figure how to spot them as "soliciting."

At this point the desk sergeant appeared in the door behind our visitors, grinning and nodding his head as he held up a fan of small calling cards. I knew from this that the cards had been found in their car and would have a business address—also possibly a commercial, including price. Thus no further delay was needed.

So I said, "All right, ladies, the traffic violation will go in our records. But there is more to it than that.

"I know who you are and the location of your business, and we all know why you were on the post. No further action will be taken against you now, but if you come on the post again charges will be filed in federal court. If there are no questions, an MP will escort you off the post."

The little black-haired one with the snapping dark eyes glanced at the inch-high brass donkey on a pedestal in my ashtray, and asked, "Lieutenant, are you a member of the Honolulu Jackass Society?"

That caught me with my wits down, so all I could manage was, "I have never heard of that society, but feel sure I can qualify as a member."

"Well," she replied, rising, "I just wondered." And the three of them exited, smiling.

After they left I looked at the little donkey on my ashtray pedestal and reflected, "You gave her that bright idea, my friend. And she is correct, because not all donkeys are made of brass — and not all of them have four legs either."

Remembering about the Honolulu Jackass Society reminds me of another club referred to in my day as "The Association of Aides, Asses and Adjutants" (AAAA). To examine that subject further we will look at some case histories.

My first observation of aides and adjutants was as a cadet at West Point. The two lieutenants I remember as aides to the superintendent became general officers. Also, both of the officers who served as adjutant at West Point retired as major generals. Finally, as records of their early service show, both of the superintendents of my era — Brig. Gen. Douglas MacArthur and Maj. Gen. Fred W. Sladen — served as aides when they were lieutenants.

So my first exposure to aides and adjutants put them *per se* on the side of the angels. But that view did not go long unchallenged.

On my first duty assignment, with the 29th Infantry at Fort Benning, the adjutant of my battalion was an outstanding officer and gentleman. But my contacts with the regimental adjutants were quite different. Consider my last day in the regiment.

In the preceding two days I had been busy clearing the post preparatory to going on foreign service. In the process I missed an officers' call and was unaware of the dereliction when I went to regimental headquarters to sign out. After signing the book I reported

out to the regimental adjutant — and he handed me a goodbye present: a piece of paper signed by him, taking me to task for missing
that routine officers' call while clearing the post.

All very military and according to regulations, but hardly necessary under the circumstances. It is such unnecessary "official" and
"military" things that do much to establish the unofficial AAAA.
That adjutant qualified for a charter membership in the Honolulu
society we were talking about.

On the other hand, the adjutant of the 31st Infantry in Manila
would have been rejected for membership in that Honolulu society.
A year after my arrival there I managed to break my right hip
playing on the regimental basketball team and was hospitalized for
six weeks. Before returning to duty, I requested two weeks' leave
at the Baguio rest and recreation camp in the mountains.

It is pertinent to know also that in my year in Manila another
second lieutenant and I had become close off-duty friends. In fact
we were known as the Black Label Twins in such places as the
Army-Navy Club bar, the Manila Hotel pavilion, and Tom's Dixie
("Dirty") Kitchen downtown.

So when I hand-carried my leave request to the adjutant he said,
"All right, Mistuh Newman, your leave is approved. And tell your
friend John it will not be necessary to submit his request for leave.
I'll put his name on the order with you."

This was no isolated incident, for most adjutants were pleasant
and helpful. Like the time I got in the doghouse with my regimental
commander, resulting in an accumulation of extra duty assignments. When my name was published to go on guard as officer of
the day, I reported to the fine major who was our regimental adjutant and said, "Sir, there is no lieutenant in my company, so when I
go on as officer of the day tomorrow it will limit my capabilities for
training my company, supervising the rifle range, training the regimental recruits, and running the all-day school for the twenty-
two newly joined second-lieutenant Thomason Act officers.* It
occurs to me you might want to designate an officer to assist in
officer supervision of these operations while I am on guard."

He looked at me with a quiet smile. He knew that I was surrep-

---

*A law passed by Congress prior to World War II bringing selected ROTC gradu-
ates on active duty for a year, then commissioning some in the regular army.

titiously pulling his leg, but that I was also calling attention to the imbalance of supervisory responsibilities charged to me. So he said, "Captain Newman, wouldn't it be simpler just to take you off the guard roster?"

Unfortunately, neither he nor the adjutant of the 31st Infantry ever pinned on stars. But of the five officers who served as adjutant and personnel adjutant of the 19th Infantry during my assignment there, four of the five became general officers — one a four-star man. But none of them would have taken me off that guard roster — so there is more than one side to this AAAA idea.

Now about aides. Some of them qualify for membership, although more from youth and inexperience than any donkey element in their makeup. A few become a bit presumptuous, but usually this results from two causes. The first is that, unlike adjutants, they have so little to do that they get into things where they have no business. A second motivation stems from the fact some generals ask them questions about matters outside the province of aides. So the aides try to keep informed in order to give their bosses the answers. This sometimes leads to a kind of semi-spy system, with the aides drifting into being talebearers. As a result, their personality profiles acquire the two long ears and a tail that are AAAA characteristics.

Some comments are:

- All adjutants are selected men, based on known ability. When generals select aides from their own personal knowledge they are nearly always men of high potential. Sometimes, however, aides are assigned on second-hand information, primarily because they are "available." These last are the best candidates for AAAA membership.
- Because of this selective angle aides — and especially adjutants — have a better-than-average chance to reach higher rank later. The most successful aides and adjutants gained broad experience from their jobs but did not make a career of such assignments.
- One reason aides and adjutants are criticized as being more high-handed than their rank would justify is that one of their duties is to shield their superiors from unnecessary interruptions. Since most of those with whom they deal are senior to them in rank, human

nature gets into the act — and the legend of the AAAA is thus continually nourished, for it is inherent in the situation.

- Among other things, sour grapes may be involved on occasion. But the AAAA generalization, like most shotgun maxims, is founded on some fact and much distorted thinking. Aides and adjutants do their jobs like everybody else, sometimes a little better. But I have known a few such gentlemen over the years who, if they had lived nearly 2,000 years earlier, could have offered Balaam a ride out of Jerusalem.

10
Day-to-Day Personal Interest

DURING MY FIRST foreign service tour I met an amiable overage company commander who, because of his general physical appearance, we'll call Capt. Little Joe Cueball. His company was not shooting well on the rifle range, so Captain Cueball came up with a novel idea for a leadership angle that he thought would inspire higher scores in marksmanship than he had been able to command.

He acquired a small goat which was taken out to the rifle range and tethered to a stake behind the firing line. Then, in his amiable way, Little Joe explained his goaty gambit: "Men, our shooting scores are below par. Some of you have been letting the company down by not giving your best efforts. This goat is a reminder to every man to do his best because, on the way back to barracks, whoever shoots the lowest score today will march in front of the company — leading the goat."

When the shooting smoke cleared and the red flags were stilled and the arithmetic totted up, it was found that the company commander's leadership gimmick had indeed paid off. Some thought, however, this gain in marksmanship was offset by the loss in discipline when Capt. Little Joe Cueball trudged along in front of the company on the dusty march back — leading the goat.

Thus, while the intangibles of effective leadership are invaluable in attaining the finest results in command, tricky gimmicks should be viewed skeptically so as to avoid possible undesirable side effects.

During my five years as company commander many minor difficulties were resolved one at a time, with not much thought being given to the principles involved. However, this experience, when examined in retrospect, reveals some interesting facets of command and leadership. Consider the following two ventures in supply supervision.

After taking command of my first company I made a drill check of our .22-caliber indoor rifle range in the barracks attic. Firing was in progress, so I took my turn at bat. Then I moved to the rear, still holding the rifle.

The targets were lighted, but the attic was dark so I found myself at the head of the stairs, apparently unobserved. Of course accountability for weapons is an important command responsibility, and it looked easy for somebody to walk out of that dark attic with a rifle. So that's what I did, and placed it behind my orderly room door.

When afternoon Recall sounded (not a static-marred loudspeaker noise but a clear, lifting lilting sound blown by a real live bugler) there came a knock on my orderly room door.

"Come in," I said. Supply Sergeant Jessie marched in, halted and saluted.

"If the Captain has finished with .22-caliber rifle 12345," he said, deadpan, "I'll check it back in the supply room."

No doubt the company got a good grin out of that one. But then I had not really expected to get away with it. After more than ten years of service I knew an officer seldom does anything around a company without the men knowing it. Still, I had accomplished two positive results:

1. I had determined there was an effective check, by number, to account for .22-caliber rifles in use on the attic range.
2. A message had been broadcast via the company grapevine system that the new captain was supply-conscious.

Some days later I noticed my lieutenant sitting at his desk, not only doing nothing but apparently content to continue that way. This suggested the idea to issue these instructions:

"Lieutenant Lassitude, go down to the supply room and inventory the pistols, compasses, automatic rifles, and our field mess equipment. Report the result to me in a pencil memo."

Another time he was directed to inventory blankets, sheets, mattress covers, and pillowcases. Still another day it was check all rifles by number — and so on, periodically. Thus the chance observation of a lackadaisical lieutenant turned up a simple and easy way to keep tabs on the many supply items for which I was responsible.

At Saturday inspections I spot-checked special things myself, such as verifying the contents of Browning automatic rifle spare-parts kits against the regulations. Or maybe the status of cleaning and preserving materials. This became an unspoken game of double solitaire between me and Sergeant Jessie (the Army never had a finer supply sergeant).

The fact that I never found any shortage of consequence made no difference; it's important to know there are none. Nor did Jessie or any of my outstanding noncommissioned officers resent my checking on them. When good soldiers are doing a superior job they like for you to inspect and find it out. Finally, all of them were aware that this method of constant checks created an atmosphere of supply discipline in the company that made life easier for all of us.

My next company was as poor in supply discipline as my first had been good. On taking command after the previous CO's departure, higher authority required me to sign for much cracked and chipped china in the kitchen, plus some shortages — and to "make it up from the breakage allowance." Also, I quickly discovered the mess itself was below standard. Soldiers who do not eat well are not happy about it.

The company commander cannot be the mess sergeant, but he can do other things — like getting a new mess sergeant. It soon became apparent, however, that this alone could not cure the sick china situation. Reason: with all that chipped and cracked stuff mixed in, it was hard to discover new damage so that we could charge it to KPs or others responsible.

After my repeated instructions failed to remedy conditions, the question was, "Do I give up, or is there a way to eliminate cracked and chipped china?"

One afternoon I had the mess sergeant collect all damaged china on a table in the mess hall. Then I sent for the supply sergeant to bring a GI can and a hammer. When the mess sergeant saw the GI can and hammer, and the supply sergeant saw all that cracked and chipped china, both began talking at once.

"Captain," the mess sergeant warned, "there will not be enough china left to set the tables for dinner!"

"Captain," the supply sergeant cautioned, "you are signed for that china — and we're short now!"

But I was adamant. "My instructions were to make some progress toward getting rid of chipped and cracked china, but that is not happening. Break it all. I'll watch."

They filled the GI can until it was heaping, and a fine dust in the air made a kind of acrid tickling sensation in my nose.

At dinner that night and at breakfast the next morning, some men ate from soup plates, others drank coffee from water glasses. But none were or became chipped and cracked. Thus it was more or less impressed on the company that the business of cracked and chipped china was a live issue.

Then, as I had previously arranged to do, we drew from post supply over my signature an advance issue of new china, thus obtaining a full set of pristine china in the mess hall. Now my orders were explicit:

- When KPs came on duty each morning they would check the china and report any damage during the day — including names of men responsible.
- At day's end the mess sergeant would check the china. Any chipped, cracked, or missing — not covered by names of men responsible for damage or loss — would be charged to KPs.
- If the mess sergeant failed to make sure these measures were carried out, he would be charged with the damage or loss.

You have to fix things so you can put the bee on somebody by name. Overnight the slapdash handling of china stopped, and in due time our breakage allowance reestablished a healthy balance — without a chip or crack in a table load.

Leadership is the art of inspiring desire in men's hearts to do what you want them to do; command is the knack of making them do what you want them to do. A company commander must understand both, especially since when properly synchronized they often blend one into the other to get the job done up to the highest standards.

Each reader can codify and evaluate for himself the various command actions and leadership angles in these little military vignettes out of the past. The same principles apply now as then. Let me point out two:

- A constant spot check requires little effort, and is cumulative in effect. It is a basic command and action technique.
- Leadership gimmicks, gambits, and grandstand plays, if used with judgment and selectivity, can be helpful in special circumstances. But nothing can replace the most effective principle of company-level leadership: the day-to-day personal interest of the commander.

11

Social Contacts Are a Duty

AN IMPORTANT ELEMENT of strength in our Army is standardization of techniques and procedures through constant changes of station among officers in peacetime. This also makes for greater cohesiveness through the ever-spreading circle of friendships among officers as their service lengthens.

This policy of rotating officers around the Army requires a means to shorten the time lag for new arrivals to get acquainted at their new posts. Official calls and unit parties serve this purpose — functions largely supplemented and in some measure replaced by cocktail parties since repeal of Prohibition.

My first official call has been chronicled (in Chapter 3), when I backed into and butted over a potted plant in my regimental commander's house at Fort Benning. On that same post a young second lieutenant got married, and the newlyweds moved into one of the unpainted shacks in an area known as Block 40. After their "At Home" card went up on the regimental bulletin board, the bride and groom received their first caller: the lieutenant's company commander, a middle-aged bachelor captain. The captain was the rough-diamond type, so they expected a routine fifteen-minute call.

Sure enough, after fifteen minutes, there was a loud insistent ringing outside the front door on the porch. The captain rose to his feet, deposited two cards in the tray on a nearby table, and said, "Well, time to go. Good night!"

Then he paused briefly on the front porch to pick up his clock, turn off the alarm, and continue on his way.

This demonstrates how official calls help people to better know and understand each other. How else could the young lieutenant and his wife have discovered the crusty old captain was human enough to have a sense of humor?

Several years later, on another post, a friend of mine we'll call Frank had a different experience. As a young bachelor, he was living in the BOQ (bachelor officer's quarters) when a newly arrived lieutenant colonel — a very senior officer in those days — moved into married quarters nearby. The BOQ occupants were expected to call on the new arrivals. Thus, when one of the BOQ residents noticed there were no lights in the colonel's house during calling hours, he decided to "drop cards."

After ringing the bell, then leaving his cards, the angle-shooter passed the word in the BOQ. That's when Frank — in bathrobe, pajamas, and slippers — decided that since it was dark outside, he could duck over and slip cards under the door. Several others handed him their cards to take along.

That's how it came about that Frank was stuffing cards under the door when the light went on in the living room, and the door was opened by the colonel. As Frank straightened up, but before he could dash away in abject rout, the colonel said, "Nice of you to call, Lieutenant. Come in!"

So Frank shuffled in with his bedroom slippers and met the colonel's wife, who received him as though there was nothing unusual about lieutenants calling in pajamas and bathrobe. They chatted blandly with Frank, said how happy they were to serve on this post again where the colonel himself had once lived in the BOQ. Also the colonel asked Frank to tell the others whose cards were in the doorway that the colonel "hoped" they would call again when he was home to receive them.

Eventually Frank escaped from the house, staggered back to the BOQ, and reported the calling card fiasco — along with the colonel's "hope" they would call when he was home. Since the wiser part of valor indicated the sooner they faced up to the issue the better, the bachelors waited until lights showed in the colonel's house during calling hours and went over in a group to ring the bell. Their initial embarrassment was quickly replaced by the pleasant surprise of finding the colonel's lady a lively conversationalist, and the old boy himself quite an interesting character.

The age gaps will always exist, but this illustrates how off-duty social contacts can establish the effective liaison of better human understanding between them.

After repeal of Prohibition, my first cocktail party was at Schofield Barracks. Among those present was a junior first lieutenant — we'll call him Joe — recently arrived in Hawaii without his wife. Another lieutenant from our regiment named Andy met Joe at the dock in Honolulu.

"Listen, Andy," Joe said, "my wife is not with me. The ladies will want to know why. Tell them you asked me, and that I said it was none of your business."

Joe was sure the word would be passed around, and that local biddies would pry no further into his personal affairs. Of course that was his mistake, as Joe found out halfway through the party when one long-nosed biddy decided it was time to get a little more information on the record. So, during a lull in the conversation, she called to Joe from across the room, "When is your wife coming over?"

Unexpectedly backed into a corner, but buoyed up by a couple of drinks, a sort of spontaneous-desperation sixty-four-dollar answer popped out: "Not being curious, I didn't ask her."

You might say that clarified the situation, for nobody asked Joe any more personal questions. If it had not been for that cocktail party there's no telling how long it might have taken to arrive at such a clear understanding between Joe and the biddies.

Of course, it is not only among the younger generation that after-duty hours social contacts can be interesting. Consider the time, after I became a general officer, when a multi-starred VIP visited our post. One of the local generals was host at a stag affair at his home for the VIP, attended only by other star-wearers. Thus it was a small gathering, with eight of us present.

Atmosphere at such assemblies will usually be on the carefully controlled side, just how stuffy depending on personalities of the seniors present. In this instance it was neutral, as though each waited for somebody else to get the party off the ground with a good story. Perhaps this prolonged restraint resulted in one of the many-starred generals losing interest, to the point that his eyes closed. In fact, he was dozing.

The visiting VIP, who was what the British call the SOP — not standing operating procedure, but senior officer present — noticed the dozing general. The VIP quickly raised a finger to his lips, and began to tiptoe from the room—motioning us to follow. Perhaps it was the silence, or maybe the rustle of seven generals tiptoeing. Anyway, the dozing general's eyes opened, everybody had a good laugh and another drink, and the party finally got off the ground. Not under a full head of steam, of course, because the watchful restraint was still there which seems to inhibit stars—it just receded a little.

The examples of off-duty social contact I have mentioned may be on the offbeat side. But when viewed in relation to uncounted thousands of more orthodox off-duty social contacts that currently take place Army-wide, they provide the leaven to make four ideas rise into clearer focus:

- Since our Army is made up of people, a basic element of overall efficiency is the ability of individuals to understand and get along with others. This can never be done during drill hours alone; thus, duties and responsibilities of soldiers of all ranks extend to off-duty contacts with military associates.
- Shifting around of people accentuates this need and multiplies the benefits that stem from it. The results are not only an invaluable technical homogeneity within the Army, but also an equally invaluable cohesiveness among men in uniform that only multiple friendship can engender.
- For each soldier, playing his full part in this vital phase of military life is a duty he cannot delegate. Virtually every man's situation is a special case, and only personal initiative based on intelligent thought and perception can get the best results.
- In some measure, each man's military career is either enhanced or retarded, depending upon how well and truly he meets this intangible obligation.

12

Best Damned Company in the Army

NO PROFESSIONAL ASSIGNMENT is more rewarding than command of a company. You are responsible for valuable equipment, weapons, and supplies — but it's men you command. And it's the men of Company G, 26th Infantry — my first command — who live in memory.

We had wonderful noncommissioned officers and fine soldiers in Company G, but the most unforgettable character among them was a wizened little middle-aged private. We'll call him Manchester; the company called him Butch. From him I learned a fundamental lesson.

In those days company commanders paid their men personally, in cash. On our first payday I directed that they report in dress uniform with side arms, and said no man would be paid for being a soldier unless he looked like one.

Several did not get the word, among them Pvt. Butch Manchester. When he came back for his third try, I took a good look at him.

Butch had come into the Army during World War I, and so had nearly twenty years of service. It had been tough getting him reenlisted the last time (the first sergeant said) because Butch had shrunk a little, and was under minimal height and weight. Also, he ⸺ not very smart, always seemed slightly worried, and his ⸺ther-beaten face made him look older than he was. But Butch ⸺ conscientious air about him and did his modest best.

⸺xt payday it took him three tries again.

The third payday, on my way to the finance office for the money, I saw Butch going into the post exchange—shirt collar unbuttoned, tie pulled loose in an unmilitary manner. So I made a mental note to take this up with him at the pay table.

The first sergeant leaned against the orderly room door and watched each man march in, halt and report, draw his pay and leave.

Finally Butch came in. He was perfect. Clothing pressed, brass polished and leather shined, fresh haircut, clean-shaven, carefully correct salute. So I gave him only a small-sized growl about that loosened collar and paid him, and then Butch left. The first sergeant chuckled, and went back into his orderly room.

After paying the company I called for the first sergeant. "What," I wanted to know, "is so funny about Manchester having his collar unfastened?"

"I'm sorry, Captain, but I was taken by surprise. You see, the company decided to get Butch paid first try this time, without getting bawled out. So they organized things, with the corporal of his squad in charge. One man got Butch's uniform pressed, another shined his brass and leather, still another made sure he got a haircut —and the corporal had him practice reporting and saluting. While he was in the hall waiting his turn to get paid they dusted him off from top to bottom—and you gave him a growl for something that had happened hours ago. It just looked like Butch couldn't win."

That's the way the Army is—full of people who act like human beings. No commander would want it otherwise, yet every commander listens to the tone of reactions. And humor has a good tone.

The company loved Butch, who seldom smiled but was loyal and friendly. When I asked why Butch was not a private first class, the sergeant said it was because he had never qualified with the rifle.

Of course, rifle season came around that year, and with it trouble for Butch. His arms were too short, his score book got fouled up, and his body wouldn't fit into the right positions. But he sweated and tried, the NCOs helped him—and he failed to qualify again.

After the range season, I called for the privates who had made Expert—and for Butch. They lined up in my office with Butch on one end, eyes downcast.

"A vacancy for private first class has been held until after range season," I said, "not only because rifle shooting is important to infantrymen, but it brings out other things in a soldier, too."

I paused, then continued.

"You experts have my congratulations, and I'll remember you for future vacancies. But there are other considerations besides marksmanship, including character and length of service."

Then, to the first sergeant: "Publish an order promoting Manchester to private first class."

In taking this action I didn't figure what effect it would have on the company. It just seemed the right thing to do. When assigned as dayroom orderly, Butch kept the place spotless and the company happy.

Of course, range season came again the next year. This time I fired in the first echelon, made a record of my sight settings, and it is necessary to know I qualified in the Expert bracket.

When the second echelon started I assembled the company lieutenants, all NCOs, and Butch.

"Manchester," I said, "use my rifle and score book. Your corporal will check the sight settings for each range. And do not change them, no matter what."

To the others I said, "No one will give Manchester help or advice. He has been told for years all there is to know about shooting. His rifle is a good one, his sights will be set properly, and whatever score he shoots will suit me."

For the first time nobody was bothering Butch or going to be mad at him. Also, he didn't have to worry about sight changes. And he qualified. Not by much, but he qualified.

So I went home to the BOQ and had a drink in celebration. But next morning when I saw the first sergeant I knew something was wrong.

"Captain," he said, "Butch is in the guardhouse."

"What for?"

"Drunk and disorderly. He slugged the sergeant of the guard. What does the captain want to do about it?"

"As soon as you get court-martial charges prepared, I'll sign them."

The first sergeant smiled. "Well, sir, you ought to hear the whole story first." And he told me.

The company had returned from the range; some of the men took Butch to Plattsburg for the biggest steak in town. Also, everybody bought him a drink; they met new friends, told them about Butch qualifying, and the new friends bought him drinks too. Finally they convoyed Butch back to barracks, undressed him, poured him into bed, and all went to sleep. All but Butch.

Apparently he lay in bed, thinking what thoughts in his loyal soul no one will ever know. He was really qualified! But there was some high-pressure steam not yet let off, because Butch dressed quietly in the dark and walked across the parade ground to the guardhouse.

"Where's the sergeant of the guard?" he asked.

"Here I am," the sergeant answered, noting that Butch had a load aboard and was incautiously coming up close to him. "What do you want?"

"I'm in the best damned company in the Army!" Butch announced. Then he slugged the unsuspecting sergeant and knocked him down. "Now," Butch said, "lock me up."

So they did.

"The captain still want to sign charges?" the first sergeant asked.

"You know I don't. You have just been playing me like a violin," I said — and left for headquarters to get Butch sprung from the jug. And that took some real talking.

This is not all of the Butch story, but it's enough to make clear the lesson I learned from a wizened little middle-aged private who always tried so hard to please: when a soldier gives his best, what more can you ask?

It's then up to the commander to assign him duties that will make the most of his capabilities. That I chanced to accept Butch in this way was surely a factor in the loyalty and support given me by his fellow soldiers — how could it be otherwise?

The way any one soldier is treated is viewed by others as a weather vane of the commander's judgment, fairness, and personal interest in his men. Of course goof-offs and eight-balls must not be tolerated. But there are also a few men of limited ability whose loyal, willing hearts can contribute something to their units above efficiency and beyond military skills. Thus, what happens to the Butch in your outfit may have a far-reaching effect on the esprit and sense of serving together that make men feel they are in the best damned company in the Army.

13

Your Mess Sergeant: An Important Man

SOLDIERS STILL LIKE to eat three times a day every day, as they did in my time, and if they don't eat well they are not happy. When I took command of Company F, 19th Infantry, in the late 1930s, the regimental commander told me there were problems he expected me to clear up. He was right, for I discovered more trouble than he knew about — and soon decided the first major move was to get another mess sergeant.

So I promoted second cook Katz to mess sergeant. Overnight there was a change of atmosphere in the mess hall and kitchen area, from a grumpy place to a cheerful one. A change for the better in chow was the main reason, but the personality of the new mess sergeant was important, too — an eager beaver who liked people.

As often happens, chance let me see which way our new mess leadership was leaning. Several days later, while approaching the kitchen serving table from a side door, I heard this exchange:

"Hey, Katzy," a soldier said loudly as he came up with his plate, "how about seconds on that goulash?"

"It's Sergeant Katz to you, soldier!" the new mess sergeant said sharply but without rancor, at the same time stepping forward and himself ladling out a generous helping of stew, making sure there were good hunks of meat in it.

"Thanks, sergeant," the soldier said, grinning.

This answered the only doubt I had about my mess sergeant. The fact that Sergeant Katz had been a fine cook would not alone make him a good mess sergeant, nor would his administrative ability and flair for planning meals be enough. He also needed certain intangible and undefinable qualities in his daily dealings with the company —a special type of low-key leadership to go with his "take charge" attitude to make them like it.

During my years as a division chief of staff in World War II, there were headaches within headaches, pressures great and small. But our division headquarters mess was a place where I could relax and enjoy my chow three times a day, without worries.

The two men mainly responsible for this were mess sergeants Shorty Scherer and Steve Stevenson. Like many fine soldiers who do their jobs superbly, it's not until later that you realize how much you owe them.

Of all the mess sergeants I knew, one holds a special place in my heart and memory: mess sergeant Long John Smith, in my first command. The first day I walked into his mess I didn't know I was meeting one of the finest soldiers in our Army. What I saw was a tall and rangy, rawboned sergeant in olive drab uniform.

"'Shun!" he announced, and gangled over in his loose-jointed way.

"Sergeant Smith reports to the company commander," he said, rigidly at attention as he saluted. Then, "Your mess sergeant, sir."

In those days we had a money allowance to run the mess. Long John did our buying and kept the records, so it was a measure of the man he was that throughout the company he was called Honest John. He never seemed to realize how much he was respected, still thinking of himself as the young farmer who had turned soldier in World War I.

One day I said to our first sergeant that maybe we should have hot tea during meals for those who might want it, with tea bags and hot water so each man could dunk his own.

The first sergeant doubted that soldiers would go for such a high-falutin' business, but he sent for Long John. The door to my office was open, so I heard the conversation.

"What's up, top?" Long John asked.

"The captain thinks we should have tea bags and hot water in the mess hall, for men who might want hot tea instead of coffee."

In the silence that followed I could imagine the puzzled and unbelieving look on Honest John's face as he stared back at the topkick, whom I knew was grinning back at him blandly. There was a slight scraping sound, like a man shifting from one foot to another.

"OK, top," Long John said finally, and I could almost see him gulp as he swallowed the idea. "The cap'n wants tea bags, we gonna have tea bags — tomorrow!" Then he added, "We'll have hot water in one of them coffee urns (only he said "coffee urines"), and a batch of them tea bags handy to it."

But loyalty and running a fine mess were not all there was to Sgt. Long John Smith. At Saturday inspections he was wearing the Distinguished Service Cross and Purple Heart, along with his World War I ribbon encrusted with battle stars.

Briefly, here is the story the first sergeant told me, for he too was a veteran of that time, nearly twenty years before, when young John Smith fought his way as an infantry soldier over some of the bloodiest battlefields in history with the famous 1st Infantry Division.

In one desperate battle, after his company officers and senior noncoms were killed or wounded, young John Smith took command of the remnants of his company and continued the attack for the rest of that flaming day. For this he got his DSC.

But that was not Long John's greatest pride, the first sergeant said. It was the day in an earlier battle that young Corporal Smith's squad had worked its way forward to a raised road that had to be crossed. The road was wide, pocked with craters from constant observed artillery shelling, and swept with machine-gun fire.

The tremendous responsibility for the lives of his men rested heavily on the young corporal. But he had orders to advance, and did not quail. That was his greatest pride: in his first battle test as an NCO he got every man in his squad safely across that ribbon of death.

Honest John was usually a teetotaler, but on special occasions — like Armistice Day or New Year's — if they could get an extra beer or two into him, he would relive that time again. To get him started one of the older noncoms would say, "John, tell us how you got your squad across that road in France."

It was (the first sergeant said) the damnedest thing you ever saw. The years would fall away and, before their eyes, mess sergeant Honest John Smith was gone and young Cpl. John Smith was staring this way and that over the battlefield.

He ordered his squad to stay down, shouted that each man would move only when and how he was told. Then he paused to study the enemy fire again before he said sharply, "Bronski, get ready," directed him which way to zig and zag in a desperate dash for life over the road, into a selected shell hole for protection on the far side, and shouted, "Go!" In turn, each man, by name, was given instructions, ordered across and into a good hole at "Go!" until, finally, young Smith himself leaped forward between bursting shells, across the road and into a muddy hole. Thus, all were over, safe.

This was the signal for one of our veteran noncoms to bring a final beer, saying, "OK, John, one for the road."

A subdued feeling always lingered in the mess hall, with kibitzers breaking up quietly, each man with his own thoughts, because they knew that's exactly the way it had been. They knew also, from company scuttlebutt, why Long John sat in unhappy silence when he drank that last beer; some of his squad who made it safely across that road never saw their homes again.

All too often we take our conscientious and efficient mess sergeants for granted, not realizing most of them would be equally outstanding in other less thankless assignments. Here are some reflections it is well to keep in mind:

- The mess sergeant (mess steward, if you prefer) holds a unique place in any company. How well he does his job affects every man in the company — personally, every day — to an extent true of no officer or other NCO.
- It's often difficult to get the right man as mess sergeant, not only because it's a tough and demanding job, but also because many good men try to avoid assignments where their best efforts are subjected to constant and unreasonable criticism.
- Everybody in the company needs and wants a good mess sergeant. So everybody in the company shares a responsibility: let *your* mess sergeant — and his cooks — know they are not on thankless jobs.

14

The Human Touch
in Command

SOLDIERS IN AUTHORITY, from squad leaders to the chief of staff of the Army, face the constant responsibility of influencing the future lives of individual men under them. At no level is this more true than among company commanders, who have complete command responsibility and direct personal contact with each man. Even a routine personnel action they make — or fail to make — may be a turning point in some soldier's life.

My memory file from five years as a company commander contains many case histories where I was directly concerned with turning points in the lives of my soldiers. Here are two of them.

When I assumed command of Company D, 19th Infantry, there was a private first class we'll call Roadbound, who had more than ten years of service. Most corporals were on their first enlistment and sergeants were relatively inexperienced, too. So I asked the first sergeant why Roadbound was not an NCO.

"He don't want the responsibility, Captain. Says he'd rather be a PFC. Also, he hits the booze, and maybe he thinks he can't handle stripes and the bottle too."

Since we had a vacancy for corporal — and it wasn't exactly unknown for a good soldier to tipple a little when off duty — I sent for PFC Roadbound. His weathered face had a somewhat resigned cast, though his gray eyes looked straight at you from both sides of a large reddish nose. But his passive expression came suddenly alive when I told him he was being promoted to corporal and squad leader.

"No, sir, Captain," he said in some haste. "I'm no NCO—and don't want to be one."

I explained it was the duty of every soldier to be ready to take over the next higher rank. If he was not willing to step up to corporal then he was failing in a basic requirement as a PFC. So I gave him a choice: to be a corporal, or get busted to "yardbird," which at that time meant going from thirty dollars per month back to twenty-one dollars. This made quite a difference in cash resources for bottled goods, a dollar being a dollar then.

"You can't do that, Captain!"

I said I not only could but would, unless he agreed to be a corporal. Also, that he had my permission to consult the division inspector general about the matter. He didn't see the IG, and was busted to yardbird.

Several months later another vacancy for corporal came up, and this time Private Roadbound said, "I'll try it, Captain."

He made a fine corporal—to his own surprise, I'm sure—and I had the satisfaction of seeing him wear sergeant's stripes within a a year. This was a major change of direction in his military career, and illustrates how turning points in a man's life may depend on someone else.

There are many angles to this command responsibility, like the time in Company G, 26th Infantry, that a letter arrived about a young recruit who had been with us six months. He was a good soldier, with a lively, likeable personality. I guess that personality may have been his undoing, because the letter said he had loved not wisely but too well—and then ran away from the result. Now he was wanted for child support.

When I called him in he admitted his paternity. Not sure what to do, I said I would look into the case further and talk with him again. And, in the process, I let him know that my opinion was not very high of a man who would get his girl in trouble, then run away and leave her to face the music alone.

Next morning the first sergeant brought in the morning report, along with the news that our involuntary father was AWOL.

"What in hell did he do that for?" was my unthinking reaction.

"Well, Captain," 1st Sgt. Big Jim Redding said quietly, "I guess the way he looked at it, there was no choice. And I don't think we will see him again."

I was chewed out by experts during my long service, but that was the worst bawling out I ever got; it hurt because I knew I had it coming. Instead of extending a helping hand to the young soldier, I had increased the pressure. He had run away from pressure before, so he ran again.

As Big Jim predicted, he never came back, so that was a turning point that changed his whole life. When I could have offered advice and counsel I failed, and have had to live with that memory, often wondering what became of him and what difference it might have made in his life and that of the girl and their child had I shown more human understanding.

Of course, war brings with it turning points for every man in uniform. Success or failure in battle is a major turning point in any soldier's military career, and I learned of one such case recently from a veteran of hard fighting in Vietnam. He was a highly decorated captain, who had been commissioned from the ranks and commanded a company in combat. We found an immediate plane of mutual interest as former company commanders. So we swapped experiences with soldiers in our companies, and that's when he told me about the man we'll call Lieutenant Steele.

"He was commissioned from Officer's Candidate School," the captain said, "and reported to my company in Vietnam as a replacement. He wasn't interested in his men or in taking care of them, and said frankly he had taken a commission just to get more money.

"Naturally, I gave him a hard time and tried to make him shape up. But he drifted along, doing only enough to get by. More than once I told Steele straight out he just didn't have it, and would never make a platoon leader."

The captain was silent, remembering, and his voice turned a little husky. "Then," he said, "our battalion got into a knock-down-drag-out battle. In fact, we were almost surrounded, fighting to live.

"That's when Lieutenant Steele's platoon was hit heavy, one of his squads cut off, and he went out himself to get it back. When I crawled over to check the situation he was crawling back, after covering the return of his squad—and we met nose to nose on the ground."

The captain paused again, and I knew he was reliving that battle moment. "Before I could say anything," the captain continued, "Lieutenant Steele said to me, 'Well, do you think I'll ever make a platoon leader now?'

"What I replied, if anything, I don't remember. But I do remember throwing my arm around his neck and hugging him to me like a brother, right there with our noses in the dirt."

The captain looked at me and added, "You know, I like to think the way I raised hell with him — even told him he'd never make it as a platoon leader unless he learned to take better care of his men — may have had a little to do with how he met his battle test. From that day on there never was a better platoon leader. Always on the ball, always with his men. So later, in another fight, when I was hit bad and being evacuated, I turned over command to him with complete confidence — being sure he would take good care of our company. And he did."

There are many kinds of turning points, and Lieutenant Steele was not the first soldier to find the right fork in the road after coming face to face with himself and his responsibilities for others in battle. In his case, as often happens, although he made the big play at the critical moment himself, in my score book I credit the captain with an "assist" too. Sometimes censure is the right approach. That's why leadership is an art; you can't make exact rules for it. You've got to have the touch — the human touch.

Some comments about turning points are:

- Most of us are concerned about the turning points in our own lives. But every good soldier in authority should be just as concerned with his responsibility to help those under him make the right turns.
- When taking command and administrative action, no matter how heavy your work load or how minor the decision, it is never a small or routine matter if the result may be a turning point in a soldier's life.
- It is easy to decide "in the best interest of the service" where money and materials are involved. When men are concerned, however, commanders must be perceptive and alert to see the turning points for individuals. It's like finding four-leaf clovers; they're always there, but you must look for them. Otherwise you may crush them underfoot unaware.

15
Personal Etiquette and Professional Good Manners

SEVERAL YEARS AGO, I visited Fort Benning and bought a pamphlet at the book store titled, *Etiquette*. It is the best of its kind I have seen, much better than thick books on the subject. Under "Social Calls" I found this admonition: "Do not remain less than fifteen minutes or more than thirty minutes . . ." (unless, of course, they happen to be personal friends).

That sounds simple enough, especially when augmented further: "When the time is up—rise, thank the host and hostess, and depart promptly. If an officer is accompanied by his wife, she should rise first to indicate the departure. Avoid lingering conversations."

To that I can add "amen," for not knowing when to go home, or how to get started, is a frequently violated rule of courtesy. Sometimes the trouble seems to be that young couples fail to arrange a signal for the husband to give his lady that says, "Time to go, dear. So on your feet—and remember, you do not have to wait for a complete lull in the conversation before you rise."

Sometimes the lady may fail to see the high-sign or, if she is having a pleasant visit, may ignore it. The Benning booklet does not cover that contretemps, so I'll give you the solution: slowly place your feet in preparing to rise yourself; in most instances, the little woman will beat you to it.

I can't add anything further, so I will proceed to what I believe is even more important: professional good manners in dealing with others in your military duties.

One of the basic elements of good manners for an officer is the return of all salutes. Nothing improves the saluting within your company more than to have every officer meticulously return every salute.

Which recalls the time I was traffic officer in the Hawaiian Division's military police at Schofield Barracks. The policy of our division commander, Maj. Gen. William H. Wilson, was stated by him in talks to newly joined officers: "We do not fix traffic tickets—we fix the drivers."

With that as my guideline, all verified traffic violations were forwarded through channels. Not surprisingly, the drivers sometimes got mad at me—especially those who walked a while to improve their driving skill. One of these, a chubby, middle-aged captain, became my first life-long enemy. This was evident when, on the sidewalk near the post exchange, he stared directly at me and refused to return my salute. This was a man-bites-dog situation because, though only a lieutenant, I could report him for that—but his name wasn't Hatfield and mine wasn't McCoy, so I let it go. (Besides, to have reported him would have lowered me to his level.)

Saluting is like many other things—you don't appreciate its value until it is omitted as a deliberate act of discourtesy, or after you lose the privilege to give or receive it. On my visit to Benning I passed many soldiers and officers on the streets, and we ignored each other as strangers—because I was in civilian clothes. So, naturally, they did not salute me and, though I wanted to salute every one of them, that was no longer the thing to do. I truly missed that exchange of soldierly greetings; it took an effort of will to keep my right arm at my side.

Another basic military courtesy is that the junior walks on the left of his senior. Over twenty-five years ago, a young major came to Carlisle Barracks as a guest speaker at the Armed Forces Information School there. After the major's talk, as we left Grant Hall, a personable young captain clattered down the steps and fell in step with the major—on the right.

The captain was merely thoughtless, meaning no discourtesy. But I was impressed not only with the major's awareness of military protocol, but that he exercised his responsibility to courteously require it of the captain. So, in the years that followed, I watched with interest and admiration the outstanding military career of that young major — who is now Lt. Gen. Benjamin O. Davis, USAF, retired.

There are countless less formalized situations calling for good military manners. They are not classified and summarized in manuals, nor can they ever be, but they require constant perceptive alertness to see opportunities to apply good manners in your military service.

When I suddenly found myself wearing eagles as a division chief of staff in World War II, the three infantry regimental commanders were some eight to ten years older than I. This called for certain niceties in my dealings with them, like the first time I recall having to phone one of them.

When a staff captain answered and reported his colonel not in the headquarters, I said, "Will you please call and let me know when he returns?"

Not long afterward the phone rang and the older colonel's voice drawled, "Newman, I understand you wanted me to call you."

"That is not correct, Colonel," was my reply. "I asked Captain Soandso to call and let me know when you returned."

That captain was a very able officer in many ways, but he never became a general officer. Certainly, I do not say his failure to follow my instructions, probably because he missed the significance of the courtesy point involved, was any great dereliction. But I do believe it was a straw in the wind of his future.

When Gen. Walter Krueger, one of the great army commanders of World War II, had lunch with our division in the headquarters officers' mess near Rockhampton in Australia, he asked to see the mess sergeant before leaving. He then told the sergeant he had enjoyed his lunch, and thanked him — thus showing the same good manners expected of any guest.

To return to the company, the matter of professional courtesy comes up in many ways. For example, in consideration of the privacy due the men of my company, I never entered the dayroom or their living quarters during off-duty hours unless there was some compelling reason to do so.

One of the most important elements of professional good manners is to be on time — not only in keeping appointments with senior officers but in keeping appointments in your own company. How often have you seen a company fall in for drill, the first sergeant take the report — and the company have to wait for a young captain to come strolling out late?

During field operations it is standard procedure for company officers to see that their men are fed before they themselves sit down to eat. In a very real sense the company commander is like any host responsible for feeding a number of guests; his first duty is to see they are served before he himself puts on the nosebag.

In my first year as a company commander we received a recruit (call him Private Jittery) shortly before beginning preliminary marksmanship training, preparatory to firing our Springfield rifles for record. During the aiming exercise of "making triangles" I was standing some yards away when Jittery made his first triangle — but close enough to hear his newly promoted corporal say, "That's a lousy triangle. You'll have to do better than that!" — and he walked off.

As I started that way, Sergeant Stinson beat me to it, and said to Private Jittery, "You're doing something wrong, kid, so we'll find out what it is. You can do a lot better."

In my turn I walked away, knowing things were in good hands. But when the drill period was over I said to Stinson, "You need a private heart-to-heart talk with Corporal Newstripes."

"That's right, Captain," the sergeant said. "And I'll do it today."

There are innumerable ways that polite consideration of others can make a unit better and happier. Here are some general comments:

- Professional courtesy and good manners should be carefully integrated parts of your command and leadership principles, both up and down. This is not incompatible with forcefulness and it is just as important in civilian life as it is in military service.
- Do not leave this to chance. Every man in authority, from squad leader on up, should be alert to avoid thoughtless or careless discourtesy toward those serving under him. Keeping men waiting is a fundamental discourtesy; and if you are unavoidably late, a brief explanation is in order.
- Nothing in good manners can serve as an excuse for poor discipline and mediocre standards. When the

boom needs to be lowered, lower it. But in demanding top standards and maintaining high discipline, unnecessary harshness and dogmatic orders can be self-defeating. Far better results are obtained when due consideration is given to what Richard Whately said more than a hundred years ago: "Manner is one of the greatest engines of influence ever given to man."

16
Standards for Bachelors

WHILE ON ACTIVE service I lived for years in bachelor officers'
quarters (BOQ), being a member of that often discriminated-against
minority. Like everything else in the Army, BOQ are bigger and
better now, but some aspects of life there have not changed much.
Thus my experience as a retread bachelor at Plattsburg Barracks,
New York in the late 1930s may still have some relevancy today.

Having just been promoted to captain after ten years as a lieutenant, I decided to make a pitch on arrival to the effect that it was not
in keeping with my long service and exalted rank to be relegated to
the post BOQ. With this in mind, I reported to our regimental commander, an impressive white-haired officer wearing the ribbons of
distinguished combat service in World War I.

He welcomed me into the 26th Infantry, reminded me of the great
battle heritage of both regiment and division, then announced that
I would be provost marshal. That was a disappointment, as I had
hoped to be a company commander. But he granted my request to
live off post, away from young bachelors in the BOQ—a pleasant
surprise.

I found a small apartment in the town of Plattsburg and resumed
my study of writing. One evening I decided to try poetry, and
planned to establish an atmosphere for the effort. So I put on a pair
of black corduroy slacks, midnight-blue shirt, white belt and tie, red
morocco bedroom slippers, and a blue silk brocade dressing gown.
With a rhyming dictionary on the small table by the easy chair, I

poured a glass of sherry, lit a good cigar, and settled down for an evening with the muse.

At this point there was a sharp knock on the apartment door. I opened it, to admit my distinguished regimental commander, come to call in full uniform.

The colonel accepted a seat in the easy chair. His hard gray eyes noted the rhyming dictionary, inventoried my attire piece by piece, flicked from the glass of sherry to the cigar label. In fact, he missed nothing. He didn't stay long either. (Later, his eyes always had a speculative look whenever he saw me.)

After several months of peace and quiet in my nice apartment, we got a new regimental commander. One of his first acts was to order me on the post into the BOQ to ride herd on some twenty-nine bachelors there, twenty-six of them with one year of service or less.

Being King of the Bachelors (KOB) was simply taking over as reigning SOB in the BOQ at one end of the parade ground, in addition to being supervising SOB in the guardhouse at the other end. When word gets around, however, that the new KOB will stand for no funny business, especially where alcohol and romance are concerned, life in the BOQ smooths out.

The professional tone of a BOQ is similar to soldierly standards of military courtesy and dress in a company: either poor or excellent. There's no middle ground, and one of the places to set and maintain the standard is at meals. In my first brief talk to the young denizens of the BOQ, I made this clear, emphasizing things like uniform regulations, military courtesy, and customs of the service—to include strict observance of the rule that a lady's name should never be mentioned in a gentleman's mess.

Lessons for young shavetails can be taught by indirection, too, as when one of the recruit Thomason Act lieutenants had trouble with his tuxedo tie. He first went to one of the Regular Army lieutenants for assistance, who in turn passed him along to me. Controlling my first impulse, I said, "Well, I use a ready-made myself, but I just came from the officers' club bar at the end of the hall. That bald-headed, heavy-set major in there having a martini used to run a haberdashery. He can really tie it for you."

So the budding young officer trooped down to the club bar with his tie hanging loose, walked up to the heavy-set major and said, "Major, I understand you used to run a haberdashery, and . . ."

What the major tied was about as big and loud a king-sized knot in that lieutenant's tail as the witnesses ever heard. Things like that get around, and do more to bring shavetails up right than hours of lectures.

Of course, BOQ are always of special interest to some ladies on the post—those with long noses and agile tongues. This was soon brought home to me at a social function when a major's wife remarked rather coyly that I sure kept late hours. The thought finally percolated through my mind that the lady had somehow learned which rooms I occupied, and had noticed my lights burning late— and was surmising I might not be alone.

To my reply that I sometimes fell asleep reading, thus my light burned until I awakened and turned it off, she gave me the old lifted eye brow and quiet-smile, "says *you*" treatment. When, later, another field-grade officer's wife made a similar observation, with comparable results, it seemed time to take defensive action.

So I bought a frosted red light globe, and placed it in a lamp near my most visible window. This was left burning all night every night for several months, and I heard nothing more about my late hours.

Of course the mess is always a problem. Unless the BOQ is operated in conjunction with an officers' club, the food is apt to be on the debatable side—and sometimes then, too. The secret is simple: get a good cook and establish mess records so that you get what you pay for; also, periodically, ask the mess officer the right questions to make sure he is on the job.

But the KOB is going to get beefs (pardon me) about the chow, no matter how good it is. So before long one of the first lieutenants came up with some improvements he thought I could make in the mess. To begin with, having just taken his turn at auditing the mess records for the month, he thought we were paying for more brandy than we tasted as food seasoning, and suggested that the ruddy tint of the cook's nose might explain the discrepancy.

"Well," I said, "maybe we should remember what President Lincoln said when told General Grant was an intemperate user of alcohol. In this case, so long as we eat the kind of food we've been getting fat on for one dollar and ten cents a day, it's not worth rocking the boat over an extra bottle of brandy and the color of the cook's nose."

Then, warming to my subject, I continued, "But I appreciate your active interest. Our mess officer is young and has much to learn, and we need an older, more experienced officer with ideas, so . . .''

"Oh, *no!*" he said, backing toward the door, "I wouldn't want to deprive our young mess officer of the fine experience he's getting. Besides, I like the mess just as it is—including the color of the cook's nose."

If it wasn't one thing it was another, for three years. But I lived through it—though my nice, smooth disposition became permanently wrinkled. Looking back to those days of my residence among the discriminated-against minority, these thoughts come to mind which the electronic age, the nuclear era and mutation haircuts have not changed.

- It is both hypocritical and unrealistic to believe that young officers can uphold a standard of discipline in their companies which they themselves do not live by. This is not a moral point, but is the foundation of our military way of life. Being a good soldier, in BOQ as elsewhere, is a kind of religion in itself.
- Many married servicemen harbor the idea that there is nothing wrong with bachelors that marriage can't cure. They fail to understand that while BOQ are not seminaries, neither are they havens for lost souls awaiting the salvation of marriage.
- Times and customs change, but basic standards remain. The old common law that "a man's home is his castle" should apply to bachelor housing as much as to married quarters, because BOQ remain what they were in my time: the home where unmarrieds live—the only place they have to live. Conversely, it is important that bachelors, no less than married officers, guard the good name of their home. If they abdicate this obligation they invite the command supervision it is so popular these days to rail against.

17

Getting Ahead Though Wed

UNLESS THINGS HAVE changed since my day, young bachelors in uniform tend to have tunnel vision when selecting a bride, giving little thought to related considerations—like how will she work out as an Army wife? Somebody ought to discuss this question, but Ann Landers, Dear Abby, and their sister dispensers of free advice are not qualified. So that leaves it up to me. My duty was made clear in a letter from the wife of a young lieutenant, who said she just *had* to talk to *somebody* who would understand.

Her husband loved the Army, she said, and was happy and proud when commissioned from officer candidate school. Apparently there was no incompatibility about their duty to posterity, since she was in that well-known delicate condition. The trouble was that her husband had gone off on detached service for six weeks, leaving her alone.

He had asked for the special course of study, but the Army wouldn't pay the cost for her to go along, too. On a second lieutenant's pay they couldn't afford the extra expense, and her husband failed in his duty to her by not getting his orders rescinded. Worse yet, he was being ordered overseas where she could not go, which would leave her all alone with their baby for at least a year.

So he would just have to get out of the Army, and she was going to make him do it. Now that she had written to me she felt better, because she knew I would understand.

I did understand, but there was nothing I could do about it — because the lady did not sign her name.

She was making a big mistake which, whether or not her husband left the Army, would bring them both unhappiness. The young lieutenant had made a mistake, too; he should not have assumed she would accept Army life. This should have been thoroughly discussed and settled between them before marriage.

Unfortunately, this is no rare incident among enlisted ranks and officers. So, as Ann Landers or Dear Abby might put it, "Before you marry her, kiddo, make sure she knows it's a design for living — that she's marrying the Army too."

Some forty years ago my regiment had a formal dinner dance while my battalion commander was away. As a grass bachelor, and one of his company commanders, I escorted his wife to the function. During the evening I made some remark about how unfortunate it was that Army wives were often duty widows.

"Oh," she said, "it's not so bad. Henry told me about that before we were married. He said he was a soldier, so it was important for me to be sure I wanted to be a soldier's wife. He also said he would make the decisions affecting his duty and military service — from how long he stayed in his office after duty hours, to what military assignments and stations he requested."

Her eyes had the misty, faraway look of pleasant memories, and she continued, "I said that was fine with me, for him to be the officer and for me to be the Army wife. So I kiss him goodbye when he leaves, welcome him home when he returns, and never compete with the Army and his sense of duty for his time. And it's worked out fine." In this way she shared in his success when he later reached high rank.

In another regiment I was senior officer in the bachelor officers' quarters, where we became a special project of our regimental commander's wife — who said we needed a "feminine touch" in our BOQ. Things came to a head when she decided we should fire our regular mess attendants and replace them with others, including two females.

The colonel was a dynamic and forceful officer, but she was an equally strong personality with a tendency to reach for the reins. This may explain why there was a nervous tension about him, which was more than usually noticeable when I arrived in his office to "reclama" the idea of firing our BOQ mess people.

After he listened for a while he said, "Captain Newman, why don't you just let me have my way?" Then he tapped a pencil on the desk, looked up at me and smiled as he added, "Besides, you know I must live with my wife."

So we tried integrating females into our BOQ mess kitchen, with results that were as disconcerting to our CO as they were diverting to us—until we changed back again. In the years since, I have wondered how much difference there might have been in our CO's professional career had he established the same decision-making procedures in his personal headquarters as the battalion commander mentioned above.

In more recent years I knew a colonel slated for a command in an area where family living conditions were not good. His wife objected so strongly that he asked that his assignment be changed. Thus he got a staff job with a nice house in a cushy living area—and was never offered another command. He never reached star rank, either, though he was a superior officer and must have come very close. His lack of command duty could have tipped the scales against him—though, in my view, it goes deeper than that. Something happens inside an officer that sabotages his self-confidence when his wife assumes command review prerogatives over his decision-making judgment in military matters.

Of course, there are spheres of influence where the lady's wishes should prevail. Like the time many years ago when a lieutenant we'll call Harry went out for a night with the boys. They played cards, there were colored chips for keeping score and arrangements to insure the players did not suffer from thirst.

The evening went so well it was after three in the morning when Harry got home, in time to change into field uniform and have a four o'clock breakfast before leaving to join his unit for an all-day field exercise. His wife (call her Agnes) fixed a nice breakfast: orange juice, scrambled eggs and bacon, toast and coffee. But he would eat nothing, just had several cups of black coffee.

He then strapped on his field equipment, took the lunchbox Agnes handed him, and left for the exercise. By noon Harry was hungry, so he lost no time opening his lunchbox—to find a jumbled mass of scrambled eggs, bacon and toast, just as his ever-loving had scraped them into the box from his untouched breakfast plate.

As Agnes explained later, "When I get up and cook a four-o'clock breakfast, I expect it to be eaten."

Now either Ann Landers or Dear Abby could have advised Harry to eat that breakfast, and I agree with them — for the decision not to eat breakfast was that of a grumpy, unappreciative husband with an incipient hangover, and had nothing to do with the responsibilities of an officer. On the other hand, Agnes had played her part as a good Army wife, and was staging a legitimate, symbolic protest by means of the lunchbox. That it had no damaging effect on Harry's professional psyche is evident by the fact he retired as a multi-starred general.

Countless incidents come to mind, from personal observations and grapevine reports, of how wives helped or hurt their husband's careers. Further, all ARMY readers — especially those who are married — have their own collection of experiences, observations and hearsay evidence. Each can thus formulate his own set of "Rules for Success in the Army, Though Married." Here are my comments:

- A Scottish poet wrote, "Steel-blue and blade-straight the great Artificer made my mate." And, also, "Teacher, tender comrade, wife, a fellow-farer, true through life." These are admirable specifications, but if you are a bachelor and are going to make the Army your career, before signing up with a lifetime running mate, ask yourself, "Can she take it? Will she make a good Army wife?"

- Many senior officers have attractive wives, which raises the question: did marrying these charming ladies get them selected for high rank, or was it because they started out smart that they picked those nice ladies. Well, it's like handicapping race horses: winners are always good horses, but sometimes a fine horse can be so heavily handicapped that some other horse not quite so good but less handicapped wins out. The difference is that horses can't control the weight they must carry, but a young Army bachelor handicaps himself in the rank sweepstakes if he picks the wrong partner.

- For a serviceman the chance of picking the right lady will be much better if he follows the advice of my former battalion commander: make sure she knows you're a soldier, and will remain a soldier. Also that she's certain she wants to be a soldier's wife — which includes an understanding of and willingness to let her husband make the decisions affecting his duty and military career.

18

Today's Contacts Can Influence Your Future

ONE OF MY friends arrived at Fort Benning in the late 1920s for his first duty station, and was assigned to the 29th Infantry. On entering the orderly room he handed the first sergeant a copy of his orders and introduced himself.

The grizzled old first sergeant glanced at the orders and looked carefully at his brand new lieutenant. Then he asked, "Lieutenant, was your father Col. Initials Soandso?"

"He sure was, Sergeant," my friend replied.

"Oh, Lord, Lieutenant!" the old topkick said, throwing his head back and laughing, "I wish I had a dollar for every time I've paddled your little behind. I used to be your daddy's orderly!"

This illustrates the fact that your personal contacts today may, in some unforeseen way at some future time, operate to either haunt or anoint you.

At Fort Benning there was another lieutenant, junior to me, who took himself and his career seriously. Also, he was on the stuffy side, with a tendency to pontificate. At that time I was pretty much of a jockstrap soldier, playing on several athletic teams and coaching others. One day my stuffy friend took me to task for this.

"Red," he said, "if you don't get out of all this jockstrap business you will never be a general."

"Well," was my reply, "that will make two of us."

Years later I remembered that conversation, and wondered if he did, too—when he was writing an efficiency report on me as my commanding general.

In my chapter "Forge of Experience" (chapter 7), I related how in 1930 I came out of the Manila Hotel bar, and fell off the dance floor onto the table of Maj. Gen. Douglas MacArthur—thus having a silent eyeball-to-eyeball confrontation over the end of my cigar at a range of two feet. Also included was the fact that two days later, perhaps fortunately, I left the Philippines to attend the Cavalry School at Fort Riley, Kansas.

Sometimes it does not take long for the past to catch up with you, for within months General MacArthur was designated as chief of staff of the Army. Post headquarters at Riley received word the new chief of staff would stop on his way to Washington, and address all officers in the post theater.

Whereupon headquarters notified me that in view of my recent return from his Philippines command, I was designated as his local aide. The word came by phone, so I hot-footed it to headquarters and told them about my silent confrontation with our new chief of staff over the end of my cigar. So they relieved me of my aide duties.

My efforts to keep out of sight were not entirely successful, because his aide, Captain T. J. Davis (since retired as a brigadier general) singled me out at the theater.

"Newman," he said, "you got out of the Philippines in good time. The Old Man had told me to get you by the ear and straighten you out before you got in trouble."

This is a glimpse of the human side of the man I consider the most brilliant military commander in our history, and the greatest American to live in my lifetime. He could just as easily have told his aide to call my regimental commander, which might have resulted in a hangover in writing on my record.

Sometimes a contact may come back in an unexpected fashion from a junior. In one company I commanded, a sergeant was having a bottle problem and otherwise not measuring up. So when his time came to reenlist, I told him to find a new home—and did not hear from him again for ten years.

Then one night my phone rang in Arlington, Virginia, where I lived while attending the National War College. It was the sergeant, calling from an Army post several hundred miles away, wanting to come see me. He arrived the next evening, with a problem: his health was failing, and he could retire—if he could get credit for a couple of years' service in the Navy. The trouble was that he had deserted from the Navy and so was afraid of what might happen if he claimed his Navy service.

Fortunately, I knew Col. William H. ("Big Bill") Biggerstaff was then on duty in the Pentagon. I had known Big Bill when he was a sergeant in my first regiment, and also as a captain in the 24th Infantry Division. So I said to my visitor, "I do not know the answer, but I do know the man who can straighten things out if anybody can."

Big Bill did just that, because the statute of limitations had run out on that Navy enlistment dereliction. So a chain of double contacts from years back, resulted in a solution for my former sergeant and enabled him to retire.

All these things come under the heading of human relations, for that is what personal contacts add up to. Often these are not single incidents, but an accumulation of routine contacts, like an experience I had in Hawaii in 1940.

One evening I attended a cocktail supper at an officer's home. You could get a highball on request, but they were pushing some sort of smooth-tasting tiger's milk with honey and sherry in it. So I had a few, and soon found myself feeling unusually healthy. Remembering what sherry could do if you drink enough of it—which I had learned the hard way—it seemed time to go home to my off-post cottage in Wahiawa.

Whether it was the sherry or the honey, I'm not sure, but when I turned left on Macomb Road I didn't twist the wheel enough and so bumped the curb at the right. This caused me to overcorrect, ending on the left side of the road as I approached the MP gate to leave the post. Quickly correcting that, I reached for the light switch to dim my lights for the MPs at the gate—but managed instead to turn them off.

Naturally, I reached in some haste to correct that—and hit the horn button. This series of events motivated the gate MP to step out and stop my car. He then walked around to see who was driving, and stood looking at me a moment in some indecision, for I had been going through that gate several times a day for the past year.

"Sir," he said finally, "do you think you can make it?"

"Yes," I replied gravely, "I think so."

"OK, sir," he said, stepping back and saluting smartly.

As you will recognize, that was a fine disciplined soldier, of good judgment. For the next year we shared a quiet friendship, always exchanging remembering smiles with our salutes when I came through his gate.

These unrelated incidents, when you look at them as a whole, bring out the fact that human relations today can have unanticipated good or bad aftereffects — sometimes years later. Four comments appear relevant:

- During the year preceding my erratic approach to Macomb Gate I had always dimmed my lights for the MP at night, and made a point of giving MPs as good a salute as they gave me. It never occurred to me this could be bread upon the waters of military life that would come back to me in time of need. But I am sure this was a factor in saving me from an official report that evening when I had too many of those honey-spiked drinks.
- To keep your human relations on an even keel often requires perception and thought. But this does not require you to be a soft-soap patsy, nor does it mean you should accept below-par standards. I like to remember that when my former sergeant needed advice and help from someone he could trust to be fair and reasonable, he turned to the former captain who had kicked him out of his company ten years before.
- Good human relations is nothing more or less than enlightened self interest. The man you served with as a lieutenant may be a member of the promotion board when your name comes up for selection to star rank. In my case, I served closely as a junior with five men who later wrote efficiency reports on me as my commanding generals.
- You cannot see into the future, and you can't go around buttering up everybody. But your personal presence and professional posture today in contacts with others will either shadow or brighten your tomorrow. Jean Paul Richter said it this way: "Men, like bullets, go farthest when they are smoothest."

19

The Best Course Is Frankness

ONE MORNING FIRST Sergeant Bonesteel (we'll call him), two sergeants and a corporal in my first company showed up looking like they had met a meat grinder in a dark alley some place. The grapevine gave me the story.

Sergeant Bonesteel—short on education, but long on soldierly ability—had decided, "They ain't giving me no cooperation."

So the previous afternoon he loaded them in his touring car, drove to a remote area on the post, and took them on man to man—one at a time, in order of rank, beginning with the senior duty sergeant. He was a bit leg-weary when he got around to the young corporal, who gave the old man as good as he got.

But from that time on he got plenty of "cooperation."

Few human relations problems can be solved so simply and directly—and I do not recommend First Sergeant Bonesteel's method. But meeting an issue squarely, substituting straight talk for fisticuffs, can save a lot of trouble in your military human relations.

Later I was transferred to Company D, 29th Infantry. On the second day First Sergeant Hildreth stopped me in the company street.

"Lieutenant," he said, "you have Corporal Soandso in your platoon, and he is a wise-guy type. If he gives you any trouble, let me know."

He then saluted, and went into the orderly tent.

Sergeant Hildreth was one of those top-flight topkicks of the Old Army. He did not wait to "get to know me," nor did he work up to what he wanted to say in a roundabout fashion. In those two simple direct sentences he was saying:

"Lieutenant, I have been around a long time, and you are new to this business. Also, I know the men in this company, and Corporal Soandso will give you trouble in little ways if he thinks he can get away with it. I'm giving you this warning, as soldier-to-soldier, and know you will take it that way. If you need help or advice in handling him or anybody else, just call on me."

That gave me added confidence in taking over a platoon of strangers. And sure enough, the next day Corporal Soandso started using foul language within my hearing. Being forewarned, I recognized this as his opening gambit to see how far he could push me around. So I called his hand. After that we got along fine — thanks to some straight talk from Sergeant Hildreth.

There is no limit to the variety of situations where a little direct talk can ease the pressure. Like the time in 1941 when I jumped from company commander to G-2 of the Hawaiian Division.

I had never before breathed such high-level, rarified air and was uncertain how I would measure up. Several staff officers were old enough to be my father, and their experienced poise overawed me. In fact I had to resist a tendency to tiptoe in the hallways.

After reporting to the commanding general and the chief of staff, I went to my office and began trying to figure out what I was supposed to do. I read standing orders and emergency plans, then delved into current files and manuals on staff procedures, especially those dealing with G-2.

I had no officer assistant, but on the third day my chief clerk, Tech. Sgt. Kennard S. Vandergrift, came into my office.

"Captain," he asked, "do you know who my best friend is?"

When I admitted my ignorance, he said, "Well, he is Kennard Vandergrift, but my next best friend is Captain Newman — as long as he is my section chief."

From one end of the Army to the other I found these veteran NCOs with wise eyes and the confidence of experience. They were loyal, alert, of high character, and felt responsible for their officers. Also, they had a simple and direct way of talking soldier-to-soldier that is the foundation of mutual understanding and trust so vital in military operations — command or staff, from the squad level up, peace or in war.

In the last year of World War II I got out of a stateside hospital and rejoined the 24th Infantry Division on Mindanao in the Southern Philippines campaign. My duty assignment was chief of staff again, under a division commander I had never seen before: Maj. Gen. Roscoe B. Woodruff.

He greeted me with a cordial handshake, saying, "Hello, Red. I've heard a lot about you, and am happy to have you as my chief of staff."

That's the way he was, straight and direct. He said what he liked and what he did not like, which makes life a lot simpler. Especially for a chief of staff.

When our drive reached the town of Davao, and turned inland on Mindanao, we established our command post on the edge of the Gulf of Davao. The division commander's tent was near the sandy beach, and some miscellaneous people — including native civilians — wandered right in front of his tent.

"Red," he said one night after supper, "put a stop to those drifters straggling around my tent."

So I issued orders to the headquarters commandant, telling him to coordinate with the provost marshal.

In mid-morning the next day, when I arrived with papers for his decision and instructions, the CG greeted me with, "Those people are still wandering around my tent, and I want it stopped."

So I called the headquarters commandant and provost marshal to my office, and told them to review their straggler control measures immediately, and make needed changes.

About an hour after lunch, on his way to the front, General Woodruff stopped twenty yards from my office tent and in a strong voice of command said, "Red, for the third time: I want drifters kept away from my tent — and I don't want to have to say it again."

No sweat, no reason to get uptight — just do what the man says. Now everybody in headquarters had the picture. When the headquarters commandant and provost marshal arrived at my office tent they knew what the problem was. So I told them if the matter came up again, I would personally establish a sentry system — and they would be on the guard roster.

This in no way disturbed my relations with the CG, for I never had pleasanter service anywhere than my tour as his chief of staff. When he liked something, he said so; and when he wanted something done, that is what he wanted done.

In 1952 I pinned on my first star as assistant division commander of the 82d Airborne Division. Some months later we got a new division commander. He had gone airborne before World War II, became one of the youngest generals in the war, and now wore two stars; but he had graduated from West Point nine years after I did.

One of his first acts was to call me in and say, "We might as well get this straight: if you object to serving under me, just say so and I'll ask for you to be reassigned."

I looked at him in surprise, and replied, "General, I would rather have this job than any in the Army, and would like to stay here as your assistant division commander. But if you don't want me, then, of course, it is your prerogative to ask for my reassignment."

The result was that instead of standing off and sniffing at each other like two strange dogs, that short and direct talk laid the foundation for working together in harmony.

I could cite many more times where straight talk was valuable but, curiously, it is hard to describe those cases where the absence of directness led to trouble. The silence and evasions, which breed suspicions and misunderstandings that lead to distrust, are nebulous. But they are there when you cannot look a man in the face and lay your cards on the table. These comments appear pertinent:

- In the direct approach, as in everything else, you can overdo it. There is no substitute for empathy — for understanding the viewpoints and situations of others — when deciding how direct you can be in your dealings with others.
- Long service in staff assignments inclines one toward "diplomatic" dealings with others. The result is that weasel words and on-the-fence attitudes make it harder to face issues with plain, simple, straight talk.
- On the other hand, duty with troops builds a direct manner in dealing with others. That is why too much staff duty makes it harder for an officer to be a good commander; and, conversely, it is one of the reasons why command duty with troops is so important to your military career.
- Finally, I suggest this guideline: when someone faces you directly with an unexpected issue that is disconcerting, keep in mind the old axiom: take no offense where none is meant.

20

When, Why, How to Qualify as an Expert

A WIDELY CIRCULATED definition of an expert is an SOB with a briefcase who is more than a hundred miles from home. This leaves a lot of unanswered questions: should you be an expert and, if so, in what? How do you qualify as an expert? What is the difference between a theoretical expert and a functional expert? Are there any inherent limitations on the expertness of experts?

My first understanding of how to make yourself an expert came at West Point. During the winter months each plebe fired a ten-shot familiarization course on the indoor rifle range, and my friend Bill (now a retired brigadier general) was low man on the totem pole, his score including several misses. But when he fired for record the following summer, Bill not only qualified as an expert rifleman, but was high man in his battalion.

The explanation was simple: Bill decided not just to get himself out of the "bolo" class, but to qualify as an expert. So every night before going to bed he got down on the floor with his 1903 Springfield rifle for fifteen minutes of self-imposed marksmanship training. He practiced trigger squeeze, correct breathing, aiming, firing positions, sling adjustments and rapid-fire exercises.

With this preparation he made expert rifleman in a walk. Later, as an officer, he was a member of the Army Rifle Team for the National Rifle Matches at Camp Perry. This illustrates how you can become an expert in almost anything—if you work and study and train and practice.

86

Sometimes, however, tenacity and effort are not enough to make you an expert in a specialized field, if you have an inherent limitation. Consider the time in 1934 in Hawaii when I was detailed to put on a half-hour musical radio broadcast, a field in which I had no experience. Things seemed to work out better for lieutenants if they just said, "Yes, sir!" So that is what I said—and set out to make myself an expert in producing a half-hour musical radio broadcast.

Where does the limitation come in? When the orchestra completed the closing musical medley, and we went off the air, I said to the orchestra leader, "It's too bad you did not get around to playing, 'The Song of the Islands' for the fade-out as planned."

He looked at me in astonishment and replied, "Lieutenant, that is what we thought we just finished playing!"

You see, I have the feel of rhythm in marching music, but I am tone deaf. That was an inherent limitation to my ever being an expert in producing musical shows, radio or otherwise. This also brings out another point: all of us have more natural abilities in some areas than in others, so we should channel our efforts into fields for which we are best suited.

After World War I, I was among the combat-experienced officers assembled at Fort Sill to consider whether changes were needed in our artillery support. During one discussion an artillery officer proposed that we do away with the 105mm howitzer because the 155mm howitzer could do the job for both of them. He said this would simplify training, reduce supply problems, and result in money savings.

Whereupon I took the floor, as a former regimental commander supported by artillery in combat, and agreed that his proposal was desirable from the viewpoint of those back where the guns were fired. But from the viewpoint of front-line troops where the shells landed, I could not agree, because I had been close to bursts of both 105mm and 155mm shells, and cited this case history.

At the town of Jaro on Leyte, in World War II, I was with my leading battalion when we went into a perimeter defense at night on a low, rounded hilltop. Since we were exposed to enemy attack in force during the night, it was important to range in close defensive artillery fires. However, we were so far out front the 105mm howitzers did not have the reach for the job. So the 155s ranged in, and anyone who has been near exploding 155mm shells will understand what that was like.

There was the *feel* of heavy concussions as the exploding shells crept closer to our perimeter. Also, large steel splinters came screeching back toward us, which was both unsettling and dangerous. Clearly, defensive fires with 155s could not be brought in as close as those of the 105s. Also, equally clear, infantry could not move in as close under barrages of 155s in the attack as they could under 105mm supporting fires.

So the idea of eliminating 105s, and having the 155s take on a double mission, was dropped. Now, years later (1972) the 105mms are still a basic weapon in our arsenal. (It should be noted, however, that 155s do have the direct support mission in mechanized infantry and armored divisions.)

This highlights a situation we often meet: when recognized experts in a general field disagree, it is usually because the area of their expertise covers a different part of the overall problem. Thus, the decision as to which expert's view should prevail will be evident when the terms of reference of the disagreeing experts are compared, in relation to the mission and the specific decision required.

There is an almost unlimited number of fields in which experts are needed. As a result, an officer is often given an assignment for which he has little experience. The answer is to make yourself a self-appointed expert in each duty assignment that comes your way — by working at it.

One broad field, with facets and angles within angles, was demonstrated on the waterfront in Brooklyn many years ago. My friend, Edwin M. Van Bibber, told me about it.

The occasion was the loading out of troops, equipment and supplies for a major training exercise. This included animal-drawn transport, which required hoisting mules in slings from dockside to shipboard. To quote Ed:

"It was quite a show. The civilian dock workers and soldiers had never worked together before, and the kicking, obstinate mules did not help.

"Then a thin and leathery fellow in a gray suit, wearing a coat and tie, stopped near me to watch. At first I did not recognize him in civilian clothes, but it was 'Speed' Lloyd."

Speed Lloyd was a middle-aged captain, with an uncertain temper and a fine but abrasive reputation as a company commander. For some minutes Speed watched the confusion and lack of coordination, and listened to the copious but futile waterfront profanity.

Then, to quote Ed again, "Speed couldn't stand it any longer, so he took charge. He first loosed a burst of sulphurous language that commanded the attention and respect of the dock workers, in a tone of authority the soldiers recognized. Then he issued sharp, direct instructions for who was to push and who was to pull what — interspersed with more imaginative language when his orders were not promptly executed. And, suddenly, things got lined up and working smoothly. Even the mules quieted down and cooperated."

Ed reported that when this happened the dock foreman walked over and said, "Lieutenant, I've been on these docks for thirty years, but that beats anything I've ever seen or heard!"

What the foreman meant, expressed another way, was that he had just seen a true expert in action — an expert in how to handle men and boss a job. It is one of the most valuable skills a military man can have. (Normally, of course, profanity is not good form, but it fitted this special situation.)

Three comments are:

- Techniques which must be mastered to become an expert vary mightily, depending on the field of your expertise, the level of command and the personalities involved. But the basic requirement is simple: study and train and practice until you have more knowledge and know-how than others with whom you work.
- In any field where you are an expert, there will be overlapping areas in other fields where there are other experts. When this occurs and you find yourself disagreeing with them, then the thing to do is to determine who has the controlling interest. In the case of the 105mm vs 155 mm howitzers for close artillery support of infantry, the controlling interest was the effectiveness of the artillery fires delivered, not the convenience of those who fired them.
- When I received change-of-station orders in Germany, my aide asked me to arrange a specialized assignment for him. I declined to do this but did get him assigned as a rifle company commander — for which, in later years, he thanked me. The most important field in which to become an expert is in how to handle men and

boss a job; every expert, no matter what his specialty, needs this skill. The best place to learn this art is as a company-level commander — preferably a rifle company, where men and not hardware are the primary components.

21

To Err Is Human;
To Admit Goofs Is Wisdom

IT IS SAID that pearls are where you find them. This one was in a magazine article: "Determination may be silly, like the bulldog who clamped his jaws on a trailing balloon rope, and was last seen vanishing into the sky."

That is a hypothetical allegory, but I saw a human "bulldog" make that same mistake in real life. It happened on the West Point parade ground years ago when a balloon was preparing to take off, and three soldiers were holding it down by holding onto a rope.

Suddenly the balloon began to rise prematurely, lifting the men off the ground. Two of them realized they were making a mistake to hold on, so turned loose and dropped to the ground unhurt. But the third soldier was a real bulldog, and held on doggedly until it was too late to drop safely. Finally, at a height of 150 feet or more, he lost his grip and fell. In my mind's eye I can still see the thin little cloud of dust rise around him as his body plummeted into the parade ground, ending the last mistake he would ever make.

The lesson is obvious: while perseverance and determination are wonderful qualities, they do not override judgment and common sense. So when it is clear that you have made a mistake, turn loose before it is too late.

Hitler gave the world a devastating demonstration of this principle when he refused the advice of his top generals to withdraw from Stalingrad before it was too late.

To give you an idea of the cost to the Wehrmacht of Hitler's refusal to let go before it was too late, consider these figures: the

Germans lost nearly four hundred thousand men (which does not include an equal number of Italians, Hungarians, and Romanians), with only about five thousand Germans returned to their homes years later as released prisoners of war.

Oddly enough, Hitler's decision cost me fifty dollars. Further, there is a lesson to be learned from my financial loss.

Hitler repeated Napoleon's mistake when he challenged distance, width of front and superiority of numbers. These inexorable forces made me believe that trying to capture Stalingrad was an error that could turn into a disaster — unless Hitler admitted his mistake and turned loose before it was too late.

When Hitler hung on, I concluded from news reports and a map of the war front that the German assault on Russia would end in overwhelming defeat. So in Hawaii during the early fall of 1942, I managed to bet a twenty-five-dollar War Bond with each of two friends that the German attack would end in disaster to the Wehrmacht *before Christmas* — a proviso that left me fifty dollars poorer.

This points up the lesson that when you make a basic decision that might be a mistake (in this case to bet on the German defeat), leave yourself some flexibility. It was in tacking on that overconfident and limiting "before Christmas" that gave me two chances to be wrong instead of one.

While those in high places sometimes make monumental errors, for most of us the Chinese sage, Confucius, was right when he said, "Men do not stumble over mountains, but molehills."

Consider the instructor at a service school some thirty years ago who was asked a question for which he did not have the specific answer. Instead of admitting that he did not know, he made the mistake of trying to fob off the question with a general statement.

But the student restated the question. The instructor again tried to conceal his ignorance of the correct answer by talking around the subject.

When the student still persisted, the instructor had to admit lamely that he did not know the answer. By this time the class realized he had made the mistake of trying to fool them — not once but twice — and the instructor knew that they knew. What began as a harmless question ended as an embarrassing incident that damaged the good relationship the instructor had enjoyed with that class.

In effect, the instructor made the same mistake Hitler made at

Stalingrad, and that the soldier made at West Point by holding onto the balloon rope too long. It was not so much the initial error, but his persistence in it that resulted in the real damage.

Because the possibility of making small mistakes is always with us, as is the capacity to lose our tempers, these two potentials often combine to make a mistake that would not otherwise occur. In the same lecture hall where the instructor made his mistake, I also witnessed another and more serious error.

On this occasion, a general officer gave an outstanding talk to the combined student classes. The students were inspired by the substance of what the general said and the skillful way he drove home his points with touches of whimsical humor. But all this admiration and inspiration were suddenly frozen in a matter of seconds.

As the general left the stage, the class stood for his departure. One of the junior students, not realizing the general was to leave by a side aisle, carelessly backed into that aisle and partially blocked the general's way.

That was an unwitting breach of courtesy by the student, but his error was completely overshadowed when the general lost his temper. In a loud and harshly angry voice, he berated the student unmercifully, then strode out of the hall.

No one who witnessed that violent burst of anger over a student's unintentional mistake will ever forget it. It brings to mind a line from a Shakespeare sonnet: "Lilies that fester smell far worse than weeds."

There seems to be no end to the ways small mistakes can end in big trouble. One of the notes in my files cites this illustration:

In a large wartime overseas supply dump there were thousands of tons of automotive spare parts. They were in excellent condition, carefully packaged to withstand weathering in open-air storage. But, as a result of one small error, users could not find what they wanted. The ink used for outside markings on the packages was not weather resistant, so the markings faded into illegibility. Thus, before obtaining specific spare parts, each box had to be opened and the parts identified — a tremendous job.

I know of no way to prevent that type of little mistake that produces such big headaches, except by eternal vigilance and preventive thinking. In this case, there were a large number of officers along the supply line who had had a chance to foresee this particular error and check it.

Curiously enough, sometimes there are errors that disprove the old adage that two wrongs do not make a right. A yellowing note from my files gives Maj. Gen. Emerson C. Itchner (now Lt. Gen., Ret.) as the source of this case where one mistake in war neutralized another.

In planning for the Normandy landing on Omaha Beach in France during World War II, an oversupply of telephone poles was included because it was believed Germans would cut down many of them. But the Germans apparently decided to leave the poles standing as obstacles to possible glider landings of supplies and reinforcements.

On the other hand, a planning error failed to provide enough pilings for use in developing docks in Cherbourg harbor, so the extra telephone poles filled that need nicely. But such a compensating double mistake is an oddity, not a consideration to alibi mistakes.

The ramification of various errors are endless, as are the consequences that flow from them. But these comments may provide useful guidelines:

- There is no substitute for alertness to avoid mistakes, but everybody makes an error sometimes. So it is important also not to make the bulldog mistake of holding on to your miscue too long. Most errors can be minimized by admitting them and taking corrective action promptly. Attempts to gloss over or to hide mistakes will almost always magnify them.
- I once saw this sign on a staff officer's desk: DO IT TO-MORROW—YOU HAVE MADE ENOUGH MISTAKES TODAY. The only trouble with that maxim is that waiting until tomorrow to do it may be the biggest mistake yet.
- The higher you go in rank and responsibility, the greater the need to get all the facts as the best means of avoiding mistakes in decisions, and the greater need for carefully considered good judgment. A Chinese proverb puts it this way: "When a king makes a mistake, all the people suffer."
- Stress, anger, and mistakes often go together. Confucius gives this admonition: "When anger arrives, think of the consequences." Another valuable guideline is the old supplication: "Oh, Lord, let my words be tender and sweet, for tomorrow I may have to eat them."

22

Staff Officer Syndrome

AMONG PROFESSIONAL FIELDS none is more difficult than being a good staff officer, especially on a general staff. Yet no other group is so maligned. The group's unflattering image is sometimes called the "staff officer syndrome." Is this fact or fallacy?

In late 1939 (at Schofield Barracks, Hawaii) I walked across the 19th Infantry quadrangle from Company F to regimental headquarters and sat down in my office as a staff officer, thus entering a new professional world. It was a brittle, complex, and deceptive world. Under its suave exterior were submerged strains and pressures.

When you are a commander, things are forthright and what they seem. But staff officers deal with conflicting interests, speak in the name of a higher-ranking officer, and you can't be sure how accurately they are stating his views. Further, while they have no authority in themselves, they often come to feel they have; yet it's a ticklish matter to question their orders.

Such an atmosphere makes staff officers hard to pin down, they become skillful at passing the buck. Actually, a staff officer lives on the spot because he is always getting second-guessed himself, so self-preservation calls for developing a little footwork. There's another side, too: human friction is a wearing factor on a staff, as complicated personalities often go with the facile minds of the best staff officers.

Therefore it's not surprising that a good staff officer—as the lady plaintively notes in the song—is hard to find. His job is a much harder and more thankless one than that of commander. He gets blamed for everything and shares credit for nothing. For example, news stories from Vietnam feature our fighting troops and the success of commanders in combat, but you rarely read about the efficient staff work that made that success possible. Yet our increasingly intricate military technology, and the unique tests we face as a result, make skillful staff planning more vital than ever before.

You do hear the term "jittery staff officer" — usually from some clod who has never been one, for good reason. But "overworked" would be a more accurate word. The more conscientious and able a staff officer, the more he is given to do and the more people want to see him, thus, inevitably, he is harassed.

When I walked into the 19th Infantry headquarters I didn't know these things, but I soon discovered that the spirit of mutual helpfulness that prevailed in my company was missing on a staff. One reason is that staff sections work along different lines, though they must "coordinate" what they do with each other. There is a watchful aloofness, too. Staff officers sometimes back different viewpoints to the commander, and this puts them in conflict.

My staff assignment was S-2 (intelligence was a much neglected art at the time), but "in addition to other duties" I was the regimental athletics officer. One morning the regimental executive officer, a real toughie, stopped in my office and stated his unhappiness with the progress of work on the baseball diamond.

So after lunch I went out there, picking up a cigar from my desk and lighting it on the way. Sure enough, the work detail was in slow motion. So I assembled them around the slightly raised pitcher's mound for a short pep talk. After taking a puff on my cigar I announced my dissatisfaction with the progress of manicuring the infield and weeding the outfield; in fact, I got a little dogmatic and said we would stay out until the job was finished. As I paused to let that sink in, I took another good pull on my cigar — and it exploded in my face.

The staging and timing could not have been more perfectly planned had it been rehearsed. The soldiers exploded too, in a spontaneous belly laugh. One young soldier even went down on his knees. I couldn't blame them . . . in fact, I wish I could have seen it happen.

You guessed it: one of my fellow staff officers had left a loaded cigar on my desk by way of welcome.

Another difference between staff and command was that the minor funny happenings and the uninhibited humor of a troop unit didn't exist in the rarified atmosphere of a staff. And when they did, laughter seemed well coordinated — and a little condescending. There was humor at times — but the kind that has a sharp edge.

I remember a discussion about sending one of our officers for duty at a higher headquarters. One officer voiced the opinion it was hardly fair to send that particular officer, as he was a bit off the beam and might get in trouble.

Another staff officer replied, "Perhaps he is not very smart. But we can do without him, and he'll be right at home up there!"

Cute, no doubt — and funny, in a way. But a tongue that pointed is not a nice thing to have poised behind your back when you come to work every day.

In early 1941, I decided to volunteer for the newest Army development: paratroopers — the embryo Airborne. At this time, however, they offered me a job as G-2 of the then Hawaiian Division where I would become a general staff officer. For a captain that looked like getting rich pretty quick. So like a dope, I took it.

We soon had a division review. It was an inspiring sight to see the division spread out there on the review field near the notch in Kole Kole Pass — thousands of men, hundreds of vehicles, massed artillery, and rolling tanks, all combining to engender an indefinable sense of military might.

As a company commander I had marched by, one among thousands in the disciplined moving mass of men, weapons, and machines. Now my place was in the raised reviewing stand, looking out at the panorama of passing power. It's things like that which seep into the minds of general staff officers. Knowing you are a part of the brain that controls all this, you begin to feel a sense of directive capacity. If you did not feel this way it would be unfortunate, for without this feeling you could hardly be a good general staff officer.

This sensation was heady at first. I hadn't yet realized that learning to be a staff officer is something like learning to milk a cow. The novelty soon wears off, and the job becomes burdensome, and smelly. As a boy I learned the hard way that if you demonstrated skill at milking a cow, somebody would keep you milking one. It's the same way with being a good staff officer.

For twenty years much of my service would be in a staff capacity, against my will. By nature and inclination I was a commander; but I had learned to milk the staff cow — so somebody was always setting me to milk one. This service included being chief of staff to eleven generals (from one to four stars, one month to two years per sentence). Also service on a unified staff and on two theater staffs.

Thus I believe myself qualified to draw these conclusions:

- The Army should eliminate the existing unofficial custom that permits senior officers to keep younger men on staff assignments, thus denying them other broadening service experience.
- The importance of military staffs has vastly increased with our constantly advancing military technology. Consider all the major headquarters around the world, including joint, combined and unified commands — plus many specialized and technical headquarters — each requiring staff officers with diversified know-how and skills exceeding anything imagined a generation ago.
- Command duty is, quite properly, an important factor in selection for promotion to general officer rank — but, similarly, the same should be true for adequate staff experience. (How can a general use his staff to the best advantage if he has never been a staff officer?)
- The old he's-just-a-staff-officer label is a subtle libel. Try to take him away, and his commander will quickly classify him as "a key staff officer."
- The fighting soldier in the front lines is and will remain the cutting edge, universally honored and respected as such. But combat troops need and deserve good commanders to insure success. And a good commander knows that the value of a good staff is beyond calculation.
- Whether the "staff officer syndrome" is fact or fallacy soon gets bogged down in semantics. But whatever you want to call it, why shouldn't staff officers adopt the protective coloration and defensive tactics necessary to survive in their peculiarly testing, tricky, and demanding environment.

23

Character: Index to the Makeup of Sergeants

AT THE ANNUAL reunion of the 24th Infantry Division, the first order of business for me is to visit the bar for a drink with my friend Spike, formerly Sergeant O'Donnell of the 21st Infantry during World War II.

Our 1971 reunion was at Louisville, Kentucky—in the middle of bourbon country. So we made a tour of the distillery where Old Fitzgerald is mellowed in oak barrels, then bottled for distribution to people like Spike and me. At the end of the tour we sampled the goods for our usual glad-to-see-you-again libation—the first time we had observed this ritual in a distillery.

We were on our refill when Spike mentioned my articles in ARMY magazine for July and August 1969 ("What Are Generals Made Of?"). He then lowered the level of amber fluid in his glass and added, "But you did not answer the important question: what are sergeants made of?"

It seems to me that, over the years, I answered that question by my memories of First Sergeants Big Jim Redding, Old Man Brown, Doc Dougherty, John Christopher and others. Also Sergeants Fugate, Stinson, Jessie, Kaatz, Long John Smith (as distinguished from Dirty-Neck Smith in an adjacent company), Vandergrift, Bosco—and the wonderful soldiers in our division during World War II, like my friend Spike.

But to be analytical, consider the story about the sergeant in charge of a hundred recruits for their first police detail: to clean an area between rows of two-story wooden barracks.

Facing the group the sergeant said, "You men that are college graduates, hold up your hands."

When the hands went up he said, "OK. Form a line between those rows of barracks at the end of the street and walk to the other end, picking up cigarette and cigar butts as you go. Also empty cigarette packs and chewing gum wrappers. Then drop them in the trash barrel over there."

After the college graduates moved out he said, "You men that are high school graduates, hold up your hands."

Hands went up and he said, "OK. Form a line behind the first one and pick up stuff like match sticks, candy wrappers, and other trash."

When the high school graduates moved out he turned to the nongraduates and said, "OK. You fellows sit in the shade and watch. Maybe you will learn something."

From this it is clear that sergeants know how to organize in a definite plan. Also, that when there is a chance to work in a little instruction, they do that, too.

One year, as a company commander, I managed to get in the doghouse with my regimental commander. As a result, extra-duty jobs began coming my way, until the cumulative result had me responsible for commanding and training my company, range officer for the rifle range, regimental recruit instructor, and detailed to run a two-week refresher course for twenty-two young Thomason Act second lieutenants before they reported to their first regular unit assignments.

As a matter of pride, I did not want to give the regimental commander the satisfaction of having me crawl to regimental headquarters and ask for help. Besides, while there was no officer in my company, there were nine outstanding sergeants. So I assigned one sergeant to look after the rifle range, issue targets, put up the flags and run the pits; another sergeant was delegated my responsibilities as regimental recruit instructor; still another sergeant was designated as platoon commander and instructor in charge of the twenty-two newly joined second lieutenants, following a drill schedule and using others to help as necessary—especially when orienting the young lieutenants in the supply room, mess hall and orderly room administration.

Of course, 1st Sgt. Big Jim Redding continued to run the company pretty much as he usually did. So I just circulated around — no sweat — and watched my sergeants doing fine jobs. They were wise enough to guess what was going on, so each one greeted me in his area with a little extra smartness in his salute, assuring me with a knowing look and tightly compressed smile that everything on his side of the house was going smoothly.

One day I wandered back to the company from a circulation tour, noting as I crossed the parade ground that Sergeant Stinson had his new lieutenants organized in platoon formation, with each one practicing drilling the platoon in turn. Nobody seemed to need me, so it was time for a cup of coffee in Sgt. Long John Smith's kitchen. First Sgt. Big Jim was in the barracks hallway, and I invited him to join me.

As we cuddled thick cups and sipped hot coffee, I said to Big Jim, "Dickerson has the range under control, Gancaz is riding herd on the regimental recruits, Stinson has his platoon of officers drilling each other, and Zak has our company training well organized. Maybe I should ask regiment if there are any more jobs they need done."

Big Jim threw back his head, laughed in that deep-throated way he had and said, "Captain, it is none of my business, but if it was me I would stay away from regimental headquarters until the storm blows over."

You see, among other outstanding qualities and skills, sergeants are wise advisors. Also, like I said, they understand a lot of things without being told.

No matter what job you give a good sergeant, he will soon master it, because sergeants know how to get things done. In Company G, 26th Infantry, I had the nine best sergeants ever assembled in one company — averaging nearly twenty years of service. They typified the qualities all good sergeants have.

First and foremost, they were competent and highly trained soldiers, but that is not enough to make a good sergeant. They were loyal, sincere, friendly off duty but all business on duty; they understood men and how to handle them. And mixed in with their other characteristics they had that invaluable ingredient: a sense of humor, with the touch and common sense of when and how to use it.

Just as fire tests steel, so does battle test the qualities of sergeants — as it does the rest of us.

That Sgt. Charles E. Mowrer, Company A, 34th Infantry (24th

Infantry Division), was awarded the Medal of Honor posthumously was mentioned briefly in "Who Gets The Combat Decorations?" (ARMY, Jan. 1967). But how he got his medal was not stated. Because it so graphically illustrates some of the things sergeants are made of, here is his citation in part:

Near Capoocan, Leyte, Philippine Islands, on 3 November 1944, Sergeant Mowrer

> . . . was an assistant squad leader in an attack against strongly defended enemy positions on both sides of a stream running through a wooded gulch. As the squad advanced through concentrated fire, the leader was killed, and Sgt. Mowrer assumed command. In order to direct fire on the enemy he had started to lead his men across the stream, which by that time was churned by machine gun and rifle fire, but he was severely wounded before reaching the opposite bank. After signaling his unit to halt he realized his own exposed position was the most advantageous point from which to direct the attack, and stood fast. Half submerged, gravely wounded, but refusing to seek shelter or aid of any kind, he continued to shout and signal to his squad as he directed it in the destruction of two enemy machine guns and numerous riflemen. Discovering that the intrepid man in the stream was largely responsible for the successful action being taken against them, the remaining Japanese concentrated the full force of their fire power upon him, and he was killed while still urging his men on.

That citation answers a lot of questions about what sergeants are made of. But these comments appear in order:

- The essential central characteristic for sergeants is the same as that for generals: character. ("Characteristics Of Character," Aug. 1970 ARMY). In fact some generals were sergeants long before they were generals — an honor and distinction I wish I could claim.
- As with generals, some sergeants are more experienced and better than others. But scan the list of Army men who have won the Medal of Honor (Medal of Honor,

1863–1968, obtainable from the U.S. Government Printing Office) and you will find the names of sergeants out of all proportion to the relative number of them in ranks (a quick check of World War II Army winners showed eleven corporals, eight technicians, seventy-eight privates, and ninety-five sergeants). I don't think you can get any better index to what sergeants are made of.

- Sergeants operate where the action is, in direct control of men who get the job done. That is why they need that rawhide toughness they are famous for, and why they have the human understanding that so few of the American public give them credit for.

24

Valuing People as People

MY FRIEND COL. Douglas B. McMullen suggested I discuss the theme "Importance of the Individual." My first thought was, "Everybody is equal, but some are more equal than others." That is not exactly new, and didn't clarify the idea much. But it did indicate the subject is too broad and deep for this old scribbler's capacity. So I decided to narrow it down to manageable size by searching for the cornerstone of that majestic principle.

Here are some relevant thoughts by others:

E. H. Chapin (1814-80): "Not armies, not nations, have advanced the race; but here and there, in the course of the ages, an individual has stood up and cast his shadow over the world."

Charles H. Spurgeon (1834-92): ". . . single individuals are the power and the might."

From *Eclectic* magazine: "There are three kinds of people in the world: the wills, the won'ts, the can'ts. The first accomplish everything; the second oppose everything; the third fail in everything."

From *700 Chinese Proverbs* (translated by H. H. Hart, published by Stanford University Press):

"Many men, many minds."

"There is many a good man to be found under a shabby hat."

"You may change the clothes, but you can't change the man."

"He who rides in the chair is a man; he who carries the chair is also a man."

Those are interesting philosophical pronouncements—especially the last one. Additional information is needed, however, to compress our theme to a workable guideline, so here are several case histories.

On my return from Hawaii (1935), as a freshly minted captain assigned to the 26th Infantry at Plattsburg Barracks, N.Y., I was detailed as post provost marshal. My individuality in this role was soon in conflict with the overly inflated individualities of some of the twenty-odd prisoners in the guardhouse — which was the reason they were there in the first place.

It was not a happy time on either side of the confrontation, for that is what it became. However, after five of the recalcitrants had spent "seven days in solitary confinement on bread and water" (exactly as laid down in regulations, including approval of the regimental commander), things settled down. If I may be permitted to pontificate a bit, it comes out this way: every man is entitled to recognition as an individual, within the *res gestae* of his situation, but trouble comes when some individuals view themselves as more individual than the limits of their special situation allow.

The question then becomes: in recognizing the importance of each individual in military service, how do you reconcile this with varying ranks and responsibilities?

One of the prisoners in that guardhouse was a fine-appearing but sad-looking young soldier. He was serving a year at hard labor with a dishonorable discharge for desertion, but was a model prisoner. On inquiry, I learned he had legally been a deserter, but had been motivated by family worry for his parents.

After about five months as provost marshal, it was my privilege to command Company G, 26th Infantry. One of my early actions was to put in a letter requesting that the unserved part of the sentence of my fine-appearing but sad-looking prisoner be remitted and that he be returned to duty as a member of my company. This was done.

In full uniform again, my former prisoner was a fine soldier. His dispirited, downcast look was replaced with the confident bearing that comes to those who have that intangible thing we call self-respect — which brings me to an interesting point about the importance of the individual.

How you are treated as an individual depends, in large measure, on how you play your part. In that Plattsburg guardhouse the difference between solitary confinement on bread and water, and having a dishonorable discharge set aside with return to full duty, depended on the prisoner himself.

A year or so ago, a young captain gave me a mimeographed sheet that bears directly on the importance of the individual. I do not know who composed the message it contains, or at what unit level it was reproduced, but its value speaks for itself:

Remember Me?

I'm the person who goes into the orderly room and patiently waits while the first sergeant or AST [Army Supply Technician] does everything but pay attention to me. I'm the person who goes into the supply room and stands quietly by while the supply sergeant and his assistant finish their little chitchat. I'm the person who does not grumble while I clean rifles in addition to my own while other people wander aimlessly around the center. Yes, you might say I'm a pretty good person. But do you know who else I am? I AM THE PERSON WHO NEVER EXTENDS MY ENLISTMENT, and it amuses me to see you spending many hours and dollars every year to get me back into your unit, when I was there in the first place. All you had to do to keep me was
GIVE ME A LITTLE ATTENTION,
SHOW ME A LITTLE COURTESY,
USE ME WELL.

To me, that isolates the irreplaceable ingredient, the cornerstone of the importance of the individual: self-respect. There are other facets to this elusive factor, so one more case history.

As a regimental commander in World War II, one of my first concerns on assuming command was to establish two things in the minds and hearts of my soldiers: that I was a competent officer, and that I was personally interested in and concerned for every soldier in our regiment. But there was an aftermath too.

As director of instruction in the Armed Forces Information School after the war, I received a letter from the Pentagon "for direct reply to writer." It was from the sister of one of my 34th Infantry soldiers, who had been killed the day after we landed on Leyte in the

Philippines. She was very upset over learning her brother had lost his life by our own fire.

She lived a bit less than a hundred miles away, so my wife and I drove over to see her. Thus, I was able to tell her exactly how it happened, since I had arrived on the spot just as her mortally wounded brother was being carried to the rear for medical attention.

I also explained that he had died for his country as much as had the thousands who fell under enemy fire—because such unfortunate tragedies are unavoidable in war. After hearing the facts, and understanding it was nobody's fault—but from the unpredictable chance circumstances mixed in with the violence of battle—her grief remained, but the bitterness was gone.

The real poignant point about my killed-in-action soldier is this: the importance of each individual in uniform goes beyond himself, because behind each man are his relatives and friends. He was a unique individual, loved and respected before he put on a uniform; he brings their love and respect with him, and he has a right to retain his self-respect as a soldier. But self-respect, in or out of uniform, is not free like the air; it must be earned. And when earned, it must be recognized by others.

Added comments are:

- Great commanders have always recognized the importance of individuals under them. Gen. Melvin Zais said it with eloquent simplicity: "You have to care."
- The immortal British admiral, Lord Horatio Nelson, won the admiration and respect of his sailors to an unusual degree because he honored and respected them as individuals. Soon after being promoted to admiral he transferred his flag to the *Theseus* and took immediate steps to improve conditions on board. As a result this anonymous note from the crew appeared on the quarterdeck:

  "Success attend Admiral Nelson. God bless Captain Miller. We thank them for the officers they have placed over us. We are happy and comfortable, and will shed every drop of blood in our veins to support them."

  That note translates like this: "You have recognized

our importance as individuals and interested yourself in our personal welfare. This has given us the pride and self-respect to fight for you in a way nothing else can."

- Battles take only a fraction of the time a nation is at war, and wars cover only a small period of time relative to the years of peace. Also, ways to recognize the importance of individuals in war are far more dramatic than in peace, including the award of medals. But the peacetime requirement will always be there, permeating every command from top to bottom.

  That "Remember Me?" piece is something for military men in authority to remember every day. The cornerstone guideline can be stated this way: at all times and in all circumstances remember the importance of self-respect to every man in uniform.

- Finally, no matter how much you "care," there will be times for some few men when there is no choice but to lower the boom. In other words, never let your respect for the self-respect of the individual degenerate into permissiveness.

25
Temper Command
with Judgment

NOT LONG AGO I saw a cartoon that pictured two recruits, with a scowling old sergeant in the background. One recruit says to another, "What has got into these people anyway? They were nice enough down at the recruiting station."

That brought back my recruit days some sixty years ago. When I attended the fiftieth reunion of my class (1925) at the U.S. Military Academy, I remembered how it was when I entered West Point as a plebe in July 1921.

My family and friends sent me away with smiles and good wishes, but no smiles greeted me at West Point. Nothing I could do seemed to satisfy upperclassmen. By Christmas time I was resigned to the fact that nobody loved me and my fellow plebes.

Then, on Christmas morning, we four plebes in Room 2714 were jarred awake by drums and bugles of the reveille "hell cats"—and we stared with unbelieving eyes at the mantel over our fireplace. Four two-pound, Christmas-red boxes of assorted chocolates were lined up there, and below each box was a Christmas stocking full of nuts, candy, and fruits.

It did not take long to realize that upperclassmen had played Santa Claus to the plebes (though none of them ever mentioned it). All of a sudden West Point no longer seemed unfeeling and coldly critical. This clear evidence of human understanding made demands for high standards seem easier and more reasonable. So I faced the remainder of my plebe (recruit) year with less stress and strain.

This illustrates why actions based on human understanding are an important element in command and leadership. To examine further the varied facets of this great intangible of military service, consider these two short articles from ARMY Magazine's predecessor, the *Infantry Journal*.

Molasses Is Cheap*

I feel pretty good. Pvt. Joe Spoony feels pretty good. And Pvt. Joe Spoony's corporal feels pretty good. Yes, and Pvt. Joe Spoony's corporal's platoon sergeant feels pretty good. And it did not cost anybody anything.

This is the way it happened.

We had a full field inspection this morning and the Old Man (that's me) looked it all over. Pvt. Joe Spoony was in the first squad, with barely a year in on his first hitch. His equipment looked fine and he was standing strictly at attention.

"That's a nice looking display of equipment," I said to him. "How did you get your mess gear in such good shape?"

"Cpl. Interest showed me how to scour it with fine sand, sir."

Then, as I continued on my inspection Platoon Sgt. Sourpuss said to me, "Captain, that's a good boy. Always on the job, and so is his corporal."

I think Pvt. Spoony and Cpl. Interest heard him, and I know some others did. Further, I am certain Sgt. Sourpuss intended that his remark be heard. Sgt. Sourpuss is as rough as an emery stone, but he has his smooth side too. The men like him.

Of course, I got on Pvt. Dirty Dogtag for not having his haversack properly marked, and gave his corporal a growl for not having checked it.

There were several Joe Spoonys at the inspection and a couple of Dirty Dogtags, too. But I have the feeling that, of my gratuitous issue of verbal pats-on-the-back and kicks-in-the-pants, the pats are going to do more than the

*Jan.–Feb. 1938

kicks toward producing the kind of soldiers and the kind of company I want.

It seems to me that in the Army today there is too much growling passed out and too little credit. Moreover, we try too often to hog the credit when some one has helped out on the job. "Cpl. Interest showed me how to scour it with fine sand, sir." Instead we say, "I scoured it with fine sand, sir."

It is true that, on some occasions with some men, nothing but the iron hand is going to do any good. But in any event the simple rule of giving credit where credit is due produces astonishing results, and ditto for the pat on the back.

Hence, without losing my kicking form I am resolved to improve my patting form. Or, as I like to remember it, molasses is cheap.

Of course, nothing makes me any sicker than too much molasses. But everybody likes a little now and then. It's healthy — and it is cheap.

(signed) Company Commander

The second short article takes a different look at the same principle.

We Need A Few*

There are those who say I am curdled on life and the efficiency of my digestive processes has been a matter of conjecture. But the most popular explanation of my manner in official matters is that I'm just a plain so-and-so.

It's confusing because I'm good and kind to all things that live and breathe — except maybe second lieutenants. And so I've tried to be modern and analyze the situation.

My conclusions are as simple as they are definite. Both soldiers and officers have developed feelings and finer sensibilities. You must handle them "tenderly" as distinguished from "fairly."

Once upon a time fairness was the thing that mattered.

*July–Aug. 1940

When somebody needed to get their ears bent they got 'em damn well bent. And all this stuff about "don't break his spirit" and "inspire by your example" — those were just ideas.

But when a man is caught off base the umpire calls him out in a loud and clear voice. And when a soldier or officer is out of step there ought to be hell to pay. Then a lot less people would get out of step.

I remember one post where the post commander was recognized as a brilliant officer. But he was short on discipline. That was all right, however, because everywhere he went there were a few so-and-sos to keep things stirred up.

Even so, things got slack, although the post commander was as brilliant as ever and everybody loved the CO.

Then a new CO arrived, a famous so-and-so. The results were amazing. Even before the so-and-so assumed command, officers and soldiers alike were stepping high, wide and fancy.

Yes, and those of us who served under him still brag about it. He was rough when things didn't suit him; what he didn't like he didn't like out loud. But he was fair.

Those who don't tell you your faults don't cure you of them either. The more polite and tactful an officer is with his junior, the poorer that young man's efficiency report is likely to be.

Maybe I am turning into an old so-and-so before my time, but of this much I am certain: the number of so-and-sos in our Army is diminishing — and any army is a hell of an army without a few so-and-sos in it.

(signed) Stone Borealis

The above short articles, which appeared over different pen names, seem to take different views of how to exercise command. But they were written by the same man and, when you know the circumstances under which each was written, both really espouse the same principle.

I know this is true, because I wrote them when I was a company commander. In "Molasses Is Cheap," I reflected the circumstances under which it was written — because my company was a fine outfit, and my command efforts consisted largely of going around and admiring how well things were going.

In my next company at another station, I wrote "We Need A Few." That came after I had preferred charges against my lieutenant for alcohol-induced derelictions, installed the mess sergeant in the guardhouse for stealing groceries from our company kitchen, busted the supply sergeant for not being up to his job, and taken certain other corrective actions.

Although I did not think of it that way at the time, in both cases people were involved. Human nature is the same everywhere, if you just take time to understand it and act accordingly. It would have been just as wrong to go around finding fault when things were fine as it would have been to pass out verbal posies when things were fouled up.

Some added thoughts are:

- You cannot expect to be treated the same way in all circumstances, as that recruit in the cartoon found out.
- No matter how intense the dedication and how high the standards in military service, the human touch is important, too.

  The visit by Santa Claus to Room 2714 at West Point in 1921 gave me a feeling of belonging to, and being a a part of, an elite organization that nothing else quite duplicated.
- As long as armies are made up of people, the human element will remain an irreplaceable consideration in command and leadership. Further, how you exercise your human understanding will depend not only on your perception and good judgment, but also on the situation and the kind of people involved.

  To err may be human, but to forgive some people is not always divine — it may just invite them to err again.

PART II
COMMAND TECHNIQUES

26
Quick and Needless Changes Have No Place in Command

IN A TALK to alumni of the National War College, Lt. Gen. John B. McPherson, USAF, discussed changes under way at the college. In opening his talk he said:

"We have not approached the problem of change with the tactics of the French Foreign Legion commander who, after leading his company on a grueling two-week forced march across the Sahara, finally responded to his troops' gripes about the monotony and discomfort of their routine by announcing one morning that there was good news. There would be a change. Every man was to have a change of underwear. Even this small amenity was received with enthusiasm, until the captain announced the method of change: Pierre was to change underwear with Jacques: Jean with Claude, and so on."

This makes the fine point that change simply for the sake of change is often worse than useless.

Changes in the military service are too complex and numerous for coverage here, so we narrow it down to one specialized angle: changes when a new commander takes over. As a captain, I discussed one facet of this in a short article (in *The Infantry Journal*, Dec. 1941):

". . . and Assume Command Thereof"

No two men take over a command in exactly the same way. But the way a commander does it — whether it be inimitable or imitative, arrogant or amiable—has lasting consequences.

The canned language of orders runs about like this, "Captain Dustcloud is this date transferred to Company Q, and will assume command thereof." But just how does Captain Dustcloud go about "assuming command thereof?"

First he blows into the orderly room enveloped in a haze of brusk efficiency that somehow conveys the idea he has been sent down to straighten out the outfit. You kind of get the impression he instantly sees a lot of things that need changing and that he thinks Captain Considerate, the former company commander, was perhaps a good fellow, but not so hot as a commander.

After a critical look around Dustcloud sits down at his desk—and does not like the way the desk light is arranged. So he has that changed.

In the kitchen he tells the mess sergeant to shift the meat block. In the supply room Dustcloud asks Sergeant No-Shortages how he runs his temporary receipts. This is changed, too, though it was a system that worked.

Now that he has made his presence felt Captain Dustcloud sits himself down at his desk where the light has been changed to suit him. He is now satisfied with Company Q—he has "assumed command thereof."

Yes, he has. No argument about it; everybody from the first sergeant to the KPs know Captain Dustcloud is there—but they are not very happy about it.

Captain Considerate's method was different.

He walked into the orderly room, shook hands with the first sergeant, and looked around until he saw what was obviously a new organization chart on the wall.

"Sergeant Bustle," he said, "that's a nice looking chart. It's the kind of thing I like to have."

When he inspected the kitchen, Captain Considerate found the coffee was good, and he said so out loud. He saw several things he wanted to change later, but said nothing about them. There was no hurry.

In the supply room Sergeant Everready was busy checking out laundry, so Captain Considerate said, "Go ahead with your work, Sergeant. I'll be in to check property tomorrow."

After talking to the first sergeant about the current training program, Considerate assembled all the sergeants in the orderly room (there were only eight in a company then). His talk to them lasted about thirty seconds, and was something like this:

"I have taken command of this company. It looks like a fine outfit, and I am glad to be here. I expect you to give me the same loyalty and support that I can see you have given your former company commander. For the time being I want you to go ahead just as you have been doing. Later on if there are any changes I want to make, I'll let you know. That's all. . . . Thank you."

Both Captain Dustcloud and Captain Considerate have very definitely "assumed command thereof"—but if you were a soldier, which one of those two company commanders would you rather have?

(signed) Stone Borealis

A lot of water has cascaded down the millrace since then. To examine the matter more deeply, here are some case histories.

Consider the captain who took command of a company in the Old Army before World War II, when NCOs often remained in the same unit on the same post for years. On his first barracks inspection the new commander looked with displeasure at the spotless waxed linoleum floor and the neat lines of bunks, with footlockers on freshly painted wooden stands at the foot of each bunk.

Finally, he said to the first sergeant, "Sergeant Rockbottom, I like metal frames for footlockers—the kind bolted to the foot of each bed—instead of those bulky wooden stands. Have the supply sergeant find out how to get them."

The next morning at barracks inspection the new captain was astonished to find all footlockers on metal frames, bolted to the foot of the bunks, instead of the painted wooden stands.

"Sergeant Rockbottom," the captain asked, "how did you get these metal footlocker racks so quickly?"

Before the first sergeant could reply, the supply sergeant, an old-timer who had emigrated from a European country, stepped forward and saluted.

"Sir, Captain," the supply sergeant said with a heavy foreign accent, "come to the attic and I show you."

In the attic the supply sergeant pointed to a pile of footlocker stands that had been in the squadrooms the day before—also two more piles of footlocker racks of different types.

"Every time we get new company commander," the supply sergeant said, "we got to have new kind of footlocker racks. No problem, Captain. I get fatigue detail from first sergeant and make change."

The point seems clear; nor are such changes confined to company level.

When I joined the 19th Infantry at Schofield Barracks before World War II, some men were wearing light-colored shoes as issued, while others wore shoes dyed a dark cordovan shade. On inquiry, I learned that a past commander had required that all shoes be dyed this cordovan color. Now the regiment was gradually returning to the regulation color, under a new commander, in a "wear out" phase.

In 1950, when I took command of the 511th Airborne Infantry at Fort Campbell, the regimental commander's office was approached down a narrow dark hallway, with administrative offices walled off on both sides. Within a short time I ordered the hallway walls taken down, so my office was approached by an aisle between well-lighted administrative areas that were bordered by a handrail. The general appearance was much like that in many banks, except that the neat display of individual "alert" field equipment gave it a we-are-ready look.

Two years later, when I returned to Fort Campbell on a visit, the walls I had ordered removed were back in place again.

In an overseas theater where I once served, the grapevine circulated word that the principle of personal preference on taking command had surfaced at a multistar headquarters there. The normal procedure at that headquarters had been to hold staff meetings with the commanding general seated at the head of an open U-shaped arrangement of tables and chairs.

When they got a new multistar commander, he preferred a King Arthur's round-table arrangement. So a large round table was made, replacing the open U-shaped arrangement of tables and chairs.

You guessed it: the next multistar commander relegated the round table to the headquarters basement and restored the

U-shaped conference setting. Also (you are right again), when his successor inspected headquarters he discovered the large round table in the basement, so . . .

There is nothing new about the assuming-command gambit of making changes to impress your presence on your new unit. Nor is it limited to tactical units.

After World War II, when General Eisenhower was Army chief of staff, I was chief of the training branch in the G-2 section of Army Ground Forces, in the Pentagon. This was the era of the Doolittle Board, including ideas not unlike some of those in the present all-volunteer Army — and for the same reason. While length of hair was not of vital concern, consideration was given to adopting the Eisenhower jacket as the dress uniform for officers and men.

One day my boss, a two-star (later four-star) general, designated me to represent him at a meeting to discuss the pros and cons of putting all ranks in the same uniform — the Eisenhower jacket.

"What are your views on the Eisenhower jacket as the Army's dress uniform?" my boss asked.

"Sir," I said, after a pause to phrase my thoughts in suitable words, "I do not like the Eisenhower jacket as the dress uniform for everybody. Among other reasons, we have now and always will have at all levels some fat fannies, broad bottoms, and protuberant paunches that the Eisenhower jacket will do nothing for."

"Well," the general replied, giving me a hard look that said he did not appreciate my triple alliterative levity, "that is your opinion. But you will represent me and the G-2 section of Army Ground Forces — so you are *for* it."

How many personal views were influenced by that invisible but potent force known as "command pressure," I do not know. But we did go to the Eisenhower jacket. Then under the next Army chief of staff we went back to pinks and greens for officers.

From where I sit, the basic idea and eventual result were not so different in principle from those footlocker racks, the dyed shoes in Hawaii, the walls in my regimental headquarters and the round table versus the U-shaped arrangement of chairs and tables in that overseas multistar headquarters.

These comments seem pertinent:

- The right of a new commander to make changes, within his authority, is not questioned. But a quickie change to make a quick impression on taking command is the impression that change will make—as in the case of the footlocker stands.

- It is as Alfred, Lord Tennyson said: "The old order changeth, yielding place to the new. . . ." Yes, we must change with the changing times. But change for the sake of change, as illustrated by that change of underwear in the French Foreign Legion, is not the answer. The first requirement of any change is that it must be for the better.

- In general (there will be exceptions where circumstances warrant), a new commander should be slow to make changes that have far-reaching implications, or that affect many people—like the change in color of dyed shoes, or a new uniform style. Such things require careful study and evaluation in the light of the best interest of the service, rather than the opinion of one person—especially when the effect is polluted with a "change of command" tag.

- Finally, any new commander who brings with him no new ideas, content simply to go along with the status quo, is a weak officer or at best a mediocre one. The point here is a simple and basic principle: beware not of changes, but of premature changes—particularly when those changes are based on personal preference, motivated by a desire to create an impression rather than to fill a need.

27

Avoid Issuing Unenforceable Orders

MORE UNNECESSARY UNHAPPINESS results from duty you don't welcome than from anything else. This takes many forms. One is the soldier on KP, as pictured in cartoons and comics, like Beetle Bailey peeling a mountain of spuds under the glowering supervision of Cookie. I have chronicled my unhappiest job (cheerleader, in Chapter 3, "The Big Decision"), but the subject needs further examination and analysis.

One of my problems on joining the 29th Infantry in 1925 was to learn how to handle the officer's saber (a skill now obsolete). Since I had been a cadet officer at West Point it was not a difficult transition from the straight cadet sword to manhandling the more cumbersome saber. After practicing a while I managed to whip it around pretty good, which our battalion commander noticed, and detailed me as saber instructor for officers of our battalion.

At first glance that may not sound like a bum job. Not, anyway, until you consider I had only a few months service, which meant that all of my "students" were senior to me—half of them veterans of World War I (including my scowling company commander) who didn't exactly like the idea.

At my hour of instruction I demonstrated and explained how to flip the saber with relaxed precision, including how to coordinate hand movement with marching cadence while passing in review. My class watched and listened with amused smiles. But there was no dodging the next step: to have them march by one at a time and salute, so I could make individual corrections. Somehow that erased the tolerant smiles.

When the time came for my most inept pupil (a heavyset World War I captain with a little duck waddle in his walk) to march by and salute a second time, he said, "Mistuh Newman, show me how to do it again."

As I marched by and saluted him, he stood there grinning. Others got the idea and asked for demonstrations, claiming they, too, learned better that way. Somewhat red in the face, I did my best to play it deadpan. So my saber hour ended pretty much with me marching up and down saluting their smirking smiles.

The next day I met one of my veteran captain pupils on the regimental street, who was ready for drill, wearing his saber. On seeing me approach he drew his saber and returned my hand salute with it — to the considerable amusement of some soldier witnesses.

It would be nice if I could say my expert instruction resulted in marked improvement in the manual of the saber among our battalion officers, but that would falsify the record. In fact, I could see no difference, proving the old adage you can lead a donkey to water but you can't make him drink. However, it cannot be said that my assignment as a battalion saber instructor was a total loss, because it is well known that stress and adversity develop and strengthen character.

At Schofield Barracks in Hawaii during the 1930s we had a fine boxing bowl, which played to capacity crowds on fight nights. Since booing is the usual tactic of fight fans to register disapproval of anything that happens in the ring, it was not surprising we had some boo-birds at our fights. Nobody paid much attention to them, until a new commanding general decided to put a stop to what he considered unsportsmanlike conduct.

He announced that Bronx cheers at the fights would stop. Also, that to ensure compliance with his order, a military police officer would be present in the bowl on fight nights. Since I was an MP lieutenant at that time, it fell to my lot to serve as Boo Officer.

When I arrived at the bowl on fight night, spit-and-polished like a good MP, my mission was known, so that blue-and-white MP brassard on my sleeve drew scattered experimental boos — a kind of warming up, maybe. When the fights started some lusty Bronx cheering erupted on the far side of the bowl. I dutifully walked over to stop it, and the booing ceased where I was headed but began where I had been. When I started back, the yo-yo booing was reversed. In effect, I was the booing coordinator, encouraging more and louder razzberry noises than ever, synchronized to my movements.

This didn't exactly improve sportsmanship, or enhance military discipline, and the Boo Officer detail was soon eliminated.

Once again, however, a bum job had its tangential training value for a young lieutenant because from it I learned two lessons. The first was an adaptation from some Chinese philosopher: When undesirable situation is inevitable, relax and enjoy it. So when boo-birds opened up my arrival at the bowl, it was either smile or scowl.

Since to scowl in the face of the inevitable seemed a futile gesture, a smile came naturally — because actually I was merely the fall-guy in a comedy situation. When the fight started I played it that way in my role as booing coordinator and synchronizer, moving toward any strong booing, but with good-natured deliberation and not in a towering huff. As we continued our little farce the booing did seem to die down a bit — which, I like to think, came more from sympathy for an embarrassed lieutenant than from respect for the authority that ordered him there.

The fundamental lesson was unforgettable: don't issue needless and unenforceable orders.

All bum jobs are not of brief duration, for some bring long-lasting and soul-testing frustration. Like my assignment on graduation from the National War College in 1947, as director of instruction at the Armed Forces Information School. That was a wonderful school, but my interests were with troops and operational matters. However, public information was a vital function of high priority in the radically changed worldwide military situation after World War II. So I mentally thanked the Chinese philosopher for his guidance and resolved to give it my best.

On reporting to AIS at Carlisle Barracks, I discovered the position of director of instruction had been created out of thin air; thus there was no office for me. So a desk was moved into a corner of the assistant commandant's office, which did not make him happy. Also, I shared the services of his secretary, which did not make her happy. Finally, there were no duties for me not already being performed by the commandant, the assistant commandant, and the department heads; so I was told to attend centralized lectures and otherwise wander around to see if there was anything for me to do.

It hardly seemed like an assignment for a new graduate of our nation's highest military college.

However, still mindful of the Chinese admonition to relax and enjoy it, I tried, but managed only a prolonged sickly smile. The Chinese gentleman had not contemplated an undesirable operational situation that would continue for a year and a half of your professional life.

These personal case histories may seem isolated minor incidents of no significance. But I could cite others, not only my own but those of many officers, where the same principles were involved. So these comments appear relevant:

- In that saber instructor detail I believe the major who commanded our battalion should have been present. Thus he would have been the instructor, and the young lieutenant an assistant and demonstrator. While I would have operated in the same way, the result would have been quite different.
- As to the Boo Officer chore, this shows the danger of seeing something you don't like and issuing hasty arbitrary orders that cannot be enforced. In my view, a carefully phrased notice in the daily bulletin — not worded as an order to cease and desist, but calling attention to the unsportsmanlike nature of unrestrained Bronx cheers — would have been far better. But to say nothing, recognizing that whooping it up in the stands is part of the boxing game, would have been the best solution.
- Nothing in my service ever frustrated me more than that make-work-do-nothing duty as director of instruction. But this in no way reflects on the great value of that outstanding school at Carlisle Barracks (now the Army Information School at Fort Hamilton, New York). It was just that, like most soldiers, I wanted to do more than wander around the fringes of the action blowing evanescent soap bubbles.
- When those in authority (from squad leaders to generals) want something done, among the things they should consider before issuing an order is what adverse effects might result for those ordered to do the job.

Then decide whether or not the good to be gained out-weighs those adverse effects — or think of a new way to get the job done, or perhaps a different man to do it. In my book it is seldom necessary to embarrass a good soldier, or condemn him to waste his time on soap-bubble-blowing jobs.

28

Accessibility to Leaders is Vital

SOMETIMES YOU MAKE a decision for completely wrong reasons, yet end up on the right road, anyway. That's what happened when I requested Fort Benning for my first post; not for the career advantage of being in the school troops of the Infantry School but because they had a college-level post basketball team, and officers could play on it.

It was fun to play on that team but, like blowing soap bubbles, nothing was gained that was of value later. At the same time, however, serving in the 29th Infantry, including participation in all kinds of demonstrations for Infantry School classes, became of incalculable value to me during the rest of my service. One of the greatest benefits was seeing how company commanders of the three companies in which I served exercised command and leadership.

These officers were as different as men could be in appearance, manner and personality, yet they had one outstanding characteristic in common: they established an invisible rapport with men of their companies, a feeling of contact, accessibility, and mutual understanding between commander and soldiers.

Consider the implications of the little scene I witnessed in the orderly room one day — orderly tent, really, for two adjoining wood-floored pyramidal tents served that purpose. A soldier came in, halted at attention, saluted smartly and said, "Sir, PFC Smiley [we'll call him] has permission to see the company commander."

He had a present for the captain, he said. It developed that the package under his left arm, which looked like a large piece of folded black oilcloth, was a repair cover that would fit the top of a Model T Ford sedan — along with a can of stickum to fasten it down.

What gave this a point was that the captain was driving the most beat-up looking car on the post, an old Model T Ford sedan, which was parked outside of the orderly tent. The top was cracking and coming apart in several places, and had long been in need of repair.

Capt. Ross MacKechnie, a wonderful officer, gentleman, and soldier, leaned back in his chair with a slow, quizzical little smile.

"Thank you, Smiley," he said. "That should do the job. My car is right outside, so will you please put it on for me?"

PFC Smiley, and several others who just "happened" to be outside, did a fine job of stretching the cover free of wrinkles and used that stickum to fasten it down neatly. For weeks afterwards soldiers would look at that nice new black cover on the captain's car, and grin.

As a young lieutenant, that was a lesson to ponder on. It focused my attention on the human-relations element in command and leadership, because that little byplay between the captain and his company — for the whole company got a kick out of it — could take place only when there was mutual trust, respect, and understanding between them.

Since that day it became an article of faith with me never to be isolated from those who serve under me, but to establish a feeling of contact by talking with individual soldiers — as I saw these three captains of that day do. This paid dividends in many ways.

Years later, after I took command of Company F, 19th Infantry it became clear that the supply sergeant should be replaced. But the problem, naturally, was who should get the job? While I was trying to find the answer, Acting Corporal Petro came to see me with some ideas he thought would improve our weapons maintenance and the system of accountability for them. In due course he ended up as my new supply sergeant, and made a fine one, too.

So, obviously, my problem was solved because Petro felt free to approach me with his ideas. Otherwise I would never have thought of him for that assignment.

A contact activity I remember with pleasure from my five years as a company commander was the softball game on company weekend picnics and in slow spots during field maneuvers — the privates against the officers and NCOs, usually with the first sergeant as umpire. There was always a lot of chatter, especially if the privates thought the umpire had blown a decision.

The last such game I recall was in Hawaii about a year before Pearl Harbor. When I came to bat one of the outfielders yelled, "Hey, pitcher, he can't hit it anyway, so give him an easy one!"

The pitcher then went through elaborate motions of serving me a little pooped-up pitch. Knowing what was coming, I got set, took a little crow-hop out to meet the ball, and nailed it over the center-fielder's head for a home run.

"Naw, he can't hit it!" one of my sergeant teammates yelled back, loudly seconded by others, and the officer-NCO team lost the game by a lopsided score, as usual. But the company won, also as usual, because those little ball games helped us to be a closer-knit outfit.

As officers climb the rank ladder they vary widely in how much personal rapport they maintain with those under them. As you rise higher this gets really complicated, for so many more people are involved. And, of necessity, you are isolated more from the rank and file — just how much is a personal matter.

After the active stage of the Hollandia operation in New Guinea during World War II, our division commander, Maj. Gen. Frederick A. Irving, wanted all officers and men to understand the after-action problems of rehabilitation and preparation for our next task. So he directed a schedule be arranged for him to talk to the division, in battalion-size groups.

This was a very effective plan, not only insuring that the information reached everybody in the division, but building those intangible values that only his presence and personal talk could achieve. In effect, since all of them could not come to see him, he went to see them.

After I became a general officer there was a tendency of headquarters people to "screen" those who wanted to see me. So as G-1 of U.S. Army, Europe, one of my first orders was that nobody who came to my office door could be turned away without my permission.

Of course, this matter of keeping in touch with those under you can boomerang if ill-considered means are used. Like the case of the company commander in the Philippines years ago who fancied himself as an amateur actor, and decided he could use this skill to find out what went on in his company when he was not around.

Since at that time the men in the company chipped in to hire natives as KPs, he dyed his skin and otherwise disguised himself as an old Filipino looking for a KP job. Thus made up, he arrived at the company late one evening and wandered around talking to several soldiers in broken English.

The result was that the first sergeant called the company lieutenant on the phone and said, "Lieutenant, you had better come down here. The captain has gone crazy!"

As with everything else, "keeping in touch" requires judgment and common sense. These comments seem pertinent:

- Beginning at the squad, commanders should be approachable — within the time available and as circumstances permit. This does not mean undue "familiarity," for a definite professional posture is required, which each leader must determine and establish for himself.
- Obviously, as you rise above company command, you cannot keep in contact with every man. But you *can* talk with a cross section of your command, and to groups; you can also use the written word and other means to retain this all-important sense of "being in touch." If you have this feeling toward your command, they will have it toward you.
- This was one of the major factors in Gen. George S. Patton's great battle success. His famous "Prayer" to abate the rains during the Battle of the Bulge — published to his command, along with a Christmas greeting, on a separate card for each man — was an inspired effort of a great leader, reaching out for contact with his soldiers at a time of struggle and crisis. Every unit, every commander, and every situation is a special case. But how well a commander avoids isolation and fosters this feeling of contact between himself and his men is, in a very real sense, the measure of him as a leader.

29

Good Memory Is an Asset

TO PARAPHRASE THE famous comment often attributed to Mark Twain about the weather: Many people complain about a bad memory, but they never do anything about it. Since a good memory is a fine professional asset, it is worth investigating to see whether or not there is any way to improve a poor one.

When I was a second lieutenant in Manila in 1929, an item in the local newspaper reported "one of the seven greatest memory experts in the world" had arrived in town and would give classes to show how "you too can develop a good memory." One class was scheduled for the American-European YMCA gymnasium at 7:30 the following night. I was living in the Y, so decided to get the promised good memory, for the price of five pesos ($2.50 U.S.).

At 7:30 the next evening, quite a group of us were seated on folding chairs in the Y gym—but no memory expert. After waiting fifteen minutes, somebody called the expert's hotel and learned that he had forgotten about the meeting, but would be right over.

Of course other residents of the Y gave us a jumbo-size heehaw about our $2.50 donation. But, looking back now over forty-two years, I can say that was the biggest money bargain of my life.

He gave us three principles:

1. You must want to improve your memory, and make a continuing effort to do so.
2. Nobody can remember everything he sees, hears, or

reads, so be selective; focus your mind on things you want to remember.

3. In focusing your mind, think of how you can relate what you want to remember to other things.

To illustrate this "relate" principle, here are some examples:

- My automobile tag number is 16 W 8397. The 16 W is our county designation, so no problem. When signing a motel register while traveling I put down the last four digits by remembering: "Nine years younger than Tennyson, one year older than Grandma" — because Alfred, Lord Tennyson died at 92 and my grandmother at 96.
- My Social Security number is 251-64-2815, which I associate with, "Class plus one, retirement, Olympics-Eisenhower." Translation: I graduated from West Point in 1925; the retirement age then was 64; I was on the 1928 Olympic Team; and Eisenhower graduated from West Point in 1915.
- My younger daughter's zip code is 01944 — and 1944 was the year of the Leyte invasion, in which I participated.

It is a little game of solitaire anybody can play. The principle is a simple one: relating the selected point you want to remember to other things forces you to focus your mind on that point, thus fixing it in your memory.

Not long after that memory lesson I was at the dock area in Manila harbor to see an Army transport off, the old USAT U.S. *Grant.* Stateroom baggage was piled on the dock ready for loading, each piece numbered with chalk to identify the stateroom for which it was destined. So I practiced my $2.50 lesson, picking a few numbers and committing them to memory by relating them to other things or ideas.

After visiting friends on the *Grant,* I was again standing on the dock as departure time neared, with all baggage now loaded aboard. Suddenly a middle-aged captain charged down the gangplank, looked wildly around at the empty dock, then rushed over to me and said, "Lieutenant, I had a pigskin briefcase in my stateroom baggage. In it were my orders, personal papers, and money. Did you see it, by any chance?"

"Are you assigned to cabin 303?" I asked.

"No," he said.

"Well," I replied, "there was a pigskin briefcase here, and the chalk mark on it was 303."

With that he charged back on the ship, then back to me again to say, "That was it. They just put the wrong number on it. I don't know who you are, Lieutenant, but if you ever need a friend, call on me!"

There have been times since then that I needed a friend, but I have never called on him. Because when he wheeled and dashed back aboard he forgot to get my name or give me his.

The principle of "relating" as a memory aid rests on the same foundation as tying a piece of string on your finger as a reminder. One of the best memory aids is a notebook, because to write down a note you focus your mind on it. That also enables you to recheck your memory, especially for figures or details.

This touches a vital element of command and leadership: when you promise to do something, whether to a subordinate or superior, and forget to do it—*he* does not forget that you forgot! And if this occurs very often your effectiveness and professional standing are seriously lowered.

One of the most important leadership techniques is to remember names. To just say, "I have a poor memory for names," and let it go at that, is more than a defeatist attitude. It shows mental laziness because anyone who makes the effort will greatly improve his facility at remembering names. As a priority project, platoon and company commanders should make a practice of learning to recognize and call by name every man in their commands.

Our finest officers do this. You will notice, when introduced to them, they often call you by name; "Glad to have you in my command, Newman." Using a name at once is a way of focusing your mind on it, and of relating the name to the face. The next time you see such officers it is more than likely they will address you by name.

In the Old Army of "square" divisions my brigade commander (later division commander), Brig. Gen. Durward S. Wilson, made a point of knowing every officer in his brigade by name. His method included having officers photographed on arrival, so he could study the pictures and relate the face to a name. You can be sure that I was impressed when, before I had been introduced to him, he walked up to me on the drill field and called me by name.

Of course there is some hazard in using a name if you are not sure of it. One of my civilian friends once used the "relating" method to fix the name in his memory of a "Mr. Lamb" he met at a cocktail party. Some time later he met Mr. Lamb again, and addressed him as "Mr. Goat."

"Advance thinking" is a fine technique to aid memory. For example, before visiting lower units search your mind for things you should remember while there. Not merely major training matters; that is automatic. But also minor things — especially those that affect people — so that you do not fail to comment on them. Then, when you leave, they may say of you what I have heard said of several division commanders under whom I served: "The Old Man has got a memory like an elephant." But they did not leave remembering to chance; they took time to think and remember in advance.

This is not the place to go into the far broader subject of remembering what you read, or what you hear in oral orders and lectures. However, that "focus your mind" is still the secret, but the "relating" takes a different form. When you read or hear something you want to remember, rephrase or summarize the idea in your own words. This fixes it in your memory more clearly. Also, to twist an old metaphor, you visualize the size, shape and nature of the woods without trying to remember all the trees. The effort must be to remember ideas, principles, and salient facts, and not to jam your brain with minutiae, statistics or parroted words.

To summarize, consider these comments:

- Some people are born with better memories than the rest of us, but anybody can develop a good memory by planned and continued effort.
- Practicing techniques and using memory aids will develop habits that form a regular thought-memory process.
- Remembering names is important. The more we do it, the better we become at it.
- Where accuracy of facts is vital, your memory will make checking easier. But a good memory is no substitute for careful verification of key facts.

- Sages through the ages have realized the importance of a good memory. This quotation from English poet Martin Tupper is my favorite: "Memory is not wisdom; idiots can by rote repeat whole volumes. Yet what is wisdom without memory?"

30

Fill Key Jobs with the Right People

HOW WELL YOU succeed in a difficult assignment depends heavily on the abilities of those who do the work for you. That is why there is a never-ending search to find the best officers to fill key positions. Three basic ways to find the right men are by reviewing personnel records; having personal knowledge of individuals; and from recommendations by others who know the persons concerned.

Sometimes, however, you may need an easily applied test to identify the right officers — like the housewife who wanted the eggs laid by black hens from a bin of eggs in a country market.

"Lady," the proprietor said, "I can't tell what color hens laid any of them eggs. Pick 'em out yourself."

So she did, selecting the twelve largest eggs in the bin — because the larger the eggshell the more egg it contained. But that criteria will not work in picking key officers because, often, the bigger the head the less brain it seems to contain.

When I was a division chief of staff in Australia during World War II, we needed three liaison officers (captains) for our G-3 section, one from each infantry regiment. Our division commander told me to request each regiment to send us the required officer, but not to ask for them by name.

Theoretically, that is the right way to do it because it prevents division from "skimming the cream" of officer talent from lower units. Regimental commanders, knowing their officers and respecting division's need, were supposed to send men well-qualified for the duties involved. That is the theory, anyway. But after a week or ten days it became clear that the three captains we received were white hens' eggs in general capacity. So we had to send them back.

Our division commander then approved calling for three candidates from each regiment, permitting me to select one of them. The problem then was to devise a test that would reveal the intangibles inside their exterior shells. This is the test used:

- After an initial interview, each candidate was given a clipboard, a pencil and two sheets of typewriter paper. He was then told to write on one sheet a summary of basic qualities of a successful staff officer.
- On the second sheet, each man was to make a freehand sketch of the floor plan of our headquarters where they were interviewed. The idea was to show the layout of the office space — not to make an artistic drawing.

Obviously, the written summary revealed legibility of handwriting, ability to express thoughts in clear readable language, and whether or not the officer had a good concept of a staff officer's job.

But it was the little freehand sketch that separated the good prospects from marginal warm bodies. It revealed such intangibles as:

- Ability to see things as a whole, evidenced by centering the sketch on the page — not drawing one room at a time and ending with a distorted picture, or one that ran off the sheet while some of the page remained unused.
- Capacity to see things in proportion to each other. If the G-3 office was twice as large as the G-2 office, it should show that way, not vice versa.
- Taken together, the two pages revealed whether or not the officer could portray an idea on paper clearly and simply, an essential quality for staff work.

The test worked, and we got three good liaison captains.

Of course, this is a specialized case. But seeking the right officer for a key job is always a specialized case, depending on the particular facts influencing the situation, and there is no one way to find him. It is quite different from overall policies and methods that regulate Army-wide duty assignments by the thousands.

The easiest way to get the right men for special jobs is to pick the best qualified officers known to you, if they are available. We see this principle applied when a senior general takes over a command and immediately begins pulling strings to get selected officers transferred to his command. In coffee-call parlance this is known as "assembling his team."

In general, however, you cannot get the men you want from outside sources. It then becomes a question of shifting personnel around within your own area of responsibility. To have the perception to see each person's capabilities and the judgment to place each where he is best suited are major elements of command and leadership.

There is, of course, another side to the question of which officers should get the important jobs and that is the right of every good officer to have his fair share of key job assignments. This runs counter to the procedure whereby a senior officer tries to keep putting his "fair-haired boys" on special assignments, and is one reason the Army promulgates a career management program.

The need for such a program is illustrated by a case that hit my desk as G-1, U.S. Army, Europe (USAREUR), when a vacancy came open for a regimental commander. The division commander requested this vacancy be filled with one of his battalion commanders, a fine lieutenant colonel who was due for promotion to eagle rank. The corps and army commanders approved his request on its way to USAREUR.

To have granted this fair-haired-boy request would have been a gross violation of the Army career management program, bypassing every eligible eagle colonel in Europe for this much desired "command assignment." So we sent a letter to the chief of the infantry branch of G-1 in the Pentagon, asking that he send us the names of ten colonels in Europe—arranged in order of preference—whose records most entitled them to consideration for this choice professional assignment.

The top man on that list was an outstanding colonel who would not otherwise have been considered because he was a military attache and his records were not in USAREUR. He was designated as the regimental commander, in a letter signed by the Commander in Chief, USAREUR, because this overruled the division commander's request — which had been approved by the corps and army commanders.

It is interesting to look back now at this case because the division commander who initiated the request became a four-star general; the lieutenant colonel who did not get the regiment became a lieutenant general; and the colonel who became the regimental commander retired as a major general. If the colonel had not received that "command assignment," would he have become a general? We can never know the answer to that, but it is a question to ponder.

The point to note here is that, while it is essential to put able men in key assignments, it is also important that these assignments not be motivated by favoritism. While seniority alone is not the answer, it should be weighed along with other considerations. As in so many aspects of command and leadership, there is no substitute for insight and good judgment.

On several occasions I visited the Pentagon to see my efficiency reports, which might be called marks received in the school of experience of my active duty years. The best reports were those rendered when I had the finest officers on key jobs doing the work for me. And, not surprisingly, the lowest report covered the time when one of my key officers was not up to par — but I left him on the job anyway.

This barely touches the complexities and ramifications of finding the right officers for important duties. Added comments are:

- The fine art of selecting the proper men for vital jobs is a primary requirement for success in command and leadership.
- Military capacity is not the only requirement for officers filling key positions; personalities are important, too. That is why a general officer is usually allowed to select his own chief of staff.
- Every commander should keep in mind that his selections for key assignments ought not be made in the vacuum of his own opinion, without regard to how others in his command may react to his appointments. Others have an interest, too, especially if a clique atmosphere develops.

If the view permeates a command that key job placements are unduly influenced by favoritism, personal friendship, religious affiliations or—on high-level staffs—branch bias, then a serious officer morale situation may build up.

- To young officers I suggest this little game of solitaire (note the word is "solitaire," not coffee-hour discussions to second-guess your boss): observe those selected for key positions and try to understand why they were selected. After years of watching how success or failure depends on selecting the right key officers, your perceptive evaluation of others will be keener. Thus, in later years, you will be better qualified to select the right key officers to get the job done for you.

31

A Staff Officer Must Be Able and Flexible

SOMETIMES YOUR STAFF-DUTY past comes back to haunt you, as it did for me at the 1974 reunion of the 24th Infantry Division held in the Hotel Thayer at West Point. When it happened my wife and I were with Fred Zierath (Maj. Gen., Ret.) and Lester Wheeler (Brig. Gen., Ret.) and their wives, about to start down the line for the Friday night buffet supper.

"Hold it!" we heard, and a tall handsome man with a fine head of hair and an impressive mustache hurried up to us. "This is an opportunity I can't miss!"

Fred, Les, and I recognized Ross Pursiful, who had been a captain on our division headquarters staff in New Guinea during World War II.

"What I want to say is this," Ross continued. "When I was in the G-3 section at Hollandia, I finally decided I could not take working for that G-3 anymore. He was a real slave driver, and I had had it up to here [pointing to his throat]. So I went to see the chief of staff, told him life was not worth living for me in G-3, and that I wanted to be transferred."

He paused for effect. He had our full attention because Fred and Les had both served as G-3, while I was the chief of staff.

"So what do you think the chief said?" Ross asked.

Nobody offered to guess, and I could not remember, so he told us that the chief said, "Ross, you are just batting your head against a stone wall — and the only thing bleeding is your head."

Those within hearing laughed at this fresh evidence labeling me the villain of those days, the redheaded SOB of division headquarters. (Well, anyway, every good headquarters needs at least one.)

The point here, however, is that after twenty-nine years Ross still carried the memory of staff duty as a tough life. What did not seem to enter his mind was that it had been a rough life for Fred, Les and me, too. Staff duty is a special kind of complex world, which I discovered as a regimental staff officer (chapter 22).

Recently I exhumed some notes and quotes out of my files from notebooks of my active-duty years. One quote was from the book, *The Mature Mind,* by H. A. Overstreet: "It is not good for a child to have too many toys, so that he never has time to love one; or to be too constantly surrounded by people; or to be too constantly on the go; or to have so many activities organized that it never has time to be itself in a kind of divine idleness."

This principle is applicable for staff officers too. When I had been a general staff officer for three years, the last eighteen months as a wartime chief of staff, I found myself feeling punch-drunk from the constant pressures of people and projects, along with the increasing tempo of training and staging in Australia for our coming New Guinea campaign.

So I asked the division commander for a three-day pass and loaded a jeep with a mosquito-proof jungle hammock and enough food for three days. Then with a driver and back-up driver, so two people would know where I was, we set off for the Pacific Ocean twenty miles away. There, in a little fringe of trees bordering an isolated beach, with no human habitation anywhere around, we hung my jungle hammock between two trees and unloaded my supplies. That accomplished, the jeep and the somewhat puzzled drivers returned to division headquarters with orders to come back in three days. This left me in that "kind of divine idleness."

On schedule, three days later and much refreshed, I returned to division headquarters far better prepared to play my part in the coming amphibious Hollandia operation. The point, of course, is that staff officers have a duty to themselves and their organization to recognize when they need rest and "divine idleness," and take the necessary steps to get it.

Other items from those old notebooks about staff duty include:

- A British major general said to me, "United States,

United Kingdom and French staff officers are different in the way they operate. The UK staff officers tend to be slow and deliberate in planning, talk with others, and come up with a well-considered plan. But it may be a bit late.

"The French want to lock themselves in a room, with no coordination, and do it all alone. But the Americans take right off, and want to get it done quickly, thus things may not be fully coordinated as they go along."

- There is nothing more dangerous than a sailor with a rifle, except a young, inexperienced staff officer with a pencil.

- One of the most important angles to staff work is the requirement to answer questions. A little girl once asked her mother where she came from, and got the birds-and-bees routine. "Mother," the little girl said, "I know how I got here. What I want to know is where I came from, because Louise says she came from Peoria."

  The staff principle involved is that before you begin answering, be sure you understand the question.

- Military assignments today include responsibilities not just on the drill field and in combat, but also in the vast areas of logistics, procurement, mobilization and international diplomatic and economic policies. This requires high commanders and their staffs to have broad knowledge, infinite tact, delicacy of judgment and flexibility.

- An internationally known lothario was asked, "What is the secret of your success? You not only have married, or otherwise had, some of the most beautiful women in the world, but also married the richest woman in the world. How do you do it?"

  His reply was, "I make them happy."

  The requirements to try to keep everybody happy — especially his commander, other seniors and subordinate unit commanders — often transforms a fine, competent officer into what is known as "a jittery staff officer." It is not a happy life for an overly conscientious officer.

- It has been said staff officers and politicians are much alike in that they strive to keep everybody happy. Consider this apocryphal story about a senator who visited President Franklin D. Roosevelt, when Mrs. Roosevelt was present, and expressed his views on a controversial subject.

  "You are so right, Senator," the president said, "you are so right."

  After the senator left, another senator came in, and expressed opposite views on the same controversial subject.

  "You are so right, Senator," the president said, "you are so right."

  Whereupon, after the second senator left, Mrs. Roosevelt said, "Franklin, you agreed with both of those senators when they stated exactly opposite views. You just can't do things like that!"

  "You are so right, my dear," FDR said, "you are so right."

  Such a gambit may work sometimes for politicians, but it is fatal for a staff officer to try to keep everybody happy that way.

- As in other areas of human endeavor, there are invidious definitions for those who have responsibility but cannot satisfy everybody—like this definition of an assistant staff officer: a mouse studying to be a rat.

These general comments appear in order:

- There is a saying that the whole is no better than its component parts. Similarly, it is hard for the effectiveness of a commander to be better than the staff that serves him. A weak commander can, if he has a good staff, appear better than he is—and the reverse is equally true.

- High-level, long-range staff planners are alleged to look in crystal balls for answers. This is the basis for a plaintive little rhyme (reported to have been composed by a former chief of staff) which begins, "We planners are a sorry lot, bereft of sword and pistol." All too often, able staff officers are denigrated by the inference that they do not play their part in the fighting front. But the reverse side of the coin is that those at the fighting front will really find themselves in trouble unless they have good staff officers behind them.

- After my retirement, we had a small lemon bush in our Florida yard that produced an enormous lemon, as large as a grapefruit. Naturally, this big lemon bent its slender limb heavily downward. To correct this I propped up the limb — and it broke where I placed the support. This illustrates the principle that staff officers who carry heavy loads should remember: bend under the load and sway with the wind to gain maximum strength and endurance. Try to stand too rigidly, and you will break like that limb. In other words, the heavier your staff work, the more important it is to stay loose and relax.

32
Some Points
on Training Problems

MY ROOM IN a hotel near Verdun, France, was spotless, as was everything else about the hotel, including the community bathroom nearby. But when I traipsed down the lighted hall that night to use the facilities, I could not find the light switch in the bathroom. Finally, deciding the star-glow seeping through the window was enough for my purpose, I closed the door, turned the old-fashioned iron key in the lock—and the light came on.

The thrifty French had solved the problem of how to save electricity by making it impossible to go out and leave the light on. In our military service there are countless problem situations in the management of men, money and materials, large, small and middle-sized, where problem-solving thinking pays dividends.

In my first year on active duty I qualified with the rifle as a Sharpshooter. The second year my goal was to make Expert, and my first score was at 200 yards rapid fire. I stood on the firing line, waiting tensely for the target to come up with its silhouette bull's eye. My rifle was the old bolt-action Springfield loaded with five rounds, and another five-round clip in my belt. When the target appeared I would have sixty seconds to sit down, take a firing position and fire five rounds, reload and fire the other five.

When the target popped up I plopped down on my fanny, came into firing position—and buck fever grabbed me. The bull's-eye danced in such a wild frenzy it was impossible to hold my sights on it. But I absolutely *had* to fire ten shots before the target dropped after sixty seconds. In desperation, I focused my eye on the front sight and my complete concentration on keeping the front sight in the middle of the rear sight — getting off the tenth shot just in time.

Then I wanted to dig a hole and hide before my target came up to disgrace me. But when it did I stared, unbelieving, because white spotters were scattered around the bull's-eye — with only one "wart four" out over the left shoulder.

That night I figured it out: the regulations were wrong about where to focus your eye in aiming, and where your concentration should be. You should focus your eye on the front sight (*not* on the bull's-eye), and your primary concentration should be on keeping the front sight in the middle of the rear sight, not on keeping the sight *precisely* under the bull. It is a matter of *angle:* whether or not your front sight is *exactly* under the bull's-eye is relatively unimportant.

That discovery in 1927 posed the problem of how to convey the information to others. The usual reaction was, "Yeah? You mean you don't look at the bull's-eye? Know any more funny stories?" So I just became an Expert rifleman, and let it go at that — until I was honored with command of Company G, 26th Infantry.

Now it was my responsibility to pass the word to others, including my earnest, conscientious second lieutenant. He, as I had, faced his second rifle season as a Sharpshooter with strong ambitions to make Expert. So I discussed eye focus with him and the company, without, it must be said, noticeable results in scoring.

Then, like that Frenchman must have done in figuring out his door key–light switch, I gave more than a passing thought to solving the puzzle. This resulted in a gimmick to try on my lieutenant (knowing very well that I need say nothing to the company, because anything out of routine is always viewed by many eyes, digested by many minds, and judiciously discussed at length).

We were firing in practice that day at 500 yards slow fire. I explained the procedure to my lieutenant; it was clear he was not happy to be a rifle-range guinea pig, right out there in front of the curious and interested company. But I knew he was a loyal, dedicated soldier, who would carry out instructions to the letter and to the best of his ability.

A phone call instructed the pits to have his target taken down and reversed. Thus he could not see the bull's-eye, only the dirty gray canvas behind it and the frame on which it was stretched. His instructions were:

- Focus your eye on the target, and line up your sights on it.
- Shift the focus of your eye to the front sight.
- With your front sight clear and sharp, center it *exactly* in the rear sight.
- With your primary concentration on keeping the front sight exactly centered, squeeze the trigger.

The target was left up while he fired five rounds, with no bull's-eye view; then marked — showing three white spotters in the bull's-eye, with two "wart fours" barely out at seven and two o'clock. The principle was clear.

Did my young lieutenant make Expert? Yes. Did that little exercise help him? He said so.

Are our shooting regulations still wrong about where to focus the eye? No. On my return from World War II, they had been corrected. But it remained hard to get young soldiers to believe the way to hit the bull's-eye was to focus your eye on the front sight (anatomically, your eye can focus on only one point at a time).

Since the aimed rifle shot remains a valuable combat skill, the reversed target training idea is still valid. The principle is even more important in pistol shooting.

An ever-present training problem in routine basic subjects is to develop an interest-provoking angle. Here is a case history with a different type lesson.

At the time I was discovering how to make Expert with the rifle at Fort Benning, we got a first lieutenant in our company. Henry (we'll call him) was an enthusiastic, imaginative fellow who devoted much thought to enlivening training in routine subjects.

One day I entered the dayroom where he was holding forth in a scheduled hour on the court-martial manual. Everybody was paying close attention, and I soon learned why: he suddenly digressed to discuss the place in the legal hierarchy of our Supreme Court.

He painted a picture of nine all-wise old men with long white beards, each with his own shiny, oversize spittoon conveniently placed for use, and all apparently dozing while lawyers argued the case under consideration. But when a lawyer made an error in his presentation, all nine pairs of eyes popped open instantly and the long white beards bristled. Then a couple of them would use their spittoons, set the record straight for the erring lawyer—and all lapse again into their relaxed appearance of somnolence.

You got the idea we had a fine legal system, with some basic facts about our court-martial procedures worked in. He definitely held the interest of and instructed his audience, although, on reflection, the method does not appear applicable for general use.

Another day we were having gas mask drill, livened a bit by passing through tear gas from grenades. And Henry had figured out a fillip to heighten interest for his platoon.

After they passed through the small, wind-driven gas cloud successfully, wearing masks, Henry went a step further. He explained how, for short periods, you could pass through gas unharmed by closing your eyes, holding your breath, and running through the gassed area.

Then, with gas masks off, Henry tossed out another grenade. As the breeze wafted the smoky-looking fumes downwind, he said, "Follow me!" and took off through the gas at right angles to the relatively narrow smoke ribbon.

The only trouble was that he stepped in an uneven spot and fell down. Members of his platoon, eyes closed, stumbled over him, and others over them. Some got gassed pretty good in the tangled mass of arms, legs and bodies when they ran out of breath and when, disoriented in their falls, they opened their eyes. A few unfortunates ran downwind, thus continuing to be gassed. But nobody suffered real damage.

Some comments are:

- The lesson from Henry's gas training idea is that in puzzling out new ways to make training interesting, careful review of bright ideas is required. Enthusiasm and imagination are fine when tempered by second thoughts and common-sense consideration of possible side effects.
- The young lieutenant who fired on the reversed target is now Brig. Gen. Lester L. Wheeler, USA (Ret.). Recently he said, "I needed 44 on the last range at 500 yards slow fire, and got 46—with an assist from First Sergeant Redding. It was cold that morning, and he brought out canteens of hot water wrapped in a blan-

ket. Before I went up to my firing point he made sure my hands and fingers were warm.''
- That's the way it was with our Top Kick, always thinking of ways to help the company get things done better —and he considered young officers his special responsibility.
- Looking back now, one of the surest marks of an officer who is going places is that he tries to improve the way things are done in whatever assignment he may have: more effective visual aids, new ideas in field exercises, more perceptive solving of personnel problems — anything that gets his job done at a higher standard, but no attention-grabbing, poorly considered ideas.

33

Safety Checks Should Never Be Routine

IN THE LATE 1930s my regiment participated in major maneuvers at Fort Drum, New York. One weekend, as a community relations project, the field bivouac was opened to civilian visitors and a number of those who circulated through the camp were females.

One group of three curious young ladies, noticing what looked like a canvas fence around a small rectangular space, decided to have a look. Since they approached this mysterious canvas-enclosed area on the side opposite the entrance, they could not see the sign OFFICERS LATRINE.

At this time a middle-aged captain was astride the slit trench type facility in the partially undraped state necessary. He looked up as small hands pulled down the canvas low enough for three curious female heads to peer over it.

The captain's reflexes impelled him to rise upright and snatch his trousers from around his knees in a single spasmodic motion—with the result that he fell in the trench, wrenched his knee severely and emerged in a somewhat tarnished state. Of course the really serious injury was to his dignity when the story spread on the hotline of the camp grapevine.

The point here is that there are some accidents that cannot be charged to failure of safety programs; you just have to accept them.

But command alertness should recognize dangerous conditions and correct them—which I failed to do as a lieutenant in Company I, 31st Infantry, in Manila in 1929. On two occasions I saw conditions that were inherently dangerous, yet took no action—and in both situations fatal accidents resulted.

In the first instance I noticed several men using a kerosene flame to delouse metal-frame Army cots outside of barracks. The procedure was simple: a rag was wrapped around the end of a stick, dipped in kerosene, and lighted with a match. The flame was then run along the cracks, crevices, and springs where bedbugs or lice could hide.

I did not know what they were doing until I asked. The explanation included the fact this was the way they had always done it. So I walked away, failing to ask what if any safety rules were followed, or to notice there was no NCO supervision.

Later that day one soldier's torch burned out and needed more kerosene. So he picked up a half empty five-gallon tin and—instead of pouring kerosene in the shallow dish available for that purpose, then dipping his burned-out torch in that—poured kerosene directly from the five-gallon tin onto the rag part of the torch.

There was still a live spark on the torch, and it ignited the kerosene, which flashed back into the big can, exploding it and enveloping the soldier in burning kerosene. He lived less than twenty-four hours.

About six months later, I inspected the coffee in our kitchen one afternoon and noticed a soldier painting the high ceiling in the mess hall. He was standing on the next-to-top step of a short stepladder which rested on the concrete floor. A second look showed his feet were on the step far enough so that his shins, about two-thirds the way to his knees, were braced against the top of the ladder. The set-up did not look very secure to me, but the soldier seemed relaxed and unconcerned, and had already painted more than half of the ceiling. So I completed my coffee inspection and left the soldier still painting the ceiling from his precarious perch atop the stepladder.

The next morning, just before he finished painting that high ceiling, the soldier lost his balance momentarily. As a result the ladder kicked out from under him and he was killed instantly when his head hit the concrete floor.

In all the years since I have had to live with the thought that I could and should have prevented those two accidents. "We have always done it this way" is not a valid reason for failing to correct an accident-prone situation.

Army-wide, we have major programs and detailed regulations covering such broad safety fields as fire prevention, operation of motor vehicles and varied and complex safety regulations governing the firing of weapons. Here are two incidents that illustrate principles that apply to all areas of command alertness in preventing accidents:

At West Point our field training included firing live ammunition. One day, when the first round was fired from an artillery piece, the air was filled with yellow smoke, fine wispy particles drifted slowly downward, and there was a bulge in one side of the gun barrel.

Of course there was an investigation. From this it was concluded somebody had left one of those cottony swabs in the barrel when cleaning the gun, and no one had looked through the barrel to see if it was clear before the first round was fired.

Since we were firing high-explosive ammunition, that could have resulted in a serious accident. And all because one of the most elementary safety rules was not followed: look through the barrel of a weapon to be sure it is clear before you begin firing it.

The principle involved, which applies in all phases of accident prevention, is that there is no substitute for constant command alertness to enforce simple and obvious safety precautions — even when the danger seems remote.

Many years later, after I left one large post, an infiltration and battle indoctrination course was set up there. This included crawling under close overhead machine-gun fire, which was a mental hazard as well as a tough physical test.

Safety regulations required that a mechanical stop be built for each gun, with a bar supporting each gun barrel, so that the barrel could not be depressed low enough to hit men crawling under the band of fire. Also, the guns were to be test-fired and bore-sighted each day to ensure the path of bullets was safely above the men. For several days there was no trouble; then tragedy struck with devastating unexpectedness when one gun fired low and two men died.

Investigation revealed that the bar under that machine gun barrel had been subject to the vibration of firing in a way that gradually sunk its supports into the ground the small distance required to change its angle. The checks had been made, but — and this is the crux of many accidents — the checks were routine. The new safety officer "assumed" — since everything had been going fine before he came on — that the mechanical safety stops were properly installed.

So he went through the motions but failed to spot that one unsafe gun.

The principle is this: no safety check can ever be routine, no matter how often performed, when the lives of men are involved. It is an insidious temptation to slight checks on regulations when things have been going safely for days — but this is the danger, because it dulls alertness.

To conclude this safety review, here are four comments:

- In peace as in war, the lives and welfare of men are constant responsibilities of every commander. The commander cannot do all the checking, but he can institute practices and personally spot-check to set the example of safety awareness. That motivates others to check, as Gen. Bruce C. Clarke expressed it: "An organization does well only those things the boss checks."
- A new company commander can make a good start on his safety program by taking positive steps like these: call a fire drill and inspect the fire extinguishers; inspect the storage of ammunition, paint and combustibles — and check local safety regulations in force. Also call on the first sergeant to search his memory and the sick book for accidents that had resulted in injuries during the past two years. Then check to see if unsafe conditions that caused any of them still exist.
- Near the end of my last duty tour, as chief of staff for U.S. Continental Army Command at Fort Monroe, Virginia, an old concrete casemate on the post was broken into. Several pre-teenage boys had pried off the lock with a crowbar, so they could use the casemate as their "clubhouse." The MP report reached my desk late that afternoon, and stated the casemate was used for local storage of explosives. So I sent for the officer who investigated the incident. He reported that the explosives had been inventoried and there was a shortage of three blasting caps. He was sure, however, there was a mistake in the records because the casemate was searched very carefully — and every boy said he did not have any. I then directed the officer to proceed immediately to the homes of the boys and ask that parents

personally search the pockets of their sons — and the three blasting caps were found in the jacket pocket of one boy. The costly lesson learned from those two fatal accidents in Manila thirty years before may have saved a maiming accident as well as prevented other accidents over the years.

- Safety awareness has continued with me in retirement. But my wife likes to prune the citrus trees in our yard and pick the fruit. So my command safety directives have failed to keep her off our stepladder. This illustrates a principle worth remembering: there is a limit to how far you can go to prevent accidents.

34

Prepare for Inspections

BEFORE WORLD WAR II an inspiring review of troops was held for a high-ranking general, climaxing his command inspection of a large post. When the review ended the general appeared favorably impressed. Everybody relaxed in self-congratulatory satisfaction as the old boy, a tough cookie, was ready to get in his car and take off.

Just at this moment an escort wagon drawn by two mules came slowly out of the dirt road from a wooden area on the far side of the review field. The general saw it, and a sudden quiet settled on the group. This was not on the program.

One reason the general reached high rank was that he understood the Army and the men in it, and didn't miss many bets. So now he wanted to see the escort wagon.

Earlier that day the first sergeant of a service company had decided to get out of sight the company 8-ball, a conglomeration of extra stuff in the supply room, an unpainted escort wagon, and a couple of ratty-looking mules — all in one master stroke. To do this he loaded the unsightly junk into the escort wagon, including the disheveled 8-ball, and told him to drive the wagon out into the woods. This was the wagon that now ground to a stop as the general's car pulled alongside.

"What have you got in that wagon, soldier?" the general asked.

"Well, sir," the 8-ball said, turning his head to one side and letting fly a stream of tobacco juice to make talking easier, "mighty nigh everything, I guess."

One glance confirmed this as perhaps an understatement, and the general inquired, "What are you doing here?"

"The first sargint, he told me to drive this waggin into the woods, and stay until after five o'clock. It's after five o'clock naow."

The general turned to the post commander and said, "Thank you again for all the effort I know went into getting ready for this inspection. You have a fine command." He then drove away without further comment.

On another post a rough-and-ready type regimental commander made an unannounced spot inspection. As he approached a company barracks, the old first sergeant saw him coming and barely had time to take emergency action — including getting his coffee-drinking company commander out of the mess hall and into the orderly room.

Because of the first sergeant's quick action, things had not gone badly. The colonel had just checked the supply room, and was outside the barracks and in the act of exchanging final salutes when his eyes fixed on an oversize GI trash can nearby. His salute froze in midair.

The lid of the trash can was slowly rising, resting on the head of a man inside, then it slowly settled back in place. The colonel strode to the can and tossed the lid aside. A very small, very dirty soldier stood up in the can. He needed a shave and a haircut; his uniform looked as though it had been slept in on the city dump — which was not far wrong, for this soldier was the company pig's ear who had just returned from AWOL.

The regimental commander, the company commander, and the first sergeant all looked at the soldier. The colonel asked, "What in hell are you doing in that can, soldier?"

"Well, sir," the soldier looked at the row of unfriendly eyes focused on him, and couldn't think of anything but the truth. "I was talkin' to the first sergeant, when we seen you comin', sir. Quick-like, the sergeant says to me, 'Git lost! Git out of sight!' Then he run in the mess hall to tell the captain. There wasn't hardly much time, sir. So I did the best I could."

The colonel did the best he could, too, in telling the company commander what he thought about the incident.

These are but two of countless incidents that have, over the years, given inspections an aura of unexpectedness; you are never sure what will happen next. They are not just something to laugh at (or cry about if you are one of the victims), but form part of endless complications in dealing with people and human nature—which is inherent in inspections. Thus leadership angles are often involved.

Some years ago a study was made at West Point to determine what qualities a successful leader must have. Leaders in all lines of human endeavor were examined—not only soldiers, but educators, businessmen, industrialists, politicians, engineers and members of other professions. One basic characteristic was found in all successful leaders.

"Courage," was my reply when asked to guess what this essential was. The correct answer was: *human understanding.* When you stop to think, that makes sense; how can you be a successful leader if you do not understand those you lead?

Military inspections are a vital technique of command designed to check many things: status of training, discipline and morale; completeness of equipment and readiness of weapons; alert plans and living conditions; and others. To accomplish the greatest benefit, however, it must be kept in mind that inspections deal primarily with people—thus they should be made with human understanding, the key element in leadership.

You Gotta Have Empathy

In the case of the escort wagon containing "mighty nigh everything," the senior general showed that he understood this. That post—and all the people on it—had made a tremendous effort to get ready for his inspection. Had he ignored this and as his last act created a stink over a minor matter, everybody would have been the loser. The general would have been lowered in the eyes of the garrison; the pride and enthusiasm of both officers and men would have been dampened had a small happening been allowed to nullify long and careful preparation for the inspection.

As it was, however, the general's alertness in discovering the errant escort wagon and his restraint in reacting to the muddy little misadventure—without rubbing their noses in it—gave officers and men a new respect and loyalty toward him. By his human understanding, the senior general insured that the Army gained the greatest possible benefit from his inspection.

The case of the soldier in the GI can was entirely different. To begin with, the inspection was unannounced; thus there had been no effort to get ready. Also, the colonel was not a visiting dignitary, but concerned in direct daily training and command of his regiment. Further, the captain had obviously been drinking coffee in the mess hall during drill hours. It all added up to a "hell-raising bee" situation, and had the regimental commander treated it as a joke *that* would have been a lack of human understanding.

Finally, it should not be overlooked that human understanding is a two-way thing at inspections: the colonel knew that his men had a right to expect their regimental commander to exhibit the temper of his steel under those circumstances.

Understanding Strained Through Peach Juice

Of course there are times when the quality of human understanding becomes strained during inspections when strong personalities meet head-on — like the confrontation witnessed by a friend of mine.

One of the Army's truly great "characters," a lean and leathery overage captain, was commanding an infantry company being inspected by a visiting bellicose general who specialized in bluff and bluster. No delicate nuances of human nature cluttered *his* inspections.

By the time the inspecting party reached the kitchen, the company commander had been repeatedly pushed around with needling questions. "Captain," the general finally said, pointing to cans of peaches on a shelf in the pantry, "how many peaches in one of those cans?"

Without change of expression the captain reached for a can and put it on the meat block. Then, picking up the meat cleaver, he dealt the can a tremendous blow — exposing the peaches, which he proceeded to count.

"General," he said deadpan — peach juice all over himself, the general, and everybody and everything within range — "there are thirteen peaches in this can."

Speechless, peach juice dripping from his chin, the general turned on his heel and withdrew from the battlefield.

Soon the battalion commander came hurrying back, but the captain beat him to the punch.

"Well, Major," he said, "that's one general who won't ask me any more damnfool questions!"

Failures in human understanding by an inspector do not often explode in a nice clean eruption of peach juice. It might be healthier if there were more such direct actions — because the smouldering resentment from ill-considered inspection procedures can corrode the human spirit.

When I was assistant division commander in the 82nd Airborne Division, the division commander directed me to check infantry regiments to insure they were ready for the Annual General Inspection by army headquarters — a detailed team-inspection affair.

In one regiment I considered the kitchens below par, and said so — and later inspected them again. Still unsatisfied, my remarks to the regimental commander were quite definite.

Breakfast Picnic Style

On the day of the formal inspection I stopped by the kitchen line of that regiment again, and it was in perfect order. But something new was wrong: I sensed the kitchen help were not happy. As I stood in the last kitchen an idea struck me.

"Sergeant," I asked the mess steward, "did the company have breakfast this morning?"

"Yes, sir!" he answered, looking me in the eye with no hint of a smile at my question, but with the ring of truth in his voice. So I left. But I too was now unhappy — for good soldiers in a good outfit ought to be happy about it.

After I returned to division headquarters I called in my aide and said, "Go back and find out *where* that company had breakfast."

He returned with the report that the company had had a cold picnic lunch for breakfast, and had not entered the mess hall.

That regiment got a high rating on its messes in the formal inspection by army headquarters because the inspectors did not discover what I had found out — or the messes would have been rated *Unsatisfactory*. The only reason for being of a mess is to feed the best possible food — and that means hot food, well served. So I bent the regimental commander's ear.

From this incident, you can do quite a bit of philosophizing about inspections and human understanding, but the big lesson is this:

never forget the soldier, his welfare and training—but especially keep your extrasensory-perception antennae sensitive to how he *feels*.

The next time I was in that kitchen, the mess sergeant had the indefinable, barely perceptible expression around his eyes and mouth that makes you know when a good soldier is glad to see you. After I looked around and was about to leave, he asked, "Would the General have a cup of our coffee and piece of cake?"

"Yes," I said, "I would like that, Sergeant."

So we had a short soldierly visit, within the relaxed yet correct protocol in such cases—and a little unspoken communication passed between us.

He was letting me know he understood my demands for high inspection standards—but mostly he was also letting me guess he had found out that I had learned about the cold outside-the-mess-hall picnic breakfast. In this I gained much face with him, for he did not like that procedure either—no good mess sergeant would.

Once again there was this interplay of human nature and human understanding during an inspection, on both sides. The current erudite word for this is empathy.

Buck Up from the Top Down

It isn't always clear how far human understanding should go in the face of below-par standards. That's where judgment comes in, which must include knowledge of personalities and the special situation. An interesting inspection operating principle was once explained to me by a four-star general this way: "When things look good I pat the sergeants and soldiers on the back, but when somebody's arm needs twisting, I look around for the senior officer present. To get things bucked up, I work on the top."

There is no intent here to make inspections (or any other aspect of command and leadership) an inhibited semineurotic exercise—for there are many times when only a heavy hand will meet the situation. But when demanding efficiency is mixed with judgment and human understanding, then and only then is the Army gaining the greatest benefit from inspections.

35

Trust Everybody but Check Performance

FORTY YEARS AGO I went shopping in Wahiawa, the small town near Schofield Barracks, Hawaii. As a pipe smoker, I paused at a pile of cheap briars on a counter and noticed the hole bored in one pipe stem did not reach the bowl. That seemed unusual enough to be worth fifty cents.

At this time I was squiring a tall blonde around, so I took my new pipe along to the officers' club on our date that evening. It chanced we had been making bets on various things — a cigar for me if I was right, a carnation lei for her on our next date if she was — and by curious coincidence I had won all of these bets. When we were into our second drink, it seemed a propitious time to promote another bet.

"Well," I said, stuffing tobacco into my new pipe, "let's bet about something.

"About what?" she said, taking a dainty sip.

"Oh," I said, clamping the pipe stem in my teeth, "I'll bet there's a hole in the bowl of this pipe to let the smoke out."

She took another dainty sip in silence.

"All right," I mumbled, trying to sound frustrated, "I'll bet it does not have a hole in the bowl to let the smoke out."

More silence, and another delicate sip. So I struck a match and reached up to light my pipe.

"All right, I'll bet," my blonde announced firmly. "You bet there is no hole in that pipe bowl. I bet there is one!"

When I blew out the match and used it to dig tobacco from my pipe, she saw there was no hole in the bowl. Her reaction was instant and positive: "I'm not going to bet with you any more!"

The repercussions from that evening have followed me through the years, because I married the young lady. The principle involved is a basic consideration in human relations. Two hundred years ago Laurence Sterne expressed it this way: "Trust that man in nothing who has not a conscience in everything."

Once you "put one over" on others—in uniform or out, from privates to generals—they never quite trust you again. Thus, a minor and questionable advantage today will be paid for by loss of confidence and trust in you thereafter.

In one company of my regiment (511th Airborne Infantry) at a command inspection, I noticed that garbage cans were unusually clean. This led to the discovery that they had two sets of garbage cans: one for inspection, and one for garbage. Can anyone imagine that would not stick in my memory, coloring my opinion of that company commander?

Early in World War II, I was made chief of staff of a division. Soon after taking over I carried a relatively routine paper to the CG, prepared in final form for signature—if there were no changes. When I told him the nature of the paper, he picked up his pen and signed it without delay. As I stood, uncertain what to say—for he had not read the paper—he looked up at me and smiled.

"Newman," he said, "you've been on my staff nearly a year. If I had to read and check papers like that when you brought them in, you would not be my chief of staff."

That motivated me to do my best to justify that empirical vote of confidence. When you think about it, Maj. Gen. Durward S. Wilson was using trust as a command and leadership technique to inspire the best efforts of a subordinate.

That technique must, however, be used with caution. Even the Old Testament—from more than 2,000 years ago—gives this warning: "He that is surety for a stranger shall smart for it." This limitation on trust was a lesson painfully learned by the time I took over as the new chief of staff of the 11th Airborne Division in 1949. Thus, one of my first considerations was to find out who could be depended upon—another word for trust.

Consequently, when I fished a G-1 buckslip out of my IN basket about arrangements for a visit by the chief of staff of Second Army

— including quarters for him in one of our guest cottages — I did not just initial and toss it into the OUT basket. I'd been bitten by the VIP bug before, so I sent for the G-1.

To my question, "Are you sure that VIP cottage is ready?" the G-1 said, "Yes, sir."

"How do you know?" I asked, and he replied, "Sir, the headquarters commandant is responsible for that, and he reports it ready."

When the headquarters commandant arrived, by request, he answered the question, "How do you know?" by saying, "Sir, Lieutenant Slipshod is personally in charge, and says it has not only been cleaned but painted, too."

On Lieutenant Slipshod's arrival his reply was not unexpected, "Sir, Sergeant Fatbottom . . ."

So I went on a little personal reconnaissance, and found the cottage an oven under the summer sun. In addition, all the windows were frozen shut by dried paint from that quickie job.

There were appropriate bottles in the refrigerator for cooling drinks, but no glasses to drink from. Also, no toilet paper in the bathroom and no glass there, either. Further, there were no coat hangers in the bedroom clothes closet; in fact the painters had removed the rod for hangers, and the shelf above it, but the floor was still there. Somehow this suggested that I turn back the bedspread, thus uncovering a greasy area on the pillow, along with two black hairs.

This called for an instructional seance with my helpers. But after this administrative contretemps I was able to trust them more, because it established their awareness that they could trust me to check up; thus it behooved them to do likewise.

This trust angle comes up in many ways, some of them quite esoteric. Consider my horse-trading while in temporary command of Company M, 27th Infantry — when machine-gun companies used mule-drawn gun and ammunition carts, and officers were horse-mounted.

One day 1st Sgt. "Doc" Dougherty brought in papers to transfer a mule to Service Company. As I picked up my pen Doc said, "Lieutenant, we're sending them that kicking mule."

When I looked up old Doc was grinning, his gold tooth gleaming. He was giving me a chance to direct that some other mule be transferred, but I ignored my conscience and signed the paper.

Later, after my horse went lame, Service Company transferred us a replacement. Doc's gold tooth showed again when he said, "Lieutenant, the word is, that mule we transferred them kicked their stable sergeant, and he says this horse will make the swap even."

Sure enough, it took two men to hold his head before I made it into the saddle. Then the ornery animal—call him Revenge—tried to buck me off, with our company kibitzing my unscheduled rodeo. Fortunately, a year in the troop officers' equitation course at the late lamented Cavalry School enabled me to stay on until he settled down.

After that Revenge and I always put on a little floor show when I mounted, which the company never seemed to tire of watching. One day he reared like he was going over backwards; then when I pulled his head down to the right, he came down to the left instead. That strained a muscle in my groin and had me limping around for a while. Scuttlebutt reported the stable sergeant of Service Company had said, "This will teach him not to send me any more kicking mules."

After I was in the saddle again, the division scheduled a review, so I rode at the head of our company. Things went fine, until my salute. As the saber blade flashed down, Revenge shied away from it, turning his south end toward the reviewing stand, leaving me saluting in the opposite direction. Then we danced by, with Revenge doing some fancy sidestepping and keeping his south end pointed at the stars, so to speak. Finally, he put in a couple of extra bucks with sound effects—which, an eyewitness told me, produced an unprecedented result: the stars in the reviewing stand smiled.

But none of them knew they were watching a young lieutenant learn a fundamental lesson: If you throw a curve ball to somebody, you can trust him to throw a curve ball your way the first chance he gets.

These are minor footnotes to experience, but they may make three comments more meaningful:

- Trust is a many-splendored thing which pervades human relations at all levels in the military service.
- Trust also has many operational facets, not just that you can trust a man to be fair, but that you can trust him to be harsh when the occasion calls for it; not just that you can trust his judgment in decisions, but that you can depend on his follow-up in implementing those

decisions; not just that you should be slow to trust strangers, but that you must be quick to trust those who have earned your confidence in them.

- There is an old saying: "Trust everybody, but cut the cards." In command, staff, and leadership this translates to: "Trust everybody, but check the facts in things that matter."

36

Don't Telephone, Don't Write, Go!

THE VALUE OF personal reconnaissance, in garrison and in the field, is recognized — but there's another allied procedure which is often overlooked. It is called "foot coordination," but I think of it as "Get off your duff and go see the man."

As a company commander, for example, sometimes when a supply requisition that I wanted to know more about hit my IN basket, I picked it up and walked to the supply room. Regulations and other pertinent information were readily available there, and in many instances this was the quickest and surest way to coordinate my thinking with facts before signing the requisition. There were other times when I sent for the supply sergeant or attached a note to him, but as often as not I foot-coordinated the paper.

This added a personal reconnaissance angle, too. It didn't have to be a special trip, but a detour on the way to drill or a brief stop on the way to lunch. Also, often such foot coordination was combined with a mid-morning inspection of the mess hall to make sure our coffee was up to standard.

This go-see-the-man principle seems to come naturally in company-size units, but many fail to see that foot coordination pays big dividends in larger units too. Early in my first staff assignment, chance showed me that the best staff work is not always done by sending a paper out to do the job.

As S-2 of the 19th Infantry in Hawaii, my "in addition to your other duties" job was regimental athletic officer — a major "staff" responsibility in those days. When our baseball team needed some practice games before the regular Schofield Barracks League started, somebody said the Navy cruiser *Houston* had a good team. Since the *Houston* was anchored in Pearl Harbor, ten miles away, normal staff procedure would be to write a letter—but the old company level foot-coordination reflex was still strong.

Anyway, I got in my twelve-year-old Model A Ford and drove down to where boats from ships in Pearl Harbor docked when shuttling people ashore. Several boats were tied up there, manned by sailors in middy blouses and bellbottoms, so I stated my mission and asked how to get out to the *Houston.*

"Come aboard, Captain," one fine-looking petty officer said. "We'll take you out." I never discovered whether it was a captain's gig or an admiral's barge, though the boat's shiny chrome and brass fittings indicated that ferrying itinerant Army athletics officers was a bit on the slumming side.

As we approached the massive steel hulk of the cruiser the head sailor asked, "Do you want honors, Captain?"

Not knowing what that meant, I played it noncommittal by answering, "Whatever is customary is all right with me." Apparently he sent some kind of signal that I didn't see.

As we neared the ladder leading up the *Houston*'s towering side, I suddenly realized it would be up to me to salute the national ensign —but it was too late to see at which end of the ship it was flying. So on arriving on deck level I left out the salute as being better than saluting in the wrong direction. Besides, things were happening.

Sailors came running from all directions to line both sides of where I would step on deck, a chevroned sailor began tootling on some kind of whistle (boatswain's pipe?), and a ship's officer stood facing me with hand raised in salute. So I stopped at attention, too, and came to the salute.

And there we stood—the shrilling whistle going full blast—and stood and stood. Finally it seeped into my Army skull that maybe I was supposed to do something, so I dropped my salute. That relieved everybody, especially the chevroned sailor doing the tootling who had just about run out of wind. Then the deck officer stepped forward to shake hands; I came on board without further fouling up Navy custom and quickly arranged details for a ball game with the *Houston*'s team.

Thus the whole business was coordinated far better than could have been done by paper-pushing — and was finalized in one morning. There were also fringe benefits: a joyride in Pearl Harbor on some goldbraid's fancy boat, my first visit on board a major ship of war, and a practical education in the protocol of how to board a Navy warship.

There are many ways that "go see the man" can work to your benefit. Consider the time, less than two years later, following the Japanese attack on Pearl Harbor, when I was G-2 of the 24th Infantry Division as a recruit lieutenant colonel.

After making an intelligence estimate of the situation, it appeared that our troop dispositions should be modified in the light of methods used by the Japanese in the Philippines and at Singapore. Prior to final typing of the estimate for submission to the commanding general, it seemed logical to check with the major unit commanders concerned. This included the 21st Infantry, then commanded by Col. Gilbert R. Cook (later a corps commander under Gen. George S. Patton).

My paper could have been sent down for written comment, but I was not much over a year removed from being a company commander, and the old foot-coordination impulse was still strong. So, setting up an appointment with Colonel Cook by calling his S-2, I jeeped down to his headquarters.

"Well, come in, come in and sit down!" Colonel Cook said, giving me a quizzical half-smile, half-stare. "To what do I owe the honor of this visit from the Great General Staff?"

We had a most satisfactory discussion, with a more comprehensive exchange of ideas than could have resulted from written communications. Also, the whole matter was concluded in a single relatively short visit.

Even more important, a direct personal relationship was established between us. As I rose to leave, the colonel said, "You are the first member of the division staff to visit me. Come back, any time." It was clear that foot coordination was as effective at higher headquarters as it had been in the company. Only the scope, nature and frequency were changed.

There are many variations, from the Pentagon on down; like the reverse English used by Maj. Gen. (later Gen.) Guy S. Meloy, when he was commandant of the Infantry School. We were due for a new multimillion-dollar hospital at Fort Benning, but Stan was unhappy with its planned location: right in the main post near the old hospital — and displacing two holes on the golf course *(no, no, a thousand times no!)*.

So he handed me the project, as deputy CG of the Infantry Center. The main post was greatly overcrowded and off-center in relation to population distribution, so I dreamed up the idea of combining the new hospital with a new exit from the post. When the technical planners discovered this proposal, with the hospital on a centrally located hilltop having a commanding view over rolling wooded areas, they said *no (a thousand times no!)*. Neither that location nor the new road were in their master plan.

So I hand-carried my paper to the commandant, explained the opposition of his planners and their conviction that higher-up technical planners would turn thumbs down, too. "But I like it, Red," Stan said. After a pause he added, "I'll get Alex [Lt. Gen. Alexander R. Bolling, CG of Third Army] down here without telling him why, feed him a good lunch, then take him out to see for himself — before the paper nitpickers sabotage his thinking."

That was successful reverse foot coordination, because the multimillion-dollar hospital and the new entrance road have been there now these many years — a monument for the "talk-to-the-man" principle.

We've covered enough ground to make these observations:

- Foot coordination cannot replace paperwork, but there are times and situations when there is no adequate substitute for getting on your two feet and going to see the man — or getting him to come see you.
- The higher the rank level you reach, the more you must rely on paper procedures and the work of subordinates. But the time will never come when you get too high to gain from well-considered foot coordination.
- There's no space to relate them here, but I've seen instances where lack of foot coordination had a direct bearing on command and staff failures. It is not merely a matter of rewards if you do, but of possible penalties if you don't.
- Many young officers look for fancy, specialized jobs, failing to understand the tremendous value of service with troops. There's no better preparation for higher command responsibilities than command of a com-

pany-size unit — not the least of the rewards is in developing an instinct for and understanding of how and when to apply foot coordination.

37

Never Forget Value of a Pat on the Back

ONE OF MY most interesting assignments was on a board of general officers to select colonels for promotion to star rank. Reviewing records of all eligible colonels, knowing that only about one in fifty could be selected that year, was a demanding and heavy responsibility.

Individual records were in manila folders, with efficiency reports fastened on the right side, and other pertinent correspondence — recommendations for promotion, letters of commendation and the like — attached to the left side. Since letters of commendation are considered in selective promotions, we will backtrack my trail as a case history.

During my second year in the Army (Company A, 29th Infantry), officers of our regiment ran the bayonet course with student officer classes of the Infantry School — about three hundred in all. Having missed some bayonet instruction (while coaching athletics), I decided not to run with the first group, because the bayonet course of that time was a dilly — as much an obstacle course as a bayonet test. But my company commander discovered my intent at the last minute and emphatically changed my mind.

So an hour later I was lined up at the starting point, rifle in hand, bayonet fixed, and worried that I might not qualify. But since my legs worked pretty well my plan was to step on the gas between targets to keep within the time limit, then not be too hurried in making proper parries and thrusts, be careful to jump into the shell holes and trench with bayonet leading the feet—and be sure to skewer the little white spotters.

That program, along with keyed-up tension from fear of failure—and the kind of luck that protects new second lieutenants—enabled me to complete the course without a penalty, the only one to do so. That was a surprise. But the real surprise came later in the form of a letter from battalion headquarters. The first paragraph read:

"The fact you have made a perfect score on the bayonet course, generally considered by all to be very difficult, is a source of great satisfaction to the battalion commander."

This was followed by more kind remarks and, though I did not realize it then, I had my first lesson in the value of a pat on the back in contrast with a kick in the behind. The kick motivates you to do well enough to avoid future bootings, but the pat inspires you to do your best. There is a vast difference.

Two years later, before leaving for foreign service, there was a letter of commendation to me about my participation in sports as a player and in coaching various athletic teams. Again I did not give it much thought, or recognize an application of that well-known leadership formula: "Kick 'em in the behind, and pat 'em on the back—but not too much of either."

In due time the two officers who took the interest, time and trouble to write those letters to a young lieutenant with more brains in his legs than in his head, were selected to wear the stars of a lieutenant general. Some may call that a coincidence, but I do not.

If there was a turning point in my career, it came from a commendation of a totally different kind. In 1933 in Hawaii my company commander (Company M, 27th Infantry) got sick, thus making me acting company commander. My guide and mentor was 1st Sgt. "Doc" Dougherty, veteran of World War I, bald to the ears, with a gleaming gold tooth, a penchant for chewing tobacco—and one of those wonderful old soldiers who considered young lieutenants their special responsibility.

We had some troubles in the company but, with old Doc's advice, things worked out all right. Then orders transferred me to the Hawaiian Division military police company. So I checked out at Company M, thanked Doc for his help, and went to regimental headquarters to sign out of the regiment.

After that I stopped at the rail on the upstairs headquarters porch. From there I saw old Doc leave the company and come up to where I stood. He had a bright glint in his eyes and his gold tooth shone in his wide grin as he went through an elaborate look-all-around to be sure no one was near. Then in a conspiratorial, lowered voice, he said:

"I don't think you know it — but you have got it on the ball, kid." His grin got even wider as he added, "And I don't tell that to all the girls!"

I had never addressed him in any other way except as "Sergeant," but now I could muster only two words, "Thanks, Doc," and held out my hand.

It was my first real vote of confidence in more than eight years of service. (If you should read this, wherever you are, old-timer, let me say again, "Thanks, Doc.")

No formal written commendation from a multi-starred general could have meant as much. It gave me a belief in myself as a troop commander that, two years later, enabled me to take command of Company G, 26th Infantry, with full confidence I could do the job.

Too often the emphasis is on getting credit, then failing to pass it down. I faced a special situation in this regard toward the end of my second year in Company G.

It happened that, after a year-long competition in various tests to select the most efficient rifle company, our company won the cup, and was designated "The Honor Company of the 26th Infantry." Further, we carried a special guidon at all formations, and men of our company were excused from regimental fatigue for a year.

But there was a problem when a formal letter of commendation arrived for me. At first there seemed no way to endorse that letter to those who really won it: our noncommissioned officers and soldiers. Then the idea came to have a certificate printed for each man in the company, leaving a space to type in his name. The wording certified he had participated in the tests, summarized them, then expressed my thanks and appreciation for his part in winning this honor for our company. My signature as company commander authenticated it.

Another commander might have assembled the company and thanked them, and maybe some would have said nothing. But I like to believe my soldiers appreciated those certificates. When and how to commend those who do a fine job is a matter of personal judgment. Methods available vary from a kind or appreciative word to a formal letter of commendation, with in-betweens from a penciled note on a staff buck slip to a personal letter of thanks, or official letter of appreciation.

Since I've said that Doc Dougherty's "you have got it on the ball, kid" was the highest and most valuable commendation of my career, perhaps I should mention the informal letter of appreciation that touched my heart the deepest.

As G-1 of U.S. Army, Europe (in Heidelberg), I had an official car and driver. To help me learn German I asked for a driver who could speak the language. The trouble was he kept crowding people on the streets with our car, apparently expecting star plates to clear the way.

After several cautions failed to cure this tendency I arranged for his transfer to a good assignment, for which he was better qualified. When told of this, tears streamed down his face, but he thanked me for arranging his new assignment.

Two weeks later I got a letter from him, saying he was getting along fine in his new job and that he wanted to express his appreciation for my kindness to him. Also that he had learned a valuable lesson from me that he knew would help him the rest of his life — to be more considerate and helpful toward others — and he wanted to thank me for that.

I am now clearing my files, thus reducing the mass of paper others must dispose of when Father Time blows the whistle on me. But that letter will stay where it belongs: in the file folder marked "Commendations."

These comments seem pertinent:

- The best way to give credit, when it is due a subordinate, is on his efficiency report. But this does not replace a letter of commendation for outstanding service in special situations, for those do not fit into the limited space on ERs.
- Situations that warrant a letter of recommendation do not occur often, which makes them all the more important when deserved. But occasions that call for commending others in less formal ways are as countless as they are varied.
- In command and leadership many qualities, attributes and techniques are required — including drive, force,

judgment, perception and others. But nothing can replace the inspiration and lift that comes from commending a job well done.

38

Supervision: How Little?
How Much?

THERE WAS A story in the Old Army about the captain of Company A who was promoted to major, then assigned as the battalion commander. When he got the word of this double promotion the new major smiled, rubbed his hands with satisfaction and said, *"Now, finally, I can command Company A!"*

The idea of how, and how much, a superior should supervise and control his subordinates remains controversial. "Give me a job and leave me alone to do it," the young fellows say. But neither age nor youth are always right, so we'll search some case histories for guidelines for both sides.

My first battalion commander seemed to have an instinct for turning up just as things went wrong. It was said in the battalion that "If you tie it up, about-face and salute—because he will be right behind you." I soon found this almost uncannily true, for during the first drill period that I failed to have proper equipment on the field, there he was to receive my red-faced salute.

But he was not omnipresent. Looking back now, I realize his command visits were carefully thought out, usually to make spot-checks of an important activity, especially when he did not know the ability of the officer in charge or had reason to question his effectiveness.

However, all command checks do not zero-in that accurately. Like the time, ten years later, when I was a company commander and Brig. Gen. (later Lt. Gen.) Walter C. Short, commanding the 1st Infantry Division, arrived on short notice for a training inspection of the 26th Infantry.

It was raining as the hour approached for his visit to my company, so a phone call directed me to set up landscape targets on our .22-caliber rifle range in our attic; also to have a squad ready to fire a musketry problem.

General Short arrived, unsmiling as usual, and took the squad leader up to the landscape panels. He selected a line target on the left panel, which presented target designation and fire distribution problems — a real test for the corporal's fire order, and the musketry training of the squad.

The corporal's order was good, and so was the distribution of hits on the target. But, as the firing began, a thumbtack fell from the right edge of the right panel — as far away from the target as you could get. And, by staring hard, I could see a bullet hole over there.

However, General Short commended the corporal and his squad, my colonel made a nice remark to me, and the inspection group filed out. Tagging along as the last man was our regimental executive officer, Lt. Col. Carrol A. Bagley, who sidled over toward me.

"Newman," he whispered as he passed, "I saw it, too. But I am not going to say anything, either."

Sometimes Fate is kind.

That company presented a special problem in delegation of responsibility. The sergeants were outstanding, averaging nearly eighteen years of service. Also, five duty sergeants were present at drill for the one platoon-size unit available on normal drill days of that understrength time — all that was left after guard, special duty, regimental and post fatigue, company overhead and other administrative losses.

Eventually I established a policy of listing an instructor (lieutenant or sergeant) for each drill hour, who picked his own assistant or assistants. The other sergeants were free to prepare their instruction for later hours — like setting up a sandtable, or other visual aids. Or go to the dayroom to study manuals, Army Regulations and the like. Also to take a mid-morning coffee break.

This worked fine, with the least of command supervision, leaving me more time for administrative duties, which in those days were largely decentralized to company level. Notice, however, that this delegation of responsibility and freedom came after I was certain of the high caliber of my sergeants.

My next command was in Hawaii, where I found things different. The company was a trouble spot in the regiment. Though it had some fine NCOs, several were below par, so I soon busted two of them. Meanwhile, the battalion commander was breathing down my neck, because my company was part of his battalion and he was worried about it.

For several weeks the company and I found each other kind of hard to live with. Soon one not-so-good soldier put in a request for transfer, and I OKed it. This produced three more requests for transfer, which I did not OK but went out to the drill field to discuss the matter with the company.

As I came up Sergeant Bosco, the senior duty sergeant, was falling-in the company after a drill break. So I gave them a little pep talk about a few things I felt were on a bogey level, along with instructions for raising standards. Then I said: "Several days ago I got a request for transfer from a not-so-good soldier, and I approved it. Now I've got three more requests for transfer, and they are from men who are not cutting the mustard here, either. I'm not going to pass on weak sisters to cause trouble in other outfits. Any man who wants to transfer will first have to soldier here to my satisfaction."

With that I released the company to Sergeant Bosco. Then, as I turned to go back to the orderly room, I came face to face with the battalion commander. Obviously, he had followed me out and heard my talk with the company.

When I saluted he returned it with a quiet little smile, walked away without a word, and never again "looked over my shoulder."

Now we'll move to a higher level, and look at another side of this basic command and leadership problem.

Soon after taking command of the 511th Airborne Infantry (11th Airborne Division), I decided to inspect a battalion of my new command at the scheduled Saturday inspection. Then, since the division commander was newly arrived, I called his chief of staff, invited the CG to go along with me, and so notified the battalion commander.

An angle to note here is that I knew almost nothing of that battalion or of its commander's ability, and made no preliminary inspection. I merely "left him alone to do the job." As a result I was professionally embarrassed, because our division commander did come along, and the battalion was definitely below standard.

Two years later, I took command of the 505th Airborne Infantry (82d Airborne Division) and soon after that one battalion went on the rifle range to fire for record. Once again, although I did not know much about the battalion commander I decided to "leave him alone to do the job," and planned not to arrive on the range until mid-morning.

Then, as I was leaving my headquarters for the range, this message arrived: "Report to the division commander at once."

Maj. Gen. Charles D. W. Canham said, "Colonel, your battalion on the rifle range is poorly organized, and the commander does not have the situation under control. Go down there and straighten things out."

"Sir," was my unwise reply, "I was giving the battalion commander time—"

"Colonel," that fine soldier and my former classmate at West Point cut in, "that battalion is a part of your regiment. I look to you, not the battalion commander, to establish and maintain proper standards."

You see, there is more to it than "Give a man a job and leave him alone to do it."

These comments seem relevant:

- When you give a man a job, that means he is a subordinate—which automatically makes you as well as him responsible for how well it gets done.
- You can and should delegate responsibility, but that does not include abdicating your own supervisory responsibility to see that any duty or mission is properly carried out.
- How much you check depends on the nature of the job and how well you know the qualifications of the officer assigned to do it. In the rifle range incident, as a new regimental commander I should have been there early that first day to see how things were organized—especially since I did not know the capabilities of the battalion commander.
- It is a serious mistake to assign a duty, then continually and needlessly try to guide and control in detail the hands of the man you give it to. But the subordinate should realize his superior's responsibilities and understand that the best way to reduce supervision is to let his boss see he is doing the job. Also—and not to be overlooked—the best way to get credit for what you do is for your boss to see you do it.

39

Undue Pressure: More Hurtful than Helpful

ONE DAY IN 1951, after I was transformed from the happy regimental commander of the 511th Airborne Infantry to the grumpy chief of the unified staff, Iceland Defense Force, I had lunch in the Keflavik Airport cafeteria.

On approaching the cashier with my lunch check I detoured and sat down again rather than join the pushy group of customers who, instead of forming an orderly line, were each pressuring her to take his check ahead of the others. Under this stress she made a mistake in change, which added to confusion.

When the coast was clear I walked up to the visibly upset cashier and tendered my lunch check, saying, "Looks like everybody is in a hurry to go sit and wait."

"Yes," she said, then added, "you know, I think their mommas and poppas forgot to get married."

Unfortunately, counterproductive-pressure situations develop in military life, too. When I was a company commander, one such case gave me the idea to write this "Cerebration," which appeared in ARMY's predecessor, the *Infantry Journal:*

Ease the Pressure*

In the spring a company commander's fancy lightly turns to thoughts of trigger-squeeze. Rifle marksmanship

*May-June 1939

dominates training, and the plaintive voices of weepers and wailers mingle with the discord of alibis. But most of these unwholesome sounds can be eliminated by easing the pressure.

We have all seen a standard one-act play that is presented, with variations, every year.

The curtain goes up when the commanding officer, Colonel Scowler, arrives on the range and stands about twenty-five yards back of the firing line near Major Growler—who nervously twiddles a megaphone and looks toward target 17 where a high deuce has just been disked.

The colonel glances sharply at Major Growler and whacks his leg with his riding crop. Picking up this pressure cue, the major places megaphone to mouth and bellows:

"What is the matter on target 17?"

Captain Howler, who stands about fifteen yards back of the firing line with hands on hips and feet wide apart, removes his cigar and barks in an exasperated voice:

"Lieutenant Marksman, straighten out that man on 17!"

The lieutenant pauses in the caged pacing of his post just back of the firing line and snaps:

"Sergeant Expert, you are supposed to be coaching Private Jitters. There is no excuse for that shot."

Sergeant Expert's neck grows redder and he begins to "coach" in a menacing whisper:

"You are a yellow so-and-so and I ought to tie that such-and-such rifle around your this-and-that neck. Now squeeze that so-and-so trigger!"

And a tired kid who is scared inside lowers his head, shakes a drop of sweat off the end of his nose and wishes he had never been born. The pressure is something fierce.

Private Jitters feels his muscles twitch and tremble, but he grits his teeth and comes into firing position. He lines up the sights and discovers the bull's-eye dancing around like the bouncing ball in one of those "everybody sing" movies.

In due time a red flag waves in front of his target — a miss.

Colonel Scowler slaps his leg again, and moves off without comment. Major Growler shakes his head. Captain Howler casts his cigar butt on the ground and walks in a small circle with obvious self-control. Lieutenant Marksman cuts his eyes at the captain and kicks the ground with his foot. Sergeant Expert heaves a heavy sigh. The pressure is now terrific.

Private Jitters wipes another drop of sweat off the end of his nose and plans morbidly to do something about not being dead.

But when Captain Insight was placed in the same situation, and that deuce appeared on No. 17, he walked up and said casually in a calm voice:

"Jitters, I know you understand how to aim and squeeze the trigger. Stop worrying, son — you are doing okay. A man's best is good enough for me."

Then the pressure eased off with an almost audible sound. And, with the easing of pressure, the motivation for needless histrionics in the chain of command evaporated.

Of course, care must be taken to distinguish Private Jitters from privates Indifferent, Hangover, Awkward, and Uninstructed. But there are not many of them, if you look real close.

And every man in the company who was once a Private Jitters himself will carry in his heart a deep and inarticulate loyalty to and respect for Captain Insight that the Captain Howlers can never inspire.

(signed) Company Commander

There are no rules about when, where and how to ease the pressures that are more hurtful than helpful. It is a matter of perception, empathy, and judgment. For example, if you are a company commander and a new lieutenant is assigned to you, in my view it is better not to look in on him the first couple of times he is scheduled to give drill instruction.

He will be under the inherent pressure of appearing for the first time before strangers, thus your presence will add stress for him on these initial occasions. However, when he has had a chance to get his feet on the ground, it then becomes your duty to add the pressure of your presence.

This not only exercises your command responsibility to ensure proper standards of instruction, but adds the spur of command pressure to motivate your new lieutenant toward his best efforts. Thus, what would be counterproductive pressure when prematurely applied becomes the proper and normal exercise of command and the leadership of personal interest.

In anticipating pressure situations, there is almost always more than one way to reduce the heat. For instance, if your new lieutenant is reporting to your company as his first duty assignment, one good procedure to initiate him in his training responsibilities is to use him as your assistant when you conduct instruction.

When I commanded the 511th Airborne Infantry and a new lieutenant colonel was assigned to the regiment, a very different kind of strain was involved. Accordingly, when he was scheduled to make his first jump with the regiment, I decided to make that jump, too, and had myself assigned to his plane. In this case, the purpose of my presence was to reduce the pressure.

He was senior in grade and had been away from airborne for quite some time. So I knew he would be "sweating" on his first jump after the long absence from jumping. Further, that if he were the senior officer and jumpmaster in the plane, those responsibilities would add more stress. When I went along, all he had to worry about was getting himself out of the door.

It should be noted also that this was a safety measure. He was rusty on airborne procedures in the plane; thus, in the tension of his first renewal jump, his chances of a mistake would be increased if he had to exercise authority. And any mistake he might make could endanger others. This brings out the point that avoiding needless pressure on an individual is almost always in the best interest of the unit.

One of the worst kinds of counterproductive pressure stems from personality conflicts. Among other unfortunate results, the senior may harass his junior, thus putting him under a very special kind of mental and psychological travail. The career of one of my friends was seriously damaged this way.

Oddly enough, or so it seemed to me, this tendency was more destructive the higher the rank of those involved. If you think this human failure did not extend into the star ranks, think again. Usually it was not obvious, except to those in the know, but the pressures were real.

Some comments are:

- As I sit and sip my sundown tranquilizer, reflecting on things that were and others that might have been, the idea comes clear that sometimes we must apply pressure to get things done.

  On the other hand, it is equally clear, as I jiggle the ice in my glass, that pressure is a lot like alcohol: beneficial when used judiciously, but destructive when abused.
- The variety and intensity of unnecessary pressures defy description and categorization. But every military man should strive for the perception to see, the empathy to understand and the wisdom to avoid subjecting others to needless pressures.
- One of the common ways that seniors induce self-defeating stress in their juniors is to over-supervise them. Another is to summon them repeatedly to report in person about inconsequential administrative details.
- In addition to avoiding foisting undue pressure on those under you, it is important that you develop a mental attitude to protect yourself from such pressures. In other words, don't let those whose mommas and poppas forgot to get married get you down.

40
Supply Discipline: Responsibility Never Ends

WHEN I WAS a cadet at West Point the story went the rounds about a young lieutenant who learned property responsibility and accountability the hard way. It happened when his unit was firing those Big Bertha seacoast defense guns of that time.

After the gun for which he was responsible was loaded and cranked up ready to shoot, he gave the command, "Fire!"

At that instant a sergeant noticed some unsafe condition about the gun, and shouted, "No. *Don't fire!*"

He then pointed to the unsafe condition. But the young lieutenant got real arbitrary, announcing, "When I say *Fire!* I mean *Fire!* —*FIRE!*"

So the firing mechanism was tripped, the big gun belched a thin plume of smokeless powder smoke, and the crew watched the heavy and clearly visible shell arch out to sea. Whether it hit the target area was not included in the story, but the "forceful" lieutenant was hit in the pocketbook on the installment plan for years to come — paying for damage to the gun that resulted when he refused to heed the sergeant's warning.

Whether true or apocryphal, the story made clear a basic fact you learned early in the Army: if government property became lost or damaged as a result of your negligence or carelessness, you paid for it.

As a platoon leader in my first company, I was also the company supply officer. A month after joining I was having dinner in the 29th

Infantry bachelor mess at Fort Benning when 1st Lt. Joe Hussing took his seat at the head of the table.

"Newman," he said, looking straight at me, "are you supply officer of your company?"

"Yes, sir," I replied, wondering why that question.

"Well," he continued in an accusing tone, "did you draw the runy rifles for your company this afternoon?"

After a worried pause I answered, "No, sir." Then rising to the bait, I asked, "What are runy rifles?"

His reply, slightly paraphrased here, was prompt: "You need them to fire propaganda at recruits."

Others at the table got some yuk-yuks and chuckle-chuckles out of that. What it proved to me was that sergeants are better friends to second lieutenants than are first lieutenants. Because the supply sergeant in my company had taken me under his wing, explaining about requisitions, inventory procedures, overages and shortages, reports of survey and other things helpful to me the rest of my service.

Before leaving Benning a training incident pinpointed a specialized supply lesson. It happened in another company during "dry" rapid-fire exercises in preliminary marksmanship training. A regular-size rapid-fire target was set up across the road from the filling station near Gowdy Baseball Field. The practice firing line, using dummy cartridges, was two hundred yards away, behind where the Infantry School Book Shop is now.

Suddenly, during a rapid-fire run, a shot rang out, and everybody stood still in momentary shock—except the two men working the screen on each side of the target. They pointed in grinning, arm-waving glee, signaling that the shooter had scored a bull's-eye with the bullet that passed between them.

A live round had somehow been mixed with the dummies. Nobody was hurt, but the supply warning was indelibly registered in my memory: never take chances when handling ammunition—being especially careful to keep live ammunition separate from training and practice rounds.

Several years later I was a company supply officer in the 31st Infantry in Manila when we got a new company commander. The captain had been away from troops for years, but he was a meticulous man and made a personal inventory of company property, ending with an accurate list of overages and shortages.

When the supply sergeant brought him the typed list of overages and shortages, the captain proved that being meticulous does not exactly include having good judgment. "All right, Sergeant," he said, "report all overages and turn them in."

"But, Captain! — " the sergeant exclaimed in instant alarm.

"No buts about it, Sergeant," the captain cut him off. "Turn in the overages, and report to me when that is done."

Now poker-faced, the supply sergeant said, "Yes, sir." He then saluted snappily — and left to turn in the overages.

When the sergeant reported back the captain said, "Now I want you to make up all shortages, so our property inventory will be exactly correct . . . no overages, no shortages."

This time the sergeant, still poker-faced, again saluted snappily — but in silence — and left. That left me puzzled about how the sergeant could make up shortages without overages as trading material. So I kibitzed his dutiful but largely unsuccessful efforts. However, his lack of success did not seem to worry the supply sergeant because there would be no skin off his pay when the day of reckoning came.

When that day arrived, both the sergeant and I were long gone. But I carried with me the firm resolve never to sign for property that was not there.

Years later, on taking command of Company G, 26th Infantry at Plattsburg, I signed for all property without delay, for the best of reasons: it was all there.

Nevertheless, I soon tested the temporary check-out system of weapons from the supply room, by holding out a .22-caliber rifle one day (as recounted in chapter 10). As reported, that nonpareil of all supply sergeants, Sergeant Jessie, called my hand and reclaimed the rifle from behind my office door. This was just the first of my spot checks, and many more that I continued to direct others to make.

It is not only at company level that supply discipline is a command function. Commanders at all levels have this inherent responsibility.

As assistant division commander of the 82d Airborne Division, the supply lessons learned in fifteen years as a company level officer were invaluable to me. When my division was preparing for Exercise Snowstorm at Camp Drum, New York, I remembered going out on maneuvers with Company G.

So I took a leaf out of Sergeant Jessie's book and applied it at division level, by drafting a command letter to unit commanders. A major provision in the letter was that all reports of survey for property lost or damaged on Exercise Snowstorm would be prepared before the division left Camp Drum. The division commander signed the letter.

As a result we had no lost or damaged property hangovers when we got back to Fort Bragg, because surveys were made out while facts and witnesses were fresh and available. Also, knowing this would be done was a supply discipline spur, warning that on-the-ground inventories must be taken. It also closed the door to long-delayed surveys, later, about lost or damaged property that might or might not have resulted from Exercise Snowstorm.

Obtaining property and supplies, as with everything else, sometimes includes off-beat quirks. Like the time when we got a newly commissioned medical lieutenant in the BOQ at Plattsburg Barracks. He noticed that 1st Lt. George Will had a fine mahogany bed and comfortable mattress with quilts (his own) instead of an iron-frame cot and Army blankets like the rest of us. So the new medical lieutenant wanted to be similarly equipped.

"Well," was my reply when he approached me about it, "the rest of us are field soldiers, and we like GI [government issue] equipment. But if you want a special issue of bedroom furniture, put in a letter and ask for it. Lieutenant Will will help you write it."

My confidence in George was not misplaced. A letter was soon in channels, addressed to the post quartermaster through regimental headquarters, requesting such items as: "1-bed, mahogany, special issue, Mark V; 1-mattress, heavy duty, Mark II; 2-pillows, feather-stuffed, Mark VII; 1-quilted eiderdown comforter, Mark IV." (For the uninitiated, those Roman numerals normally designated certain types of explosive ammunition.)

That letter collected some interesting and imaginative endorsements before it finally got back to the new medical lieutenant. It was what you might call practical instruction in the nature and availability of military property.

Every soldier of long service has his own collection of things that got snafued in the care, handling, safe-guarding and maintenance of property.

Here are three general comments:

- There is no substitute for troop duty in a company as the foundation for command and leadership at all levels —which includes a basic understanding of how to establish and maintain supply discipline.
- A periodic inventory at long intervals is not enough; continued spot checks are required. Also, when property is discovered to be lost or damaged, over and beyond "fair wear and tear," prompt administrative action is needed to ensure that persons responsible be made to account for it. In this way only can creeping shortages be prevented.
- The only way a commander can make certain his unit has good supply discipline is to play his part toward that end. He cannot, nor should he, try to do all the checking—he is the quarterback. His primary job is to call the signals, requiring others to carry the supply ball.

41

Never Fiddle Federal Funds

WHEN I WAS a teenager my mother returned home to South Carolina from a trip to New York City and told us about that metropolis. The story included her ride on the subway with her older brother, a federal judge from Virginia, who was making his first venture in the subway system, too.

Uncle Aubrey (whose first name I bear) put a nickel in the slot, but managed to push against the turnstile before he was in the proper place to pass through. A subway guard nearby began to berate my uncle, "Now you have done it, and there is no way you can get that nickel back!"

"But, my dear man," my uncle said, "I have another nickel."

That solved the problem nicely and illustrates a principle that every man in uniform should keep in mind: when you meet a new situation in your military duties where money is involved, remember that you are almost always "accountable." So before you act hastily, it is well to have another nickel handy.

It was also in New York City, as a cadet in uniform returning from my last Christmas leave, that I learned a supplementary principle of money management. After taking a taxi at Grand Central Station for the Thirty-Third Street ferry across the Hudson River (thence a West Shore Railroad train for West Point), I noticed the taxi seemed to take a roundabout way. On arriving at the ferry, there was a sizable amount showing on the meter.

"How much do I owe?" I asked the driver as I dismounted.

He quoted a figure exactly double the meter price. After a puzzled pause I said, "That is twice what shows on the meter."

The cabbie laughed loudly and replied, "This must be the first time you ever been in a cab. I've got to have back fare, to get back to Grand Central Station."

This had some kind of logic. But after struggling with the idea, I pointed to the policeman at the nearby intersection and said, "I'll pay it if he tells me to."

This gave him pause. Then, after I paid the exact fare on the meter (no tip), he drove off muttering, "You meet a lotta cheapskates in this business."

Maybe so — and perhaps some suckers too. Without realizing it, I followed a principle that can save a lot of grief in military service: before you authorize or spend money or use materials of money value, if you do not know the regulations involved, ask for technical advice from someone who does know.

One potent field for money booby traps is at company level. Soon after I assumed command of Company G, 26th Infantry, in 1936, 1st Sgt. "Big Jim" Redding pointed out that our mess-hall tables needed refinishing. The tabletops were of hardwood, covered with clear varnish that was beginning to chip and show scratches. Big Jim said that to do it right would require sanding to the raw wood, then about eight coats of varnish, each coat rubbed down with pumice before applying the next coat.

I sensed no money booby trap and approved the project without giving it an evaluating thought.

Two days later, when checking the quality of Sgt. "Long John" Smith's coffee, I saw the first mess-hall table getting its multi-layered varnish treatment. But I also noticed the varnish used was a high-quality commercial grade.

So I returned to the orderly room and called for Big Jim. While our company fund was healthy, regulations made it a strict no-no to purchase paint instead of drawing the issue kind from post supply. To my query about the source of the fine varnish for the tables, Big Jim replied, "No sweat, Captain. We've got everything under control."

But the problem was not that simple, for I discovered he planned to pay for it from a slush fund he administered — which was strictly against regulations. Especially so, since the source of money was the cash payments for lunches (which belonged in the mess fund) made by married NCOs who were drawing ration money.

The solution was not a happy one for Big Jim — that wonderful old soldier to whom I owe so much — because I promptly liquidated his slush fund. I also paid for that varnish myself, keeping the receipted bill and my canceled check.

Fortunately, soon after our mess tables were made resplendent with their new varnish coating, we were inspected by our division commander — a real toughie — Brig. Gen. (later Lt. Gen.) Walter C. Short. Our regimental commander and battalion commander were with the inspecting party when General Short stopped in our mess hall to admire our pristine table tops.

He stood looking down at them, then turned to speak to me — but changed his mind. There was tension in the air and I could almost feel my regimental and battalion commanders squirm in antici- pation of the imminent question, "How did you get those table tops to look like this, and was government-issue varnish used?"

The words never came, but I was not nervous. We had not used government money illegally, there was no slush fund—and I had my canceled check and receipted bill in my office. First Sgt. Big Jim Redding was standing by and I think that, for the first time, he for- gave me for taking away his slush fund and understood why I wrote a personal check.

There are countless ways of "cleverly" misusing government money or materials, all with the highest motives. But you just can't fiddle with federal funds.

A few years later I found myself G-2 (Intelligence) of the newly organized 24th Infantry Division in Hawaii, barely two months before the Pearl Harbor attack on 7 December 1941. One of my pri- mary duties, in the event of war, would be to keep a G-2 situation map in overlay form, so I wanted some of a new transparent but frosted acetate you could write on with ordinary lead or color pencils — a great improvement over the slick acetate that required thick, smudgy "paint" pencils.

This posed a money problem because the acetate was a nonissue commercial product that came in four-foot-wide rolls that cost twenty-two dollars. The G-2 section had no funds, but the adjutant general administered a headquarters fund. So I decided, as a newly minted general staff officer, that the "exigencies of the service" warranted this purchase — and so informed the adjutant general.

In due course, my roll of frosted acetate arrived—and so did a summons to the office of our fine but crusty old chief of staff.

"Newman," he said, "by whose authority did you instruct the adjutant general to spend twenty-two dollars from the headquarters fund?"

Well, I flubbed around about "need" and "being ready" and "not worrying you about such a small matter" and offered to reimburse the fund if it was hard up for money or if the purchase was illegal. It was this offer that really got me told.

"I know," the chief said, "that less than a year ago you were a company commander. There you could pay out of pocket to reimburse the company fund for small illegal purchases an inspector might find in your fund vouchers. But you are out of that league now. At this and higher general staff levels, errors are not paid for that cheaply and easily, even if you have enough money. Instead, the result can be entries on your efficiency report that will affect your career, or possible disciplinary action."

"Yes, sir," I said.

And for the rest of my service I never forgot that I was out of the league where it was possible to have a backup nickel that could rectify an error of judgment in money matters.

Personal pride or egotism—maybe a little of both—prod me to add that when the Japanese attack came about two weeks later, our G-2 and G-3 situation overlays apparently looked nice on that frosted acetate. Anyway, when a senior officer from headquarters, Hawaiian Department, visited our command post and saw the overlays, he inquired about them and discovered we had a roll of the new stuff—which he promptly confiscated and took back for his own headquarters.

Chastened judgment told me not to ask our chief why, at our general staff level, he let that man hijack property from our headquarters fund. I knew his reply would be, "You miss the point, Newman: I would have OKed buying that acetate, if you had asked me, but I cannot have individual section chiefs spending from the fund for which I am responsible—thus, not only without authority, but also without coordination and without considering the overall need for those funds."

There is no end to the variety of troubles that lack of money or misuse of it, can cause.

Other comments are:

- The nature and scope of your management of money will expand and proliferate as you progress upward in authority, but one rule never changes: always drive your money wagon — and accountability for things of money value — down the middle of the road; never, but never, fiddle the figures in your financial responsibilities or equivocate in oral money discussions.
- A good principle to remember is the one I learned by suggesting that the cop monitor my taxi fare at the Thirty-Third Street ferry in New York City: when you don't know the regulations, call for the advice of a man who does know. But he will not wear a blue uniform and brass buttons. At company level it may be the first sergeant or supply sergeant who knows where to find the applicable regulations. At higher levels, the man who knows will have such titles as comptroller, judge advocate, finance officer or engineer.

    Of course, the final decision will be yours — and so will the responsibility.

42

Your Message Must Be Loud and Clear

THERE IS AN art to the way good commanders control, coordinate and get the best efforts from others. It's not enough to speak or otherwise transmit grammatically correct words; the idea must be communicated clearly and unmistakably. But there is more to it than that. What you *do* may speak louder than words, and *how* you say or do it may be the difference between success or failure as a leader.

An officer once told me this little tale which, when you think about it, illustrates a principle in the art of issuing orders. Before World War II he had a colonel who had been graduated from Annapolis. Like some regimental commanders of that time, he was nearly twenty years older than they are today, and qualified as a "character." His foibles included carrying a riding crop and a tendency to use seagoing language.

At retreat formation one day the flag was fouled halfway down the flagpole. The officer of the day then heard the slapping sound behind him of a riding crop on leather boots, followed by this salty order: "Sweat the lee halyard!"

The OD, not sure what that meant, relayed it to the sergeant of the guard: "Sweat the lee halyard!"

The sergeant knew a buck when he heard one, so he passed it on in a commanding voice to the corporal of the flag detail: "Sweat the lee halyard!"

Whereupon the corporal gave his superiors a lesson in how to communicate when he said, "Pull on the damn rope!"

From a squad to a theater command, you've got to communicate, to get your point across. There are many ways to do this: from oral commands and pronouncements to written orders; from personal example or individual contacts to policies established by command actions; through the chain of command or by shortcutting normal channels.

Which method to choose and how to apply it in each instance depends on the situation — also, sometimes, on your perception and imagination. A veteran first sergeant told me about a new second lieutenant who joined his company in the Old Army, and faced a delicate problem in communicating.

The young lieutenant's first name was Abraham, and he became known unofficially in the company as "Abe." One soldier soon braced the lieutenant for a loan "until payday" to buy his mother a birthday present. When that oldie succeeded, the word spread. So Abe soon listened to several other touching tales and, still striving to be a good fellow, added to his outstanding loans — a practice frowned on by proper authority.

On payday young Abraham's debtors drew their money — which, after deductions, wasn't much for $21-per-month soldiers — and took off for town. The next day all but one of them, obviously enduring the withdrawal pangs of a severe morning after, gave their lieutenant some hard luck stories in lieu of repayment. The other man was AWOL, and the company scuttlebutt predicted he would never return.

Several days later, when the first sergeant was about to dismiss the company after morning drill, and the company commander had left for headquarters, young Abraham said, "Just a minute please, Sergeant."

He then faced the company and raised his voice so all could hear. "I have an announcement to make," he said, and paused for dramatic effect before adding, "Abe has been Christianized!"

Everybody got the idea, as wide understanding grins made clear. Thus Abe got himself out of a queasy situation by his forthright and singular method of communicating. Further, he not only avoided unpleasant individual conversations, but also raised his personal stature in the eyes of the company.

One of the most flexible means of communication is by what you do. There was a soldier in my company in Hawaii (we'll call him

Rufus). He was a tall, gawky, good-natured youngster, an excellent soldier when he wanted to be, which was not often.

Rufus finally decided he didn't like the Army and wanted out, so he started riding the sick book to build toward a physical discharge. When the medicos kept marking him "Duty" he decided on a new approach, which soon came to my attention.

"Captain," the first sergeant said one morning, "we got to get rid of that man Rufus. He's going crazy."

"What makes you think so?"

"The last two nights he got out of bed after Taps, turned on the hall light outside his squadroom, and practiced rolling and unrolling his field pack on the floor. It wakes the men up, and they think he is going nuts."

When Rufus stood in front of my desk his eyes focused in a far-away look over my head, his face set in his best poker expression.

"Tell me about it, Rufus," I invited.

"Well, sir, I can't roll my pack very good. That worries me, so I'm practicing to get better at it."

After some thought I said, "Maybe I can help you get rid of that worry. Since this is Saturday, there's no drill this afternoon. I'll arrange for the charge-of-quarters to supervise your practice in pack-rolling for two hours after lunch."

Apparently that session eliminated his worry. But a week later the first sergeant was back again, shaking his head. "That man Rufus is really off the beam, Captain, and the men are leery of him. Last night he was playing pool in the dayroom — but instead of powdering his hands and the cue, he dumped the powder in his hair."

Once more the tall, gawky young man in front of my desk had that faraway look and poker expression.

"Rufus," I said in my best interested and judicial tone, "you may have the company thinking you're going nuts, but I think you just don't have enough to do around here. That's why the first sergeant will put you on extra duty detail to clean and polish porcelain and metal fixtures in the latrines."

His faraway look and poker face remained impassive, perhaps because he figured he was making progress toward a psychiatric discharge. So I added, "Every time you come up with another screwball idea, I'm going to have a new idea too. The next time my idea will be to transfer you into Sergeant Bosco's platoon."

Sergeant Bosco was as fine a duty sergeant as the Army ever had. Further, he was a man with a short fuse that was easy to light. Also, as both Rufus and I knew, Bosco would tolerate no funny business, and was a man reputed to favor direct personal action to straighten out curve balls.

Now Rufus lost that faraway look, and the light of complete sanity dawned in his eyes. At last I had managed to communicate the idea it was going to be much easier to complete his enlistment than to harass the Army into a phony discharge.

The most basic way to communicate above company level is through the written word. Wise old Benjamin Franklin once said in his famous letter of advice to a young man, "There is no skill but can be improved with practice." That's how it is with skill for putting ideas on paper. The secret of success: be sure you have something to say, and cut out every unnecessary word by revisions. Further, improving your ability to write will carry over into an added facility in your spoken language.

This barely touches the vital subject of how to communicate with others in getting things done. Here are six guidelines for better command and leadership communication:

- Fancy language is not a substitute for good judgment.
- Be clear and direct, like "Pull on the damn rope!"
- Be perceptive and imaginative in special cases, like "Abe has been Christianized!"
- What you do often speaks clearer and with more emphasis than what you say.
- Constantly study how to communicate, and include human understanding and common sense in your considerations.
- Never overlook the special merits of face-to-face conversations, but also never forget what Robert Southey said: "There are three things that ought to be considered before some things are spoken—the manner, the place, and the time."

43

Actions Speak Louder than Words

IN THE LATE 1930s I was a new captain, and the senior officer in the BOQ (bachelor officers quarters) at Plattsburg Barracks, New York. There were also in the BOQ a couple of first lieutenants and a gaggle of second lieutenants, most of them freshly commissioned. One of these last, whom we will call Lieutenant Vague, was a bit gullible.

Some ten days after his arrival Lieutenant Vague said to a first lieutenant named George, "How do you go about meeting some nice girls around here?"

George, who was quick on the uptake, said, "Have you met Polly Beine?"

On receiving a negative reply, George explained that Captain Beine was a genial, middle-aged captain (most captains then were middle-aged veterans of World War I). Also, George said, "Captain Beine is a good friend of mine, so I'll tell him about you. Call him up tomorrow and ask if it is okay to date Polly."

The next evening when Captain Beine answered the phone he said, "George told me about you, Mistuh Vague, and Polly would like to meet you. If convenient, come down to the house about eight o'clock tonight."

When Captain Beine answered the door bell he said, "Come in, Mistuh Vague. We can visit a little until Polly is ready."

The captain then became the "heavy father," putting Polly's

potential swain through an interview designed to find out his antecedents and possible intentions toward Polly.

Finally, he said pointedly, "Polly is a good girl. Where did you plan to take her this evening?"

"Why . . . er," the newly minted lieutenant quavered, "to the post movie."

"Fine," Captain Beine said, with an air of now-we-have-things-straight. "I think Polly is ready and will go get her."

When Captain Beine returned, there was a green parrot on his shoulder. "Mistuh Vague," he said, "I want you to meet Polly Beine."

That got the message across, and the former gullible lieutenant was not easily made a fall guy after that. Just another case where what you do conveys an idea in a way nothing else can.

Recently, my lifetime friend, Brig. Gen. Frederick O. "Fritz" Hartel, USA (Ret.), visited me. As we sipped our sunset libations of bourbon and water, talk turned to "back when." Fritz told me of the time in World War II, when his division was training for overseas service. He was a battalion commander under Maj. Gen. John C. H. Lee (later Lt. Gen. "Court House" Lee, who headed the Services of Supply in Europe).

General Lee gave Fritz a memorable demonstration one day of how to dramatize an idea by what you do. It happened when the division commander inspected a company kitchen after breakfast and found edible food in the garbage cans — including bacon, half a loaf of bread and a sizable hunk of butter.

So General Lee turned to Fritz and said, "The division commander and the battalion commander will now have breakfast in this mess hall."

They did, and Fritz took a good swig from his bourbon and water at the memory. He then said, "You know, Red, the only thing in our breakfast that did not come out of the garbage cans was the coffee."

No publicized message or oral commander's conference order could permeate the whole division the way the grapevine circulated news of that "command breakfast." Thus, what General Lee did put everybody at all levels on notice that "proper use of leftovers" was a command policy to which they had better give more than lip service.

The late Gen. Walter Krueger was another commander who sometimes used direct action as the best way to get across a command message. Via the ubiquitous Army grapevine, I learned of two case histories about General Krueger before he went overseas to command his famous Sixth Army in the Southwest Pacific Theater.

When he heard that one of his division commanders had prevented several general staff officers of the division from going to the Command and General Staff College at Fort Leavenworth for the special "quickie" wartime course, he inquired about it. The division commander stated he could not release members of his staff just before the division went on maneuvers.

General Krueger then transferred those general staff officers to another division, with the stipulation they be sent to the first available class at Fort Leavenworth.

In another case, a division commander was required to select a cadre from his division to be the nucleus for organizing a new division. He saw this as an opportunity to get rid of a few undesirables. After General Krueger inspected the cadre, he reassigned the division commander — to organize and command the new division.

Those who served under General Krueger will tell you his actions in these two cases reflected a dominant characteristic of that fine old soldier, the highest professionalism. His message was unmistakably clear: the good of the service comes first, not your personal interest, and that he would not tolerate violations of this principle.

In some situations physical action can speak more clearly than words — like the time I arrived at Fort Drum, New York as assistant division commander, 82d Airborne Division, to assume command of our advance party and prepare for arrival of the full division for Exercise Snowstorm.

The night before my arrival one of three World War I type frame buildings, which were to house division headquarters, was barely saved from burning to the ground by the post fire department. One of our soldiers on the second floor died from intense heat and smoke inhalation.

By the time I entered the building, it was charred inside from top to bottom, like a whiskey barrel. Walls were of the pressed-board material which made those old buildings so vulnerable to fire. It was found that the fire started from a cigarette on the first floor near the stairwell, but the fire itself had not progressed very far, even though flames had burst from the windows as the fire department arrived.

This was a laboratory illustration of how fire burns, consuming the gas released from solids by heat—then becoming a self-sustaining action. You could see how the fire built up temperature inside the building, until the heat released flammable gas from that vulnerable wallboard—then the whole interior of the building exploded into flame like a firebomb.

The man upstairs had no chance, but the fire department arrived just in time to leave the wordless record of how it happened.

In past years there had been a number of fires at Fort Drum during winter maneuvers, so I directed the building remain just as it was—including the marked outline on the floor where one of our soldiers died. Then, instead of a fire-prevention memorandum, a schedule was set up for every NCO and officer of our division to visit that building and see the silent message there. And we had no further fire problem during our winter maneuvers at Fort Drum.

One of the most important actions any leader can take is to "show the flag" with his command presence. Nothing conveys the kind of message to soldiers on the battlefield as does seeing their commander "up there"—thus *they* know that *he* knows what it is like where they are.

Napoleon Bonaparte used his presence in critical situations to produce results obtainable in no other way. It was his personal presence at the "Battle of the Bridge at Lodi," early in his career in Italy, that first earned him the confidence and loyalty of his men. The Bridge at Lodi was a desperate action that kindled the first spark of that special mystique which would continue to inspire his troops. They called him *le petit caporal* as the direct result of seeing him "up there"—not from some brilliant strategic plan implemented through staff channels.

The same principle applies at all command levels, peace or war: never forget that what you do conveys a message. One of the best ways to exercise command and leadership is for the company commander to do his job up to the standards he expects from his soldiers. Every man in his company will get that message.

Some added comments are:

- Actions can never replace words, oral or written, as a means of communication. I believe, however, most experienced officers who saw that charred building at

Fort Drum would have used it as a silent exhibit to pass the word.

- When Maj. Gen. Charles D. W. Canham commanded the 82d Airborne Division he ordered a one-time personal appearance "Saturday inspection" of all officers, using the chain of command. (Thus, as his infantry brigadier, I inspected my three-man squad of regimental commanders.) His message was clear: live by the same inspection standards you demand of others.

- There is no one best way to communicate; methods used will vary with individuals and situations. Often the best way is to back up what you say by what you do. What you do, however, must be balanced by common sense and good judgment.

General Lee's command breakfast was a one-of-a-kind maneuver that worked for him in wartime. But such extreme gambits are not recommended. Grandstand plays will usually do more harm than good.

44

Harsh Discipline: Balance Justice with Judgment

IN DISCUSSING VARIED facets of command and leadership, I have omitted a vital element — perhaps because it should be seldom used. In addition to leadership qualities a good commander must have enough steel in his soul to enforce discipline with harsh measures when necessary.

I first saw this principle in action as a young second lieutenant. The commanders of the first two companies to which I was assigned at Fort Benning (1925-28) were quite different. One was a toughie about *any* violation, while the other was easygoing and tolerant. Consider these two incidents under the tough commander.

Soon after my assignment to his company, one of our soldiers, found guilty of some dereliction, was marched off to the guardhouse under an armed guard with rifle at the ready.

Not long after that I was late for a formation, and was ordered to "Take reveille formation for a week." Since the bachelor quarters were a mile from the company and I had no car, this meant I walked a mile to receive the first sergeant's report at reveille, trudged another mile back to the bachelor mess for breakfast, and returned a third mile to the company for drill call. Also, there was my uncomfortable awareness that the first sergeant and the company were witnesses to my daily penance.

But we felt no resentment against the tough captain because there was nothing personal in his disciplinary measures. He merely wanted to make it clear that, officer and soldier alike, he would lower the boom on anybody who stepped over the line. So we stayed in line, and had a happy, efficient company.

In the company with the easygoing, tolerant commander there was an avoidance of prompt disciplinary action in favor of "sweet reasonableness." Also, there were more derelictions and failures, and we did not have as happy and efficient a company as under the tough but fair commander.

During my first two years at Benning the guardhouse was no country club. Inside the wire compound prisoners moved at double-time; for any small infraction the provost sergeant would order, "On the track!" This meant the culprit would double-time around inside the barbed-wire-enclosed stockade until the sergeant felt he had proved his point.

There were no seats in the mess hall, no conversation (a man pointed to what he wanted), and no clashing of silverware or china. So meals were eaten in silence, standing up. If you entered the mess hall and closed your eyes, the only sound was a rustle of movement. There were also some restrictions in the living area.

In those two years, when I was officer of the guard, there were never more than sixty-five prisoners in the guardhouse at one time. Then we got a new commanding general and a new enlightened policy in the stockade. And I left the post for seven months on detached service.

On my first tour as officer of the guard, following my extended absence, prisoners walked around inside the stockade, and nobody went "On the track!" In the mess hall everybody was seated, there was a buzzing babel of conversation, clashing of cutlery against china, some laughter — and there were twice as many prisoners in the guardhouse as I had ever seen before, nearly 130 men.

On leaving Fort Benning in 1929, I carried with me many lessons in leadership, and memories of service with fine NCOs and soldiers whom I liked and respected — the first of the wonderful American soldiers who made the Army the professional love of my life. However, I also carried with me the understanding that in any large group of men there will always be a troublesome few who can be controlled only when the commander has the required steel in his soul to take adequate, clear, and unequivocal disciplinary action. But this does not include unreasonably harsh measures — like no seats in a guardhouse mess hall.

Another caution must be kept constantly in mind: be sure your steel is tempered with good judgment in the light of all the circumstances — a lesson I learned at West Point.

We had two parallel basketball courts in our gymnasium there. Early in my plebe year I was among those shooting goals on one court while an intercompany game was played on the other court. The major in charge gave a sharp order to keep free balls off the court where the game was in progress.

Not long after that another player lost control of his ball, and it started toward the off-limits court. Remembering the major's order, I jumped to stop the ball from getting on the court. In this I barely succeeded, but got one foot on the other court — and the major turned in time to see my foot over the line.

Whereupon he took my name, and denied my request to make a statement by saying, "I saw you myself." And he reported me for Deliberate Violation of Instructions.

This was a serious offense, as worded, so I was called up by a reviewing officer. He allowed me to talk, but failed to get the point that I got my foot over the line trying to carry out the major's order — because I could have done nothing, and thus not become involved.

However, I got ten demerits and twenty punishment tours. Each tour was an hour long, walked in dress uniform and white gloves on Saturday afternoons in the barracks quadrangle — and for every minute of those hours I seethed with the injustice of being punished unfairly.

Thus, while harsh disciplinary action was called for when I was a commander in later years, I remembered not only those disciplinary lessons at Fort Benning, but also those unjust hours walking punishment tours at West Point.

Twenty-two years after leaving Benning I commanded the 511th Airborne Infantry at Fort Campbell, Kentucky. One day, court-martial charges arrived on my desk, signed by a young company commander against one of his platoon sergeants, for being drunk on duty and going AWOL for several days.

The man was a master sergeant with fifteen years of service, a Silver Star, a Purple Heart, and battle stars from war service. But the record showed he had been transferred three or four times in the past couple of years, so it looked like he was an alcoholic.

I talked with the company commander, pointing out the sergeant's long service and war record, then asked what he thought about putting the sergeant on probation and holding the charges in abeyance. He said, "No, sir! I've already given him enough breaks!"

After some thought I told the company commander to bring the sergeant to see me, and for the regimental sergeant major to come in with them. Then I addressed the sergeant in front of these witnesses:

"Sergeant," I said, "your company commander wants these charges to go to trial. He says he has already given you enough breaks. But I'm going to give you one too.

"I know your length of service and fine war record, but I also note you have been transferred several times recently. It looks like you have a bottle problem, and have transferred to keep from being tried. But it will not work that way here.

"I will hold these charges, pending your good behavior. But if there is a next time, both sets of charges will go to trial — and you will probably end up as a private."

Within weeks more charges were filed on him. He was tried, then transferred out of the regiment — as a private — so that he could get a new start. Since he was married, this was a real hardship. But you cannot establish a policy that married sergeants with good war records have a license to get drunk and go AWOL.

These comments seem pertinent:

- Discipline is essential in military service but, unfortunately, it cannot be maintained unless stern measures are taken when circumstances call for them.
- As a commander, it is not only necessary that you be fair — especially before imposing heavy penalties — but that the men of your command *know* you are fair. I called in the sergeant major as an impartial witness to the break I gave the bottle-scarred sergeant, and to underline the seriousness of my warning to him. But I also was aware that the sergeant major would relay to others the fact that while I approved the court-martial sentence later, this was after I had checked into the facts and had given the sergeant a full warning of what would happen to him if his offense was repeated.
- The more serious the offense, the heavier the penalty — thus the greater the importance of avoiding injustice by getting all the facts straight, and tempering blind justice with judgment.

45

Apology, Explanation or Silence?

IN THE ARMY, as elsewhere, you sometimes find yourself in an embarrassing spot over some minor mental or physical miscue. The error may result from misunderstanding or stem from ignorance; also, some awkward situations lie in ambush for the unwary. Should you apologize, explain or keep a strong upper lip in silence?

Consider my first formal sit-down dinner in the Army, where I was the partner of a young lady, others present being a generation older. When the salad course came, it had a glob of mayonnaise beside what looked like a midget cabbage, but with thicker and more pulpy leaves. Having never seen an artichoke before I wasn't sure what to do about it. My lady friend didn't help when she whispered, "Now we'll see how well you've been raised."

Cagily, I waited to see what my hostess did. My side vision revealed she pulled off a leaf with her fingertips, dunked the pulpy end in mayonnaise, and put it in her mouth. So I did that, too. The taste wasn't bad, but before long I seemed to have quite a cud in my mouth that was getting bigger and resisted chewing. When I cut my eyes toward my dinner partner, her face was getting pink from efforts to keep from laughing at my problem of disposal.

After more chewing and further observation of what others were doing with that little cabbage, the answer came clear. I hadn't watched my hostess long enough to see that she just stripped the pulpy ends between her teeth, then laid aside the fibrous ends. It was a wad of fibrous ends that had me on the spot.

Looking around at the older faces, I visualized their reactions had I asked to be excused in tones muffled by my fibrous mouthful or — nightmarish thought! — if they were to notice a surreptitious effort to disgorge it. It seemed preferable to swallow my problem, though at imminent risk of choking. In fact it was a close thing — for both of us — because my girl friend understood what was going on and came about as close to choking as I did.

Like so many on-the-spot situations, this one was founded on ignorance. The real villain was false pride: nothing can make you look so silly so often as that. All I had to do was say to my date, "I've never seen one of these little cabbages before. How are you supposed to tackle it?"

Sometimes we build traps into which we fall, as I discovered when a second lieutenant named John shared a room with me in the American-European YMCA in Manila. We had a simple routine for long tropic evenings: a game of chess after supper at the Y, then a warm-up session at the Army-Navy Club bar, followed by migration to the Manila Hotel dance-and-dine pavilion, with a final tapering off at an oasis known as Tom's Dirty Kitchen. To simplify financial arrangements, one of us would be banker each evening and pay all charges. He counted his money at the start and end, then called on the other to reimburse him for half the shrinkage.

One evening when John was banker — thus my pockets were empty — we decided to make a duty call in lieu of the chess game. So in our nice white civilian suits we walked several blocks for the streetcar. As we neared the corner a car stopped, and we broke into a trot to catch it. But the motorman showed us his white teeth in a grin and took off.

In those days my legs worked better than my head, so I also took off to outrun it. It was one of those streetcars you enter in the middle where there were two steps up to a wide opening, and no doors. The cars were slow starters, so I caught this one, putting a foot on the first step and vaulting inside. But the forward motion of the vehicle threw me off balance on landing, and in falling sideways I hooked my fingers into the corner of the change-and-ticket drawer mounted waist-high on an iron pedestal. Since the condemned thing was pivot-mounted, it swirled me around in a pop-the-whip action that laid a football block into the fellow waiting to sell me a ticket, and sprawled him in the aisle.

Thanks to my grip on that revolving drawer, and slowed down by body contact in the block, I managed to stand up without falling—and realized I had no money for my ticket. This was no time for apology or explanation but for silence and action, so with virtually no pause I exited from the still accelerating streetcar the same way I entered. In a final victory of legs over judgment I was able by hard running and violent arm-waving to avoid falling, thus preserving the pristine whiteness of my nice linen suit.

Just what the people on the streetcar thought about my arrival and departure I am not sure, but when John came puffing up, he was clear and explicit about his views. Anyway, this little exercise demonstrates a fundamental idea: sometimes, when quick, impulsive action gets you on the spot, some added quick, impulsive action—like a strategic retreat—may be the best way to get out of it.

At this point I was only several years into my service as a second lieutenant, but continued to accumulate experience for more than thirty years. To prove, however, that I am not alone in this regard, I'll cite a couple of quickies about others.

One day I was on the subway in New York City with two officers on our way to Governor's Island. As we neared South Ferry we knew we would either just make or just miss the boat. So we scrambled up the exit stairs and across the street at a run, headed for the short alley between buildings to the ferry slip. An aggressive first lieutenant named George was in the lead.

When we two trailers turned into the alley the ferry was eight or ten feet from the dock. We were just in time to see George lower his head and really step on the gas, then soar over open water to land on the deck—but lose his balance and fall, his uniform cap rolling into the scuppers.

The ferry drifted in slowly and docked, since it was a bit late and just arriving, not leaving. There was scattered applause from witnesses to this demonstration of determination and agility. Of course George could have stood up, pointed to his watch, and explained that the ferry was late. But he was too sound a tactician for that, so he gave the applauders a dirty look, picked up his cap and went inside the ferry, where no one had seen his premature Brodie.

Younger soldiers are not the only ones vulnerable to bloopers. Consider the social reception held for Brig. Gen. (later Lt. Gen.) Walter C. Short, toward the end of the 1930s.

The general headed the receiving line when guests arrived, then he and others in the line sat in chairs. I was standing nearby disconsolately sipping the punchless fruit punch when several officers and ladies came up to speak with General Short. While standing to greet the ladies, the general changed the direction in which he faced about sixty degrees, a move of which he was unaware. When he went to sit down he missed his chair and landed on the floor with a thud.

Naturally, guests crowded forward, concerned that he might be injured. One officer offered a hand up, which General Short accepted, and quietly thanked his helper. Aside from a slight smile he ignored his inadvertent seat on the floor, making no effort to analyze or explain the mechanics of his misadventure. After some amiable small talk he sat down again, careful he was properly pointed at his chair.

These minor awkward incidents lead to several conclusions about the relative desirability of apology, explanation or silence:

- It rarely pays to try explaining the unexplainable or to analyze the obvious.
- In personal relations, as in military operations, there are times when a strategic retreat is the approved solution. In such instances silence — perhaps accompanied by a smile — is often the most effective rearguard action.
- Everybody finds himself "looking funny" on occasion, so such mishaps are nothing to get unduly ruffled over. From the incidents I have summarized, we see the time-tested thread of an old maxim running through them: when there is nothing to say, say it.

When there is a misunderstanding about facts, especially where official matters are concerned, we have a different type of "situation" which may call for an explanation, or even demand one. Memory takes me back more than forty years to Manila again — not on a streetcar this time but in the Army-Navy Club swimming pool.

As I floated on my back, a hand on my head dunked me under. After blowing a few bubbles I surfaced to find my fellow shavetail, Bob McCleave, grinning at the success of his maneuver.

Since Bob might pull the same stunt again, I worked my way to the deep end and resumed floating. Sure enough, a dunking hand was placed on my head but, alert for this, I quickly gulped a good breath as I went down. On looking around under water I saw that there was a foot with attached leg, so I grasped the ankle with both hands and took it to the bottom with me.

The owner of the ankle struggled, but I kept it down there long enough to be sure Bob got the idea not to try that again. Then we surfaced—and I found myself the center of excited confusion. The owner of the ankle was not Bob, but the shapely wife of a senior middle-aged captain, and she had to be hauled out on the bank half drowned.

While females fluttered around, whacking her on the back and otherwise rendering what they considered first aid, I shuffled from foot to foot waiting to apologize. Her husband, a large, powerful man about twenty years my senior in age and rank, came bustling over. My automatic reflexes launched an instant explanation, the strong-upper-lip silence idea somehow seeming inappropriate. When he got the picture, and noticed his wife was recovered enough to glare at me, the captain relaxed. I thought his faint grin indicated he was not displeased with how things worked out. Perhaps because the lady would be less playful with young lieutenants in the future.

Of course, I offered my abject apologies to her—tactfully forbearing to mention that she initiated the action. However, she was less understanding than her husband, possibly because I hadn't noticed any difference between her shapely stem and Bob's hirsute leg. This points up the fact that even the best apologies and explanations have limitations.

In some situations there may be a question on both sides of what, if anything, to say. Consider the case of a young Navy officer who married early in his career. In late afternoon one day, when his wife was visiting her mother across town and expected to remain overnight, an Annapolis classmate dropped by their small apartment for a visit. Since the sun was over the yardarm, it was proper naval procedure to break out a bottle, which they did.

Some hours later, after toasts to King Neptune, the Navy goat and everything else that needed toasting, the ensign prevailed on his visitor to remain overnight. He also insisted on sleeping on the living room couch himself, while his friend occupied the only bedroom.

Still later that evening the young wife returned home. Finding the apartment dark she came in quietly, tiptoed into the bedroom, changed into nightdress, and eased into bed alongside the recumbent form resting on its side. It was a chilly night, so she snuggled up behind the figure and began to run her cold foot up and down his leg from ankle to knee — then froze in place.

He husband had nice, smooth, almost hairless legs, but her foot met a leg covered with hair. So she eased out of bed, retrieved her clothing and retreated into the living room, where she discovered her husband on the couch. In a whispered consultation she reported the figure had not moved, and she was sure his friend had not awakened. So it was agreed she would return to mother for the night, and they would say nothing to the guest.

They did not know, however, that the question of whether or not to remain silent had also confronted the guest. This was clarified several days later when the wife received a gift package in the mail, with no card identifying the sender, containing a pair of thick, wool bed socks. Which shows that a little imagination can be helpful.

The problem of what to say, if anything, is not confined to off duty hours. One day during the late 1920s, my favorite tennis opponent, a member of the Army rifle team in training for the national matches, seemed preoccupied and off his game. So between sets I said, "What's the matter, Captain? Wouldn't the little bull's-eyes stand still today?"

Then he told me. At long range there had been quite a wind, and his first shot was wide to the right. After making a windage correction, his second shot was closer, but still off the bull's-eye. When the major in charge of the team asked if he had made a full windage correction, the captain said he had. Whereupon the major stepped up, looked at the captain's scorebook, then walked away.

"Well," the captain said to me, toweling sweat from his face, "I looked at my scorebook again. That made me out a liar; due to a mistake in mental arithmetic I had taken only half the windage correction."

"Why didn't you tell him?"

"Because that squinty-eyed runt would think I was telling another lie, trying to cover up the first one." The captain threw his towel down and said, "To hell with him. Let's play tennis."

Was silence the right course? I am not sure, because the captain did have a point: the little major was on the acidulous, unpredictable side. However, I lean to the forthright "set the record straight" policy, but without long-winded explanations that make Himalayas out of gopher mounds.

Perhaps my leaning toward explanations when in doubt stems

from my own failure, on occasions, to make them. Looking back now at three cases casting me in an unfavorable light, I decided then it would be insulting the intelligence of my bosses to assume they would fail to see the situations correctly.

What was the result? It later became clear that my confidence in thinking my bosses would see through the fog of appearances and misunderstandings was misplaced, for they did not. Thus my professional image was damaged, and in two instances my professional record was affected.

What would I do now? In one instance I believe silence was the best procedure, for time burned away the veil of misleading circumstances. In another I would still say nothing, but I would have a disloyal subordinate transferred out of my outfit. In the third I would give my boss the facts, clearly and briefly — which would have been unpleasant for me, for him and for several others. But the CG would then have got all the chickens roosting in the right coops, and in the process plucked a tail feather or two from a couple of young roosters.

My basic error was in believing my motives, like the virtue of Caesar's wife, were beyond question. With this unrealistic above-the-battle viewpoint I failed to stop, look, listen well, and ask myself: "All facts considered, what should be done in the best interest of the military service — which includes me?"

From all this it appears that sometimes the choice is wider than just apology, explanation or silence; that command or administrative action may be in order. Like throwing a rotten apple out of the barrel, thus removing the cause, rather than explaining the effect.

Of course, there are types of situations where you are called on for explanations. My initial contact with this was at West Point. One cadet was required to explain in writing this report: "Kicking horse in riding hall."

His written explanation was: "The report is correct, but the horse kicked me first."

That is a model explanation. Clear and brief, yet it clarifies the situation without extraneous details or special pleas.

A parallel system in the Army is the "reply by indorsement hereon" letter addressed to individuals. The only one to me came when I was a senior colonel, on a post where regulations required that garage doors be closed to prevent leaves blowing in and creating a fire hazard. The letter, signed by the post adjutant, read: "You will reply by indorsement hereon why there were leaves in your garage at 0930 on 13 November."

It seemed desirable to reply on the same intellectual level, so my indorsement read: "I forgot to close the garage door, and the wind blew the leaves in."

Nearly all written demands for explanation deal with your unit, however, rather than with you personally. These may allege violations or failures in an endless variety of staff and command responsibilities. One such periodic requirement is in reply to reports by inspectors general. Usually these relate to minor details, but some can have consequences vital to the careers of the officers concerned. To be specific, we'll look at one derogatory IG report on a division post.

The post (Fort Campbell, Kentucky) had been on standby status prior to arrival of the division from overseas in the late 1940s, and shortly thereafter I reported there as the new chief of staff. Before we were settled in good, much less caught up with the long-neglected post maintenance, an IG (inspector general) arrived for the annual general inspection.

The grapevine had said he was religiously inclined, and one of his first checks was an unused chapel, allegedly littered with trash. This started him out incensed, and he left no stone unturned to throw the book at us. Whether or not this motivation is true, or how bad the situation was in that chapel, I do not know. My first direct information came when worried staff officers brought me the IG report, which called for detailed explanations of a multitude of sins — and rated us "Unsatisfactory."

Our staff was disturbed not only at this grossly unjust rating, but felt that to try to dig out old information — dating back in many cases to prior occupancy when they were overseas, even before the post went on standby status — would interfere with the pressing need to get our current job done. Further, they hated for the CG to see that distorted report, which reflected unfairly on them.

So I kept the report for study. The IG had really outdone himself. Though his imposing title was "Inspector General," his actual military rank was lieutenant colonel. But that did not change the fact the report he had signed required a formal reply.

The question was *how?* In dumb humility, as though we deserved that scurrilous document? Having seen the tremendous job our staff and units had done under trying conditions, the answer was *no*.

I can't remember how the solution came to me; perhaps my sub-conscious saw some parallel to the situation where that West Point cadet kicked the horse back. Anyway, the IG had kicked us first, so I reached for paper and pencil to draft a reply. There was no attempt to explain any alleged violation, just two brief paragraphs like this:

> The above report neither mentions or takes into con-sideration that this division recently returned from over-seas for the first time since World War II, to a post long neglected on standby status. In fact, it fails completely to reflect the overall situation accurately, and gives no indi-cation of the tremendous amount of work accomplished under difficult conditions.
>
> Request another and more competent officer, of experi-ence and mature judgment, be designated to reinspect this command.

The indorsement was prepared for our CG's signature, he prompt-ly signed it — and we never heard any more about the matter.

The point is that this reply was really an overall explanation of the IG report — a simple statement of basic facts. Any long-winded reply, replete with laboriously researched, ancient administrative details, would have been a monumental waste of time, more likely to leave us condemned than to clarify the situation. If we failed to see that that miserable report reflected on the competence of the IG rather than on our job performance, how could we expect the army commander, hundreds of miles away, to get the right picture?

The number and variety of situations that raise the question of apology, explanation or silence, is so great that, like bridge hands dealt at card tables, there can be no set of rules that covers all spe-cial cases. That IG hand dealt us in the late 1940s was one of a kind, too, for I've never heard of another similar case. There is no substi-tute for taking each problem as it comes.

Every officer of experience has his own private collection of "un-fortunate situations" — some serious, some tragic, others just plain frustrating. They might be likened to ladies: every one different, each requiring different personal handling. I can't go so far as to paraphrase Kipling and say, "So be warned by my lot, and learn about special situations from me," but I can summarize several guidelines:

- There are times when saying nothing is the best solution, but there are also times when a simple, clear explanation is the only logical and sensible way to clear up misunderstandings.
- In general, apologies are called for only when you find yourself in the wrong, and then only in personal relations. In official matters, the solution is an official explanation, clarifying misleading circumstances if they are directly relevant. Also include a report of corrective action, if appropriate, but never try to reduce a matter of official explanation to a personal apology.
- Sometimes the hands Fate deals you are of the damned-if-you-do-and-damned-if-you-don't kind. When this happens, the crying towel does no good. Just pick the lesser of the evils available. Also, if some administrative action is in order, take it — and relax, because such things happen to everybody.
- It is natural to try to keep ourselves from "looking bad" unfairly, but we should also be alert to make sure our own judgment of others is not distorted by misleading circumstances. Further, if you are perceptive and see some fine subordinate cast in a poor light by perverse chance, don't leave him with the monkey of decision on his back as to whether apology, explanation or silence is called for. Let him know you see the picture. Thus you change a sticky problem for him into an opportunity for you to exercise the human touch in your command and leadership.

46
Military Tact Tactics

A PERENNIAL TOPIC of military coffee-hour conversations concerns having "The Courage Of Your Convictions." This is one of the Army's most ticklish (but not funny) problems. The solution, however, does not lie in somehow finding a way for imaginative (and infallible?) young subordinates to overrule their (they think) not-so-imaginative superiors.

The situation might be likened to a smart (she thinks) wife who wants to wear the pants of her not-so-smart (she thinks) husband — a fundamentally unsound organizational concept. If she is really smart, however, her views will influence his decisions — yet leave him wearing the pants (rank, head of household, and all the rest).

Applying this principle to the military situation, if a young subordinate is really so much smarter than his older superior, his tactics might be capsuled, "How to Correct Your Seniors and Make Them Like It." Or, "How to Disagree with Your Superiors Without Getting Squelched."

The higher up the rank ladder, the more convoluted and inhibited this becomes, complicated by conflicting interests, command postures, and personalities — especially personalities. Yet there are tactful tactics that can alleviate this touchy dilemma at all levels.

My initial lesson in this came on my first post, as a shavetail in the old 29th Infantry at Fort Benning. Our regiment was taking part in an Infantry School exercise, in a maneuver where members of the Advanced Class (majors and captains) were our commanders and staff officers. As heavy-weapons (howitzer company) liaison officer, I was present when the regimental commander (student major) issued an oral order for a night march, specifying a route that took the left fork at a Y in the road. Later he changed his order to the right fork, by written message.

That night I was at the Y to make sure the heavy weapons turned right, and noticed that the wire-laying communications people took the right fork.

Then an advance guard formation turned left. While I was debating what to do about that, the main body looked up in the darkness —led by a rough-and-ready battalion commander (student captain). Suddenly coming to life, in my best Eager Beaver manner, I rushed out to him at the head of the marching column and announced in an urgent voice, "Sir, that's the wrong road —"

"Who are you?" his harsh voice cut me off.

When, properly abashed, I told him, he said, "Well, Mistuh Newman (a second lieutenant was Mister then, especially when he had a foot off base), suppose you go back and sit under your tree as liaison officer, while I continue to command this battalion."

So the troops went up one road, communications another — and things were gloriously fouled up.

Sure, the battalion commander was wrong in not hearing me out. Certainly, the regimental commander should have sent a staff officer to that road junction to ensure his change in orders did not go astray.

The point here, however, is that I was wrong in the way I approached an older and higher-ranking officer. Though my facts were correct, my military tact tactics were not. What I should have said was, "Sir, the route of march has been changed to the right fork, and communications personnel have already gone that way."

From squad leaders on up, those who exercise authority are human beings, and a lot of intangibles come into play when a subordinate tries to set his superiors straight — particularly when there is an audience.

About ten years later, as a captain, I was an umpire with the reserve battalion in a large maneuver at Pine Camp, New York. The attacking troops were halted by machine-gun fire from an elevation called The Hogback, so the regimental commander ordered a company from the reserve battalion to knock out The Hogback by a close-in envelopment.

The reserve battalion commander (later a general) read the message, then said to his S-3: "I'm going forward on reconnaissance. Move F Company to RJ 123, and I'll give detailed orders there."

He then took off for the regimental OP to see the regimental commander, and I tagged along. There he came directly to the point: "Sir, I have a company moving to an assembly area at RJ 123. With your approval they can move wide around the left flank of The Hogback under cover of those woods [pointing] and knock out the machine guns holding up the regiment. In that way we can take them by surprise, also avoid coming under their fire—which would happen if we tried to envelop instead of flanking them."

The colonel, who had been away from troops a long time, studied the terrain again and got the picture. With a slight smile he turned back to the battalion commander: "I like your plan, Major. Cancel my message on the subject—and do it your way."

As the battalion commander turned to leave he saw me, and his eyes met mine in a level flat stare that seemed to say, "Both of us knew I had received his message—but there was nothing to be gained by trying to make him eat it. Furthermore, don't flap your trap about it around my CP."

I had witnessed a fine demonstration of professional courtesy, on both sides. As a result, their military team relationship had obviously been strengthened at a time when it might well have been weakened.

In the New Guinea campaign of World War II, I was chief of staff of the 24th Infantry Division, under Maj. Gen. Frederick A. Irving. We were part of a reinforced corps landing force, staging for the Hollandia invasion.

Our division task force would land in Tanahmerah Bay, and drive through a narrow mountain pass. The other division task force would land in Humboldt Bay, about thirty miles east of Tanahmerah Bay, and attack along a road toward the airfield complex—thus forming a pincers movement.

Our division plan called for a battalion to land in an arm of Tanahmerah Bay where it could not be supported by naval gun fire. This was a calculated risk, but if surprise were complete the mountain pass might be seized without a fight.

Higher headquarters disapproved that part of the plan. General Irving then went to see the three-star landing force commander, who agreed to take it up again with higher headquarters — which refused to change its prior decision.

Now General Irving went over the plan once more with his staff and the lower-unit commanders who would carry it out. Firmly convinced the possible gain warranted the risk, he directed that a letter be prepared briefing his reasons for requesting reconsideration — and he hand-carried this to landing-force headquarters. There he was given permission to fly back to higher headquarters and present his case in person — and was again refused.

But he left his letter, which now was of record in the headquarters that had disapproved the initial plan and had twice refused reconsideration.

Shortly after his return the pressure of that letter, with its well-marshaled reasoning, resulted in a radio approving his plan. In the actual operation, the battalion that landed without naval gunfire support stormed ashore in the little village of DePapre, and plunged into the jungle over the single narrow trail, up through the pass where a squad could have halted an army — and captured the pass without a casualty.

It was only then that hard fighting began, with Japanese forces rushing to defend the pass — too late.

Bluff and bluster would not have bulldozed a change in the decision by higher headquarters. But a calm and determined commander, convinced of the soundness of his ideas and willing to put it in writing with carefully considered military tact tactics, won his point. This not only saved lives but brought quick success in our operation.

As deputy commandant at the Armed Forces Staff College, years later, I learned of an inquiry being made to large headquarters around the world, asking for information about the effectiveness of our course in preparing AFSC students for their high level staff assignments. The only meaningful answer that came back was that our students needed to learn more about how to get along with people — another way of saying they could do with more military tact tactics.

The way in which General Irving handled his efforts to get a change in the decision by higher headquarters for the Hollandia invasion is a classic example of How to Correct Your Seniors and Make Them Like It. But one point should be added. When he returned from his last trip, after leaving the letter with his written request for reconsideration — and before receiving the radioed OK — he called me in, as his chief of staff, and said: "Red, I have done all I can. Now we'll carry out the decision — so be sure everybody understands this is final."

Two comments:

- It is often overlooked by junior officers that the same courage of convictions they consider so admirable in themselves is equally admirable when possessed by their seniors.
- When a decision is finalized, it is up to the junior to cut the mustard, quit mumbling in his beard — and make it work. To put sand in the implementing process by foot-dragging is sabotage. A smooth-running military operation requires both juniors and seniors to lubricate it with a good grade of military tact tactics.

47

Life in the Ivory Tower

WRITERS—WISE AND otherwise—fill our public prints with diverse diatribes and dithyrambs about the Pentagon and those who toil there. National and international affairs viewed in the light of military strategy, our national budget and the next election get full play—frequently as reflected in the distorted mirror of incomplete information evaluated in the vacuum of a lack of personal knowledge. As a result some fine officers avoid duty there, apparently failing to realize they are depriving themselves of invaluable professional training and experience for high rank.

Perhaps a grass roots view of service in the Pentagon is in order.

When I reported there in 1946 it was, primarily, headquarters for the War Department (now Department of the Army). The Air Corps was still part of the Army, and there was no Department of Defense. Yet certain intangible factors of life in the Ivory Tower remain the same now as then.

The labyrinth of offices and interlocking staff procedures in the Pentagon of that day encompassed another high staff: headquarters of Army Field Forces (now U.S. Continental Army Command). It was organized like the War Department staff, but a step lower on the totem pole—though the chief of Army Field Forces was a four-star general.

Within this framework I was chief of the Training Branch, G-2 Section, Army Field Forces. Under my authority were another colonel, a lieutenant colonel, a major, a secretary and a clerk-typist.

After reporting to my section chief, a two-star general, I went around to my domain of two connecting offices. There I met for the first time the Pentagon Pause, Peer and Ponder. That is, when a stranger comes in the door of an office:

There is the *pause* when everybody stops talking, typing or whatever they are doing.

Then you get the *peer* as they take a deadpan look at you.

Next is the *ponder* while everybody is obviously thinking, "Who is this guy, and what the hell does he want?"

So I answered their *ponder* by proclaiming myself their new boss, and sat down where the inevitable Pentagon field equipment was neatly arranged on my desk: an IN basket, an OUT basket, a fountain pen set, a scratch pad and pencil, and under the glass top a chart of the Pentagon staff organization. This chart listed names, duty assignments and room and telephone numbers. Without it you could do little in the Pentagon.

As I wondered what I was supposed to do, and how to go about it, our clerk-typist put some papers in my IN basket — and I was in business in the Pentagon. The physical *modus operandi* was simple: each day I took papers from my IN basket, generated something to put on the papers, placed them in the OUT basket — and that was it. It may sound monotonous but it was not, for often research was required, other people had to be consulted and there was, finally, the problem to answer on the paper.

Also, when you signed those papers some very important people would read what you wrote, so you had better be able to defend your ideas. Often there were future angles which required visualization to realize what could happen.

Early in my tour one paper had to do with a scout dog platoon — an order assigning it to Fort Podunk for station — bucked to me by our front office. It looked simple, so I gave it a simple answer: "Noted."

That seemed a safe enough action, but I sure got tired of seeing that paper — and more embarrassed each time it bounced back. First it returned with a pencil note from my boss, "Inadequate comment." Remaining casual, I said it was a good idea to keep the war-time learned art alive by retaining the K-9 unit in being as planned. Again it came back, this time with the pencil note: "Is that all?"

Losing my cool a little, but still thinking off the top of my skull, I added the sage observation that Fort Podunk was a good station, having tactical troops the scout dog platoon could train with. Also, that training should include tests to see if changes were needed in the tables of organization. This time the note said: "See me."

Thus I learned a lesson from him about what I should have foreseen myself, had I used imagination and common sense: that the scout dog platoon had positive intelligence value, and should be stationed at our intelligence center being set up at Fort Riley, Kansas — a pet project of my boss.

That was a valuable lesson. During the rest of my service when a prosaic looking paper came to me while I was on a high staff I never brushed it aside without careful thought, because it might be another scout dog platoon paper.

Of course I quickly ran into that staff procedural trap called "concurrences" on "action papers." When somebody in an office in the Pentagon decides to get something done, he starts an action paper. It works like this:

On a single sheet of paper, write the problem — what the paper is all about. Then discuss and analyze it, and end by making recommendations: the action required to get done what you want done. At the bottom of the page there must be space for signatures by those who "concur" or "non-concur" for all interested staff sections. (While that top page shows a thumbnail summary of everything, as many supporting data as you want can be added as attached papers, tabbed for reference).

Your paper goes fine so long as everybody "concurs." Then a "non-concur" goes down, with reasons in writing. That means it must go to somebody with authority to make a decision, so you consider: do I bury this paper with military honors, and forget it, or do I fight for it?

Sometimes you have to take action, can't get it OKed the way you want it, and compromise rears its straddle-faced head. But when you finally get it finished, the "action" will be "coordinated."

The fur flies, though, when you "concur" in a paper for your staff section, the action is taken — and your boss does not like it. Your education in this may come soon after you enter the Pentagon, like this:

Some smooth operator had tried to process an action paper on his pet project. (Don't look down on "pet projects" — airborne troops and atomic submarines were once pet projects of able staff officers.) Anyway, your predecessor had checked with your boss before concurring, and the boss said "non-concur." So the project died.

Then you arrive and the pet project, exhumed and dusted off, comes in to you and you "concur." You discover that an angle shooter has run a whizzer on you when your section chief wants to know why his "non-concur" was reversed. Thus you learn that when you sign your name you are not only betting your opinion is sound; you are also wagering your boss will agree.

Another hazard you learn to beware of is the paper with the so-called "weasel words" that can be read more than one way so the "concur" gets signed, and the fight is posthumous.

By now you may have put me down as critical of the Pentagon, but that's not true. I think there is a thread running through these little stories and cynical quotes that outlines the difficulties of operating on any high staff where diverse viewpoints and varied interests must somehow be coalesced into decisions and direct actions.

This was especially true for officers on the Army General Staff, who were then and still are second-guessed from all directions. Thus they require more than military ability, for there were and are political factors and pressures requiring a special kind of mental toughness and elasticity.

This once-over-lightly look at life in the Ivory Tower would not be complete without the quotation I saw in a frame on the desk of a fine Army General Staff officer (quoted here from memory): "If I tried to read, much less reply, to all criticisms leveled against me—I would have time for little else. I do the best I can, the very best I know how. And will continue this to the end."

To me, after you penetrate the smoke screen of wisecracks and criticisms, this little sign typified so many of the wonderful officers I knew in the Pentagon—and others there now. It states the motivating force that permeates those miles of corridors and the maze of offices, the basic principle that underlies the best efforts of the finest professional officers in the world who labor there—and I sleep better each night because I know it will remain that way.

If those of you still in active service have the chance, don't miss the professional opportunity and personal privilege of serving with them.

48

The Monkey Principle

AT FIRST THOUGHT it might seem that three monkeys could have nothing to do with command and leadership. But, on second thought, consider the famous image of three monkeys sitting side by side—one with hands over his ears, another with hands over his eyes, and the third with hands over his mouth. The caption is "Hear no evil, see no evil, speak no evil."

In command and leadership, it is well to keep those monkeys in mind when faced with certain special situations. No clear rule separates cases where the monkeys are right from those where they are wrong, so let us examine and reflect on several footnotes to history involving monkey situations.

The first episode concerns the Army tactical officer for my cadet company at West Point. The occasion was a full field inspection in ranks with equipment rolled in a pack on the back of each cadet.

As the "Tac" moved down the line, an alarm clock went off inside the pack of one of my roommates. The ranks stood firm and unsmiling while the Tac blandly ignored the raucous clock and proceeded with his inspection. The inspection ended, the Tac left and the company was dismissed, both sides well pleased with the quiet self-control they had managed. (All except the cadet in whose pack the alarm clock had been hidden. "All right, now," he demanded loudly, who the hell did it?")

That was a case where poor hearing by the Tac was the best part of wisdom. He knew there was virtually no chance he could find out who staged that alarm clock coup. So, figuratively speaking, he put his hands over his ears.

Here is another situation with monkeyshine overtones, involving weak hearing and poor eyesight. This occurred on my first post soon after we received a new regimental commander.

One Sunday afternoon I wandered down the hall from my room in the bachelor quarters to that of a classmate named Eddie. Several others were there with him, including an athletic pal of mine at The Point named Dudley, who was a bit nearsighted.

They were in Eddie's bedroom with a bottle of Prohibition Georgia corn and, incongruously enough, a long-necked bottle of green *creme de menthe*. The atmosphere was pleasantly jovial and they offered me a drink, but did not persist when I declined.

Not long after my arrival, there was a knock on the living room door and Dud, in slacks and undershirt, said, "I'll get it, Eddie."

He stepped through the bedroom door and I started to follow — but recognized the figure in the living room doorway and froze in place. It was our distinguished new regimental commander in white tropical uniform (seldom worn there) come to return our official social calls.

But Dud was not fazed, for he wheeled about in the middle of the living room and said, "Hey, Eddie, there's a white-haired old geezer here to see you."

I remained silent and frozen in the bedroom, feeling like the innocent bystander who sees a bullet headed his way. But by the time Eddie answered Dud's summons our visitor was gone. And shortly thereafter I was gone too.

That fine old gentleman realized his young bachelors were not expecting callers and knew his white uniform could be mistaken at a glance for a civilian suit. So he quietly faded away. Whether he guessed he had walked in on a little Georgia corn party I'll never know, but I believe he suspected it. If so, he was following the policy of those Old Army days: take positive action in disciplinary matters, but don't go snooping around for off-duty peccadilloes.

And he well knew that is what it would look like if one of his first acts was to invade the bachelor quarters unannounced, then lower the boom on that bedroom social hour around a bottle.

As for me, I never forgot the quiet consideration and understanding of an older senior officer for some young squirts. That fine old colonel (later a general officer) was following the example of all three monkeys at once: he saw no evil, heard no evil, and spoke no evil to the regimental adjutant the next morning about initiating a *post mortem* in the premises.

Years later, after assuming command of Company G, 26th Infantry at Plattsburg Barracks, I found myself with a somewhat similar monkey on my back. In fact, two monkeys: one involving eyesight and the other a question of whether or not to speak a restrictive evil.

Several weeks after assuming command I had shared a coffee break in Sgt. "Honest John" Smith's mess hall with 1st Sgt. "Big Jim" Redding. In this informal setting we discussed certain unwritten customs that I would follow as company commander. These included:

- That I might show up at the company any time, day or night, but unless there was some specific reason, I would normally confine my out-of-duty hours visits to my office, our kitchen, the supply room and hallways connecting them.
- More particularly, unless there was some direct reason to do so, in off-duty hours I would not invade the privacy of the dayroom or the sleeping areas.
- Finally, that I looked to him and our sergeants to monitor and control off-duty hours in these areas and bring me into the act when necessary.

Some weeks later, I returned to my office after supper on a payday. In passing along the hallway to the office, I glanced toward the dayroom and noticed a group standing around a table where others were seated.

Like my former regimental commander (the "white-haired old geezer") I was pretty sure I knew what was going on: that the use of cards and the exchange of money was involved. Like him, however, my eyesight was poor and I continued on my way, but the hands over my mouth slipped a bit the next day in a little conference with Big Jim Redding.

I told him that gambling was against regulations, but that if some men had to gamble and were going to do it anyway, maybe it was better for them to do it in our own dayroom than to be taken by card sharpers somewhere else.

On the other hand, I told Big Jim to pass the word to all NCOs that for an NCO to gamble with privates was strictly a "no-no." Also that I would invoke the law to divest any NCO of his chevrons who tested his skill and luck for money with privates. Further, it was the responsibility of NCOs to insure no outside sharpie invaded our barracks to "take" our soldiers.

Pertinent comments include:

- That image of the three monkeys was created by a civilian as a guideline in dealing with your fellow man in day-to-day living. However, in specialized situations, it can apply in military duties — with perception, judgment and common sense.
- There are those who will cluck in dismay at the idea of a regimental commander quietly fading away during Prohibition when he had reason to think he was privy to a violation of the Volstead Act. Similarly, they will look with dour displeasure at a former company commander who acknowledges that, within certain limits, he has tolerated gambling.

  To them let me quote Rudyard Kipling: "Single men in barracks don't grow into plaster saints." Further, to add my view: Military men in authority should keep in mind there are times in command and leadership when the idea of those three monkeys may be pertinent and appropriate.
- One of our greatest military leaders was General of the Army Omar N. Bradley. In *A Soldier's Story* he records a special command situation and his solution to it. This involved the indomitable Col. Harry A. "Paddy" Flint, who assumed command of the 39th Infantry before the invasion of Sicily.

  To help his regiment gain confidence under fire Paddy would stroll about the front, calmly rolling a cigarette with one hand and saying scornfully, "Lookit them lousy krauts. Couldn't shoot in the last war. Can't shoot in this one. Can't even hit an old buck like me."

  One day Paddy came to II Corps headquarters with Maj. Gen. Manton Eddy. When Paddy ambled off to the G-3 tent, General Eddy picked up Paddy's helmet and displayed the "AAA-O" stencil on it.

"It means," General Eddy said, 'Anything, Anywhere, Anytime, bar nothing.' Paddy has this thing stenciled on every damned helmet and truck in his whole damned regiment." Then he added, "Haven't you issued some kind of corps order about special unit markings?"

"Manton," General Bradley replied, "I can't see a thing today—nope, not even that helmet of Paddy Flint's."

Just another case where the principle of the three monkeys was perceptively applied in command and leadership.

- Where does flexibility end and permissiveness begin? Anyone who decides to break some rule or regulation will do so at his peril, and the same applies to the commander who tolerates a violation. Whether you are the superior or the subordinate in applying the monkey principle, your judgment had better be good—because you will have to live with the result.

49
Planned Leadership

IT IS ODD that after so much has been written about leadership it is still so nebulous and intangible. A thoughtful article by Lt. Col. E. C. Townsend (*Infantry Journal,* February 1948) discusses "Techniques of Command"—as distinguished from Leadership. Colonel Townsend makes a rather delicate distinction, but the techniques he outlines are sound.

He adds that we need more military writings on command (leadership), based on experience in the practical application of known techniques to specific situations—and that's where I come in. Here is one man's solution to a specific leadership problem and, while it may be presumptuous, it does not presume to be *more* than one man's solution—told in day-by-day incidents and actions. But perhaps I should review my credentials first.

I approach the qualifications Colonel Townsend desired in his authors, having had peacetime command experience—and both command and staff duty in combat. (My original magazine article was published under the by-line of "Colonel Riposte," so that I could write of personal experience without inhibitions.)

Fate decreed that I should start World War II as a division general staff officer, and then become division chief of staff. Finally my division commander conferred on me the honor and privilege of commanding a regiment in battle—and for this I shall forever be indebted to him.

The initial problem in leadership I faced was somewhat unique in that I was given my regiment barely three weeks before the division was to load out for an amphibious operation. Thus I had to become quickly acquainted with my officers and men—*and they with me.* On top of that there was an amphibious field order to prepare and a combat team to load out. And all in three weeks.

Leadership or command (either term means control of troops legally placed under your orders) should not be just an extemporaneous reflex, or instinctive action. It should be planned and considered, following definite principles but tailored to fit the commander's personality. I believed strongly in this, and so fixed in my mind a few fundamental principles, as well as a plan of the things I would do in taking over my regiment.

The basic principles and ideas on which I based my leadership plans were:

1. First and foremost, I wanted the respect of my officers and men, based upon their belief that I knew my job and was a competent soldier.
2. I felt that much of my success as a commander would depend upon whether or not my officers and men felt they knew me — I could not remain an abstraction to them.
3. A personal interest in and responsibility for the individual welfare and safety of each of my men was a duty that I had to fulfill every minute of every hour of every day.
4. I would do what I thought was right and proper, because it was right and proper — or blood flow when necessary — either mine or theirs.
5. I would not ask any man to do what I was not willing to do myself. I had to obey my own orders, to physically go where I asked my soldiers to go.
6. My men would soon come to understand that I would and could do what I ordered them to do and the natural result would be that both officers and men would risk their lives in carrying out my orders. And they would do it in a way that no threat or regulation or court could ever force them to do.
7. There is absolutely no substitute for personal knowledge of a military situation.

8. Good soldiers of all ranks thrive on responsibility, so I would use my staff and commanders to the maximum. I would not be a one-man regiment.
9. I would give credit where credit was due.
10. If any officer couldn't do his job, I would relieve him as soon as it was definitely clear. There would be no vacillation.
11. Ammunition, food, medical care, extra socks, coffee, and other material things are often as important as the scheme of maneuver, and failure on my part in these things would immediately, and justly, bring my competence as a commander in question in the eyes of my men.
12. I would frequently talk with individual officers and men, and never allow my staff to insulate me from my command.
13. I would be loyal to my superiors and to the men of my regiment. Neither was entitled to my loyalty to the unjust detriment of the other.

These, then, were the things I kept in mind as rules to follow after I assumed command of my regiment. It was a big advantage to have a clear idea of what I was going to do. I could wag the circumstances instead of being wagged.

From this point I'll put down the things I did, pretty much in chronological order. In most cases the relation of these incidents to leadership, or the technique of command, needs no explanation.

Feeling Out the New Command

When I arrived at my regiment I had a talk with the regimental executive officer. I told him that I wanted things to go on just as they always had, and that if I gave orders that would change the customary way of doing things in the regiment to let me know. I might at any time change previous ways of doing things; but when I did I wanted to know it and have a definite reason for the change.

I informed him that I would operate through him, that if I wanted something done I would tell him, and would normally leave to him the organization of how the staff was to do it. I also told him his work was known to me, and that I felt very fortunate indeed to have him as my Exec. This was very true.

My first order was to call for a brief conference of all regimental staff officers, the battalion commanders, and the separate unit commanders. In that assembly I said that I was very happy to be with them; that it was the realization for me of an ambition; that I was glad it was that particular regiment; that I would work largely through my staff, headed up by my Exec, but that I wanted to keep in personal touch with each of them, and that from time to time I would call them in individually to tell me about their problems.

Next I told my Exec to set up a large tent as a planning room in which there would be a bulletin board. It was here that we would do most of our work on the important job of getting out the regimental field order for the amphibious landing. Each part of the field order would be posted on the planning tent bulletin board as soon as it was completed—if still subject to revision, it would be marked "draft." I told him to organize the staff to prepare the order, and to consult me from time to time and keep me abreast of just what he was doing. But I made it very clear that he and not I was to be the Exec.

School for the Colonel

On the second day I instructed him to arrange a school for me—and that he was to make no bones about it with anybody. This was to be a refresher course of instruction for the regimental commander to ensure that he knew the way things were set up in the regiment. As division chief of staff I had been out of touch with a lot of changes and details in equipment and organization of a regiment. This school was to run for six consecutive afternoons, and was to be organized as follows:

> 1st Battalion—Parade all weapons (including grenades and small arms) of an infantry battalion, and be prepared to demonstrate them to me—and to let me fire each one of them.
> 2d Battalion—Set up a battalion headquarters and command post, complete with all signal installations, in-

cluding radios, and be prepared to explain everything connected with a battalion command post and how it operates.

3d Battalion — Parade all transportation of the battalion, and be prepared to have various officers and men explain every piece, its uses, limitations, and so forth.

Headquarters Company — Set up a field regimental command post, and show how it operated; describe their plans for moving — all details necessary for me to understand how my own CP was established and functioned.

Cannon Company — Parade all weapons and equipment, and brief me on what they could do, how they operated.

Service Company — Parade and explain all their stuff.

It might be well to interject here that I saw no reason to try and bluff my way. In addition to learning a lot of things about equipment and its operation, the school gave me a chance to size up my regiment, and gave the regiment a chance to start sizing me up.

Picking a Bodyguard

I had all the officers of the regiment assembled, and spoke to them briefly in headquarters. At the end of my little talk, I held a receiving line formation and shook hands with each of them.

Of course a personal orderly and jeep driver were assigned to me, and radio operator. But I wanted a bodyguard, and gave special instructions to the adjutant about how I wanted to select this man myself. To do this the following arrangements were made:

1. There would be a selected military orderly within call of my office tent from after breakfast in the morning until such time as I would dismiss him at night.

2. So that this orderly would not be worn out on this duty, there were to be four of them each day — one from each battalion, and one from the separate companies.

3. Each orderly was to come from a different company of the battalion each day.

4. They were to be picked men, and from them I would pick my personal bodyguard.

This arrangement made it possible for one man in every company in the regiment to have been adjacent to my tent in the period of four days. I knew these men would tell the men in their companies what the new regimental commander was like. They would see me dealing with my staff, checking on planning, and handling the many details incident to getting ready for the coming operation. And, since I felt I knew my job, I would carry on "business as usual." There would be no "act." If I knew my job my soldiers would come to know it.

It was SOP (standing operating procedure) for each orderly to report to me when he first came on duty. After returning his salute with unhurried precision, I asked him to have a seat in the chair outside my office. I used these orderlies as runners and thus gave them a chance to see how their regimental headquarters was working by carrying messages for me.

This arrangement gave me a chance to show them that a soldier was entitled to my courtesy. Nothing ostentatious — and it was no act. When I left my office tent I told the orderly to listen for my phone, and to sit in my chair while I was gone as it was more comfortable and convenient to the phone. At mealtime when I left to eat I asked the man on duty if he had eaten — or knew of the arrangements for his meals.

My interest was sincere, and I wasn't kidding anybody — but it did give my regiment a chance to find out before we went into battle that the Old Man was interested in the welfare of each soldier.

When I finally chose one of those orderlies as my bodyguard for combat, I had him draw every kind of small arm there was and do some practice shooting, including throwing grenades, using a tommy gun, a pistol, and Garand rifle. I told him I expected him to have his field equipment in top shape, carry his entrenching tool, and in general be ready to spend very little time in the command post. The man I picked for my bodyguard was a fine looking soldier, an athlete, apparently a man who would not shirk his duty when in proximity to the enemy.

But I was also aware that he was a man with a tongue, and not exactly the silent type. As by this time you may have guessed, my idea was that in a short time my men would know a lot about what the Old Man was like. I could have assembled them, given them a fight talk and thumped my chest — but that was not my way.

Meeting the Noncoms

I did have all the first, master and technical sergeants of the regiment assembled at headquarters. To these fine soldiers — the backbone of the enlisted strength of my regiment — I said a few simple things. I told them that I did not get canned as division chief of staff, but that I came to the regiment because I asked for it as the highest honor an infantry officer of my grade could hope for; that I had been a lieutenant for ten years, almost all of it with troops; that as a captain I had been a company commander for five years, in three different companies; that to my regret I had never been a battalion commander, and that this was my first regimental command; that I knew and understood the place they held in the regiment, and that I had assembled them so that I could meet each one of them and let them know I was depending on them; that any one of them could come to headquarters to see me at any time; that I felt a special relation existed between the highest commissioned officer in the regiment and the highest noncommissioned officers of the regiment. I then stood by the door of the tent to shake the hand of each man as he left.

I made a tour of headquarters with my Exec, meeting every officer and enlisted man in the headquarters at his place of business and had each one of them brief me on what he did, the equipment he used, and his method of operation. In addition, I had my Exec set up an after supper school for me for one hour each night. Then in turn, on separate nights, each of the staff officers — personnel, intelligence, operations, logistics, signal, surgeon, chaplain — told me about his job and answered my questions.

Let me say here again there was nothing either secret or ostentatious about this. What I didn't know I was asking people to tell me; also I was sizing them up — and I hoped, and believed, they were sizing me up.

Concurrently, a good many things were going on at once. But of course I have to tell about them one at a time, so you will have to picture mentally that a lot of these things I am telling you in sequence were actually overlapping in time.

Getting Closely Acquainted

I had the adjutant arrange for three officers, outside of the staff, to come up for lunch and supper each day and join me in the regimental officers' mess. Once again it was just so I could see them and they could see me close up — they were my guests for a meal. It was good for me and for them, I am sure.

At the first Saturday inspection, with equipment displayed on bunks, I went to every company area. And everywhere I checked a few of the standard things. I looked at the police of the area, and very carefully looked over the kitchens. And as always, I looked closely at weapons.

At this point I might add that I didn't ask soldiers if they were getting enough to eat. I knew the answer, and so did they. I had been around to company kitchens before reveille, looking at what they were getting for breakfast, and stopping at chow lines and kitchens at all hours of the day everywhere I went.

During the inspection I stopped to talk to men here and there. I complimented some on the excellent care they gave their weapons. I asked others when they had last fired their weapons, or to see their second pair of shoes. Sometimes I looked at the bottom of the shoes they were wearing. In general I tried to make my inspection accomplish something, to inform me of things that counted. When I found things wrong, they were changed that very day, if possible. That made my inspection more than just a case of parading through the regiment. When things looked bad to me I said so, without rancor, and when things looked good to me I said so, with sincerity.

It became advisable to move one of my battalions from a somewhat separated location into the general area of the other two. I carefully checked the arrangements for this, the first movement under my command, and had everything planned so that there was no "hurry up and wait." No doubt I looked over the battalion commander's shoulder more than I normally would, but I thought everybody might as well get the idea in the beginning that details had to be buttoned up when troops moved, and that included good meals.

As I rode around in my jeep the driver's orders were never to pass a soldier of our regiment when we had an empty back seat.

How, with an amphibious field order to prepare, did I have the time to do all this moving around? Well, I had a fine soldier as Exec, and an efficient staff. The deadline for finishing each part of the order was announced, the scheme of maneuver settled. Things were organized in the planning tent with the bulletin board arrangement so that I or anyone else could walk in and check on how things were progressing at any time — and I was the regimental commander, not the regimental staff. I could see that they knew their jobs so I took a pride in letting them go ahead. The result was they took a pride in my pride in them, so that all I ever had to do was spend the evening looking over what they had accomplished during the day. This gave me my days free to do things that my staff could not do for me.

A Little Matter of Salt

In the planning I made arrangements to get extra socks, extra coffee, and extra cigarettes. These are little things, but there were times coming when relatively small things were going to take on a value out of all proportion to the trouble necessary to get them. And then there was the little question of salt — which I think deserves a paragraph all to itself.

Where we were going it was hot, and we were going to need salt tablets. This could make quite a lot of difference in the endurance of individual soldiers. I checked on this and found we did not have an adequate supply. On a recheck I found salt tablets were still in short supply, and a still later check showed they still had not been distributed. I determined this by simply asking men to show me their salt. So I built a fire . . . and to make a long story a little shorter, when the men were loaded aboard ship I checked individuals for salt, and found some men still without it. So I turned over the stink pot. The men got salt. I think getting that salt helped us to understand each other better.

Supervising the loading out was a matter of course. By this time the new regimental commander felt that maybe he was being accepted, because when officers and men saluted or reported they seemed to have lost the flat expressionless look that soldiers usually give officers they don't know — or dislike. It is always the part of the senior to take the lead in getting acquainted with his juniors, and I had made careful efforts to do this. It was a great satisfaction to be recognized everywhere I went. Nobody patted me on the back, but I was accepted and I hoped I saw a friendly light in the eyes of officers and men when I came up.

Plans for Combat

In planning the landing formation, I decided to land with the leading assault battalion. I told the battalion commander that I wanted no announcement made about that, but that it was no secret and should be known to the men: the news, I knew, would spread.

I had my field equipment checked, and was dressed as an enlisted man in every particular — including pack. It was a very "stripped" pack, but in that pack went several D-ration bars along with room for sandwiches or a K ration. I expected to be away from regular messing facilities frequently during combat, and did not want to be chiseling chow from men who were doing the fighting. I had a carbine which I test-fired and zeroed. I did this because I expected to be up where these arrangements would be very practicable and sensible, but I was also mindful that word would get around that I was not preparing for combat by sharpening pencils. It seemed better for the regiment to find out from the things I did, rather than what I said, as to where I planned to go in battle.

If I had had my regiment longer — or a shorter time — perhaps I would have talked to them as a group. But under the circumstances I decided to let what I was doing to get ready speak for me.

One night when I was checking a paper that needed my OK, the field phone rang, and the battalion commander of the battalion with which I was going to land called up and said that he had wangled some extra beer, and that it was cooling in the creek. Would I drop in at his tent and have a beer?

Now that seems like a small thing, but to me it meant a lot. I dropped what I was doing and went, though it meant that I would have to check that paper before breakfast the next morning. Had I not accepted the invitation it would have, in my opinion, been a serious mistake — killing a chance to know and understand the mind of one of my important commanders.

For me to have failed to see that going down for that beer was an important duty would have been a lack of insight into a vital intangible of leadership.

As planning for the operation progressed, I sat in on staff conferences from time to time. Before each meeting the Exec briefed me on what the conference was to be about, and I made sure I understood the subject under discussion. Thus I never went to a meeting without having done some thinking in advance. This was so that I would not find myself talking, then have to say, "I'm just thinking out loud, so correct me if I'm wrong."

On the other hand, if something came up on which I needed more information, I would ask direct and specific questions. Even to know what you don't know is definite knowledge, and something that no man should hide. And a staff is there to get answers for the Old Man. In this, as in everything else I did as a commander, the regiment was going to learn through the mysterious grapevine about what kind of a soldier they had who might hold their lives in his hands — or head.

One last point on these pre-combat days. I had made an overall plan of the things I wanted to do, but I also made daily plans. Each night I thought about the next day, and what I was to do. In fact, I quite often fell asleep going over these plans in my mind. Then the next morning, as I dressed and shaved, I again went over what I planned to do that day. Then after breakfast I would tell my Exec my plans, if I had not already told him the night before.

What has all this to do with leadership?

A very great deal. By coordinating with my staff there was a dearth of sudden little emergencies; no occasion to send out runners to look for the Old Man, or otherwise putting on the grapevine the news that things were not well organized at headquarters. I wanted a certain surety about my movements, so that my regiment would begin to think maybe I knew where I was going all the time — and why.

Of course, there were other things in addition to those I have covered here, but these give an idea of how one regimental commander tried to influence his impact upon his regiment in a rather brief time. It was the solution of a specific problem. Of course every problem should be reviewed and met with a definite plan. A leadership problem is no exception.

From what I have written it is evident that I think efficiency of operation overlaps into leadership. One of the very best ways to exercise leadership is simply to deserve the respect and trust and loyalty of your command and to give loyalty, consideration, and respect in return. The best "fight talk" in the world is empty bombast if it is not backed up with action. And the best way to tell your soldiers that you, too, are a soldier is to be one — deliberately and on purpose, as the result of careful and intelligent forethought.

PART III
COMMAND IN BATTLE

50

Planned Leadership for Battle

THE PRECEDING CHAPTER outlined my experience as a leader before going into combat with my regiment—the 34th Infantry, 24th Infantry Division. It was simply a narrative of how I attempted to exert an influence on my regiment over and beyond the mere issuance of orders.

This chapter will concern my experience in combat. Most of the ideas involved were collected in little pieces of understanding through the years, and digested in battle. In my view they add up to the thing that is so often spoken of with so much respect and so much vagueness: leadership.

Some of the personal references that follow may seem overly intimate, when published without my "Colonel Riposte" pen name. Few men can openly reveal their innermost thoughts, and I am not unlike most men. However, what I have to say would be of no value unless it were true, and based on success in battle. I am sorry there is so much "me" in this. If it opens me to criticism, all I can say is that it is just my story—for what it may be worth. To be coy would make this study useless, and so I shall be unblushing in pursuing the theme as best I can.

The techniques of leadership should fit the individual leader and the particular situation. Therefore, my leadership program is only a solution by one commander to a particular problem, and presumes to be no more than that. Finally, it should be remembered that this was my first battle experience as a commander, and that I had been in command of my regiment less than a month when we entered battle together. Therefore I did some things that would otherwise have been unnecessary.

I am sure that everyone who reads this will understand that I know I succeeded only because of the magnificent soldiers in my regiment, and the outstandingly fine officers it was my great good fortune to inherit. But even the finest officers and men need competent leaders to organize their energies and give purpose and direction to their best efforts. So I hope those with whom I served will understand that I am not trying to claim credit for their efforts.

Further, I believe my officers and men will agree with me that leadership can and should be planned. In addition I believe that — if it had been possible for me to ask them — they would not object to using our common experience to try to make clearer some of the problems of battle leadership.

Shipboard Plans

Our combat team was put to sea in eight ships, as part of a great armada in one of the world's largest and most complicated amphibious operations.

Part of my leadership plan called for certain things to be done on board ship. We had constructed relief maps of the battle area for each assault battalion and, during the voyage, every officer and man was briefed on what he was to do and where he was to go.

We had a good plan, carefully worked out in detail. I wanted everyone to know and understand it fully. That way if our leaders became casualties I would have a whole regiment of men ready to become leaders; also if things did not go according to plan, everybody would know it and understand the resulting difficulties. And finally, it was good to have everybody working on something positive, not just thinking and worrying in a vague uncertain way about what might happen in the landing.

Of course we had boat drills, weapons checks, and other such details, and there was work for the regimental staff too.

My staff, under the Exec, drilled in a Standing Operating Procedure on how to get out a field order quickly, basing practice orders on our coming battle area. We would normally operate on fragmentary orders, but there should be no floundering over mechanical details when a full-scale order was required.

And what was the regimental commander doing?

Just this: reviewing the steps by which I could most effectively exercise leadership in combat. To begin with, I was going over in my mind the principles of leadership I hoped to stick to. I went over them constantly, because they bore directly on things that I, as the commander, had to get straight in my own heart. They were three in number:

I would do what I thought was right and proper, because it was right and proper, and let the chips fall where they may — or blood flow when necessary — either mine or theirs.

I would not ask any man to do what I was not willing to do myself. Thus I had to be ready to obey my own orders, to physically go where I asked my soldiers to go.

My men would soon come to understand this, if it was really so, and as a result both officers and men would risk their lives in carrying out my orders in a way that no threat or regulation or court could ever force them to do.

And to these I added four points to remember about planned leadership for a commander in battle:

1. My men would expect me to anticipate battlefield developments; they would expect me to take positive action when faced with an emergency.
2. They would look to me for *resolution.* In their hearts they would want me to order what must be ordered; they would want me to have iron in my soul, for my men were soldiers — intelligent American soldiers.
3. Therefore, if I was to be effective, I would have to win the right to issue such orders by appearing in the forefront of battle. And after I had established this right it would be my duty not to needlessly endanger the valuable soldier I would then be.
4. Good regimental commanders are hard to come by, but if the Old Man ever reaches the point where he does not go to the "hot spot" where his men need his presence, then he is no longer a good regimental commander.

I made my final preparations for exercising leadership as I leaned against the rail on deck at night. I looked down at the dark shapes of my men on the well deck below, and a heavy weight rested on my shoulders, the weight of responsibility for their lives, and for our success in battle. Then I looked at the vague shapes of other ships where hundreds of other men sprawled in the darkness, all with their thoughts, just as I was with mine.

I remembered, too, how in the brief time we had together before we embarked I had tried to arouse in them a belief in me, and I hoped that in those ships on the dark sea there were men who felt a little better about the coming battle because they believed their commander was a competent soldier. But in their hearts there would be one unanswered question:

"What will he be like when the chips are down?"

I may dwell overlong on how I felt about going into battle, but I think this is of incalculable importance to successful leadership in combat. The leader must win the battle in his own heart, before he walks into the flame of combat; he should not be just another soldier trying to conquer fear. He can be afraid — any intelligent sane man will be afraid in battle — but he must be the master of his fear.

Leader! What a truly great word.

To Become a Leader

There are born leaders. But I was not one of them. So I planned what I should do to be a leader, for I was a commander, and a man has no right to be a commander of a combat unit unless he is also a leader.

So in the darkness, as our ships moved inexorably on toward the place where our blood would stain the ground and the men would be separated from the boys, I came to this realization:

It would be better for me to come out of battle dead than a failure.

I went down into my cabin and looked at the maps and aerial photographs for the hundreth time, thinking of things that could happen, the different ways the battle could go, and what I would do in each case. In particular, I saw that the main route of advance of the division was in the zone of action of another regiment, but if my regiment captured its objectives on schedule, it might be that we would move ahead. So I thought about what we might do outside our own boundaries.

The last night before landing I wrote a letter to my wife, not saying that we were landing the next day, but saying a few things briefly that I wanted her to have as the last words she would ever have from me — if fate decreed it that way.

After finishing I took another piece of paper and wrote down on it these words that had come to me:

> I have the strength.
> From where it comes I do not know,
> But of this much I am very sure:
> I have the strength.

I then turned out the light and, there in the dark, repeated the words of the West Point motto silently, like a prayer: "Duty — Honor — Country." There was peace in my heart, because I had won my battle before we landed. So I went to sleep and got a good night's rest.

To those who have commanded men in battle I know that I do not have to explain the above in terms of leadership. To others let me say that a vital part of your Planned Leadership must be to win the battle within yourself before you face combat. Resolution appears outwardly only when you have it inwardly. There is then no hesitation or vacillation when you face the reality — you will need only to decide: "What is the right thing for me to do now?"

Amphibious Landing

There was a real thrill in the naval and air bombardment in the pre-landing softening up the next day. With every man at his post, the boats were lowered, the waves were formed, and I was in an LCVP (Landing Craft Vehicle Personnel) of the fifth wave, headed toward the beach where the shells were landing.

On the beach there was confusion and men were pinned down. The company commander had been killed where I landed, and when I called upon men to move inland, they did not respond. But we *had* to move. All that had happened was not clear to me, but there could be no question of what must be done: we simply *had* to move inland. So I stood up and moved forward. And my men went with me.

It becomes clearer, I think, that my mental preparation—fixing in my mind the part I should play—resulted in my taking what I now know was the right action without delay. I had landed with the leading assault battalion partly because I wanted to be in the assault for some indefinable reason. But also because I thought that battalion in particular, and the regiment in general, would react more positively to my orders from then on.

The beachhead was finally extended one thousand yards inland, with another battalion passing through the assault battalion to a position on the far side of a deep swamp, where they were heavily counterattacked during the early morning hours.

With the first light of dawn, I rose and shaved with a handful of water from my canteen. (There are two schools of thought—the shaved and the unshaved. I belonged to the first.) Then I had a quick breakfast, interspersed with arrangements for an air strike on the strong enemy force which had attacked our segment of the beachhead during the night and early morning. As soon as the strike arrangements were complete, I took my bodyguard and a radio operator with a 300 set, and started out in an Alligator (a track-driven, armored, open-top, amphibious vehicle), crossing the swamp to the battalion that had repelled the enemy counterattack.

My Exec could run the command post, and the 300 radio would keep me in touch with him.

At the Front

I found the situation under control. They had really laid 'em in the aisle with machine guns, and were now busily engaged in mopping up. Also everybody was jubilant over the success of the dive-bombing air strike.

But one company had been almost entirely overrun in the enemy attack before dawn, and the battalion was shaken—with a line of our dead, silent on the ground. These, naturally, had a depressing effect upon the men, so I ordered the bodies removed immediately.

I told the battalion commander that we would launch an attack as soon as he could get under way, because the enemy force was on the ropes from the effects of smashing their counterattack.

These orders were issued without asking if an attack could be launched, because I was there, not just talking on the phone. After the desperate fight just finished, our men did not feel like attacking; but it was clearly my responsibility to issue that order.

After reporting to division, I returned to follow the attack, accompanied by the battalion commander. As we neared the top of the ridge that was our objective, the company on our left reached the crest of a lower portion of the ridge — and were driven off in a fierce counterattack. I continued on to the top to be sure the company there did not withdraw, while the battalion commander — a very able officer — went over to stop the left company from withdrawing beyond a specified point.

That night, as I went over the events of the day, one thing bothered me. I did not know what it was like to be with a platoon in attack. So I resolved to educate myself on this point.

The next day when a coordinated attack, properly supported with a good fire plan, was launched to retake that part of the ridge lost in the Japanese counterattack the day before, I went along. I found out what it is like to be with a platoon attacking high ground. In two of my three battalions now, it seemed to me, I had established my right to issue orders to attack.

The next day the remaining battalion of my regiment, which had been held in division reserve, was returned to me. It was launched in an attack on another part of the ridge line, and so I went to that area.

The initial attack, on a one-company front, reached the top — and was caught in a concentration of fire. It suffered heavy casualties, including the company commander. Seeing this, I told the battalion commander to replace that company with a fresh one, and hold the ground gained. Then I went back to report the situation to division.

On my return, the relief had not been completed; and when it was, the new company was counterattacked. The battalion commander was ineffectual — a good man whom I liked, but something was missing in combat. He waited for things to happen and watched them, rather than forcing things to happen the way he wanted them to. And he had not yet been to the hot spot of his battalion — on top of the hill. So I went up there to make a personal reconnaissance for the following day.

Things were a lot different up there than they looked from two hundred yards away, because actually nobody owned the sharp crest of the hill. Our men were just below the crest, and they swapped hand grenades over the crest. If either side attacked the other, they would be perfect targets as they tried to cross the ridge line. It was not a happy situation.

So I went back to division again, to tell my commander that I proposed to pull back that night so that I could bring the full force of our fire power to bear (it could not be done as long as we were so close to the enemy).

Military Common Sense

In the exercise of leadership I had now been to the critical points in each of my three battalions. This day's action also gave me an opportunity to do something that I was very anxious for my regiment to understand: when the situation was such that common sense called for pulling back in order to save lives of men who would otherwise be useless casualties, I pulled back.

This was application of another principle: a personal interest in and responsibility for the individual welfare and safety of each of my men was a duty that must be in front of me every minute of every hour of every day.

Any officer who does not recognize this principle is not worthy of the command he holds. In no other way can a commander hope to get the energetic wholehearted effort of his men in tense situations; they must know for sure that he has their welfare and safety at heart, and that he weighs this in his plans.

Throughout the day I saw that the battalion commander just did not have something that I thought was necessary for a battalion commander in battle (although he was a good man otherwise). So that night I relieved him. I did not go off half-cocked, but waited until the end of the day when I had made sure in my mind it was the right thing to do.

I was fortunate in my Exec (now a retired major general). He was as fine and efficient a soldier in combat as he had been in pre-combat days. I could be gone most of the day and leave things to him in our command post — always keeping in contact with the 300 radio. By using double talk and a prearranged code we did very well, and I owe a debt of gratitude to him and all of my staff.

One thing that had to be straightened out in combat was that, as regimental commander, my physical strength should be conserved; there were a lot of things I might normally do for myself, that should now be done for me so that the regiment could get the maximum benefit from my efforts. For example:

Getting Vocal

The first two mornings I was the first man stirring at dawn. The first time could have been an accident, but the second time I got vocal on the subject — particularly when no coffee and breakfast were waiting for me. In my opinion, it was a duty to demand that these things be done for me, so that I could give my whole attention to the regiment. Experienced officers, for some reason, perhaps trying to be democratic, will sometimes permit such things to distract their attention.

Of course, I tried to consider eventualities that could happen days ahead. It soon appeared that a possibility I had foreseen was approaching an actuality: a shift in boundaries could place our regiment in the lead on the principal route of advance in the breakout from the beachhead.

In anticipation of this I directed a battalion to attack a small piece of high ground, using only one company in assault, preceded by a sudden short preparation by every gun the regiment had, and all the artillery fire power the division could give us. Before dark that night, I had the attacking company relieved of its objective by a small holding force from another unit — and assembled the battalion in readiness to tee off down the road if circumstances should make that possible.

Field Order

As soon as the attack succeeded, I called on the Exec to assemble all commanders for a dictated field order that same evening. If things broke our way we would be ready to jump. Now the practice our regimental staff had had in putting out a field order paid off. When I arrived back at our command post half an hour before the order was to be dictated, I found the following:

1. Our folding situation map was set up so I could use it in dictation.

2. Folding chairs, boxes, and logs were arranged in front of the map so everyone could sit down.

3. Two trained typists (well versed in five-paragraph order form and standard abbreviations) were sitting at opposite ends of a folding table, facing typewriters in which there were seven sheets of legal-length onionskin paper, with carbons.

4. The heading was already filled in except for the time signed.

5. The S-3 had another map on a board, with a legal-length onionskin sheet pinned down over the operating area to serve as tracing paper. (This was so I could sketch the scheme of maneuver for duplication, to go with the order when completed).

6. A folding drafting table was set up, and two draftsmen were ready to reproduce the overlay.

7. The S-3 handed me a slip of paper containing a station list — just a penciled list of regimental and attached units which should be covered in the order.

8. The S-2 gave me a brief note with some dope he wanted in Paragraph 1a.

9. The S-3 gave me the latest division order for a quick once-over, and a slip of paper on which he had written out several things he thought ought to go in 1b and 3x of the order.

10. The S-4 had several lines he wanted in Paragraph 4.

11. The Exec (who had stage-managed the whole setup) said he had a messenger standing by to take a copy of the order up to division — and did I want anything else?

12. My orderly was there with a canteen cup of hot coffee.

Now there may be those who will say, "What in the hell have these little mechanical details to do with leadership?"

Just this: there may be a better procedure, but this is one that worked. Everybody knew exactly what everyone else was going to do; there was no confusion, and I knew exactly what to expect and what I was going to do.

It gave me and my staff a nice feeling that we knew our signals and were on the ball. I am sure my commanders were glad to see we knew what we were doing.

In the dictation I called off the paragraph and sub-paragraph numbers, to keep the typists straight. I stopped now and then to get data from my staff or from a commander of an attached unit. In this way, by talking unhurriedly, the typists had little trouble in keeping up.

When the dictation was finished, reproduction of the order was also complete; thus distribution was made at once to unit commanders to take back with them. Also I asked that each read his copy before leaving, to be sure it was legible and that there were no unanswered questions for his unit.

I asked my Exec and S-3 to check our copy for accuracy before sending the copy to division, then went to my tent and lay down to rest.

I have taken time to outline this little procedure to bring out the point that SOPs (standard operating procedures) of this nature should be worked out and perfected by practice. They are a definite part of the way a commander gets his will across, and there should be a certainty and lack of confusion to complement the commander's tone of assurance when he speaks.

Queer Feeling

It gave me a queer feeling the next day as I stood on high ground and watched from a distance as one of my battalions attacked a towering hill mass. We had planned for that, even including the preparatory softening up by division and corps artillery and by air bombings. The queer feeling I had was because I was not going with them. But I had two other battalions, and this time there were other things to do.

As I watched, my mind was on plans for what we would do if the attack succeeded — which it did.

As I had anticipated, the division commander shifted the boundary and scheme of maneuver. As a result, we were given the "go" sign to take off down the road with the battalion that was waiting for that chance. Since that was the "hot spot," and I had no way of knowing what would happen, I went along — and one of those curious breaks of combat came our way.

Our division commander (who believed in and followed the hot-spot principle himself) was with our battalion as we began that move, assuring us that we would get full support from division if we got going. This was a critical move from the division viewpoint, and his personal presence and on-the-ground instructions made a lot of difference to us.

After bypassing a hill still held by the enemy, using the cover of trees, we passed over a mined area in the road, and found a blown bridge. The enemy defenders were taken by surprise, and soon we were on our way down the road through an area of blown bridges, where no transport of any kind could go.

It was one of those things you have to sense, to feel, and for which there are no rules — because we had gotten through the enemy lines, and the troops in his rear did not yet know this. So I called on the battalion commander to pull in its flank guards, so that we could push straight down the road, shooting at anything we saw.

The battalion commander and I were with the advanced party. It was nerve-racking business. The surprise of our appearance, as much as our fire, scattered the enemy and we punched five miles into his rear areas — with only the food and ammunition and arms we could carry on our backs. By this time, too, we were beyond effective artillery support because we were beyond radio range, due to hill masks.

The push to that depth would never have been made if I had not been there. We took some calculated risks, but I knew about the general situation so was thus much better able to evaluate the position in which we found ourselves.

It was terribly hard on the men carrying weapons and ammunition. But that drive, when we found we had broken through, saved lives even though it cost the men much physical energy — and cost me a lot of mental sweat.

We spent an uneasy night, but morning came finally with only a few shots fired our way.

No Chow

My bodyguard had come off without the chow he was supposed to carry. So I shared a single D-ration bar with him for supper, and another for breakfast — the only two we had. I gave him direct orders not to even mention chow, much less take any food from front-line troops.

That morning, just as I was ready to go back to division to report our situation and also to see that the leap-frogging battalion was en route to pass through us and keep going, our chaplain came up to me.

"Colonel," he said, "I hope I am not speaking out of turn, but I think somebody ought to tell you that you are an inspiration to these men."

I am afraid I stood there looking rather dumbly at him, for I was choked up inside. Finally I managed to say:

"Chaplain, it is really the other way around—it is I who am inspired by our men."

The chaplain, without knowing it, was telling me that I had passed the test—that the Planned Leadership to which I had given so much thought was able to replace the born instinct for command that I did not have.

Up in Front Again

Our drive continued, with another battalion taking the lead while still another came up to a position of readiness. Once again I joined the leading battalion.

This time I found them stopping for the night short of the objective set—and so directed them to get going again. It was better to suffer with weariness than from enemy fire. So we resumed the advance, and drew strong enemy fire. This located the enemy position, so that artillery fire could be massed on it during the night.

And here occurred a little incident which I think is worth recounting.

As the battalion hastily established a defensive perimeter for the night, the forward artillery observer began ranging in with a single gun. This was difficult because of the long range and poor radio reception. A couple of shells went over, and I heard the observer's sensings—and then, *wham!*

Although we were expecting enemy fire, I knew it was an artillery short. I chanced to be looking right at the point of burst, about ten yards away, and saw men go down. At least five of them—just crumpled in that queer relaxed way men fall when they are hard hit.

I did not move, but continued my conversation. The forward observer and the commander of our battalion of direct support artillery (who had come forward—another of the many superlative soldiers to whom I shall be forever indebted) made haste to check the fire data, which was all I could have done. The dead and wounded were taken away. My only action was to say clearly to the artillery commander, so that men near by could hear me:

"I know these things happen, and I know you will take all the corrective action required. You have given us wonderful support, and I know you will continue to do so."

This was just one of those things I had set my mind to meet. We had the best possible relations with our supporting artillery, and as a leader it was up to me to show my men the way to meet the misfortunes of battle. How they reacted to this I can never be sure, but here was my chance to show loyalty to higher headquarters and to our supporting artillery at the same time. I did not feel it necessary to put on an act, screaming about "them people back there!"

We were all working together for a common end, and harmony counted. I did not want the cheap popularity of a moment, bought at the expense of trust in our leadership and our companions in arms. No one can tell me that my men were not smart enough to see that this was the right and proper thing, under the circumstances. Both officers and men looked at me in that moment of sudden tragedy, with the strain of a possible counterattack brewing, and I am sure they took their cue from me. Nothing was ever said about the matter again.

Soldierly Valor

I could go on with other details, but they would only emphasize the principles which I have already underlined in one way or another. It is a great disappointment that the purpose of this story, and the space available, do not permit me to recount many examples of the skill, determination and flaming battle courage of my men and officers of all ranks—such as the magnificent valor of Pvt. Harold Moon, who received a posthumous Medal of Honor; the company commander who led a spontaneous bayonet charge; platoon commanders in action; but, most of all, the never-to-be-forgotten courage of individual soldiers.

However, we are looking here at just one case history in Planned Leadership—and so we come to something about which I have said nothing so far.

As we continued on our drive, I continued to go to the "hot spot," unless there was a compelling reason for me to be somewhere else. Generally I went where I could exercise the best control over the actions of my regiment—and, in particular, the *timing* of what we did. Also there is an indefinable sixth sense, an understanding of the situation that comes only to the commander who is where he can see.

One day I found myself with my leading battalion, well out ahead of the rest of the regiment—and thus was able to issue orders for the actions of my other two battalions with a surety that would have been impossible had I been back at the end of a telephone or radio in my command post. And once again I spent the night in a battalion perimeter that was sure to be attacked before morning.

It was a long night but morning finally came, and with it several dead Japanese within a few yards of me. Our perimeter had been penetrated during the night. I had been in the center of the perimeter, and relatively safe—not unduly exposed. It gave me an advantage because there was no reason for me to be timorous over a radio report of fighting up front in the night which I could not have evaluated had I spent the hours of darkness in my CP.

After a quick breakfast, I stood on a little round hilltop, with the snap of inaccurate small arms going by, and heavier caliber firing in the edge of the town where our leading elements were pushing down the road. I looked at the bodies of the enemy who had died not far from me in the night, and within me there was a sense of succeeding in a hard game, after long years of getting ready for the test. The thud of our tank fire came back to me, and intermittent concussions from what I thought to be enemy mortar fire.

Succeeding in a Hard Game

Messages came and went. All around me there was the ordered confusion of a trained unit on the move, and I remember noticing young faces, so often turned toward me, with the intent questioning look young soldiers have for their leaders when they are going toward danger. And in my heart I wondered if, at their age and with their experience, I could have met the test as they were doing. I felt, however, that I had their trust and that I deserved it — not because I was born with something they did not have — but because there were years of getting ready behind me. I was a trained professional soldier, and I had carefully planned to become the leader I had not been born.

The assistant division commander arrived in the area, to bring an end to my battle reverie. I talked with him and, among other things, asked him (as I had done on previous occasions) not to go beyond that point — that I did not want my regiment to become famous for having a general officer casualty in our area. Little did I realize then (as I started forward) that I had just made arrangements for a general to be at a crossroads to act as a traffic cop in speeding an ambulance with me inside.

The battalion commander was busy with some of his staff on the edge of the road near the outskirts of the town, so I passed him and continued on toward the front. There I found things stalled, and the company commander of the lead company not enthusiastic about pushing on in the face of the fire he was getting. After some conversation with the captain, and not wishing to bypass the battalion commander by issuing orders, I decided to hell with wavering and went on down the road myself.

There I found the leading platoon pinned down by small-arms fire and two tanks not advancing (it was not tank country), waiting for the infantry to precede them due to lack of visibility. It was hot, all right, but I did not think it was hot enough to stop the advance; besides, the enemy positions were not yet well enough located to bring effective artillery fire down on them. So, after a few words with the lieutenant, in which he advised me urgently to take cover instead of getting his men up and going as I had wished him to do, and disregarding the hit that had just been scored on the tank a few yards away, I started forward.

The lieutenant leaped to his feet and shouted, "Let's go! The colonel is here!"

Yes, just like in a storybook — the regimental commander fell at the head of his regiment.

Other men died in that attack, and others were wounded; and when I became a casualty with them I was worth no more than any one of them. My Planned Leadership was suddenly lost to my regiment — because I lay helpless on the ground.

No longer was I a leader, but a burden to be taken care of.

But as I lay there, the habit was still strong, and so I gave orders —but in a short time twilight settled over me. I remember lying and looking up at the sky—and talking—then memory fades. But it does not matter, because I have reached the end of the lessons I learned about being a regimental commander, and this last was a bitter lesson.

I had made a great mistake, because I had become a casualty needlessly.

The Commander's Task

I like to think that the Planned Leadership with which I had approached my job had paid dividends — that while I was on my feet I was an effective commander. It is something that no one can ever take away from me.

In retrospect, however, I can draw some conclusions about this last lesson: where *should* the commander go in battle?

That is a hard question; but, to me, the points I made in the preceding chapter, and the first part of this one, still hold: he must prove himself in the eyes of his men. If he has come up from a company grade officer, then he does not have to go about it the same way an officer coming in cold who has not been "up there."

I also think that the commander, no matter what his rank, should go to the "hot spot," to the place where judgment counts, where a true feel of the actual situation can be gained that just simply is not transmitted by telephone or radio—in fact is transmitted in no other way than through the six senses of the man who is there. How far forward this is will depend on his rank and upon the situation at the time. There is no set rule, unless the rule is that when in doubt err toward the front and not toward the rear.

So we seem to be coming back again to that fundamental principle:

"I would do what I thought was right and proper, because it was right and proper, and let the chips fall where they may—or blood flow when necessary—either mine or others."

That can solve an awful lot of questions about where the commander should go, if he will just consider it objectively that way each time.

Looking backward, the principles I have recounted are sound—but they must be tailored to fit each personality and each leadership problem. There is no one way, but there is one thing we all can do: *take some thought as to what we should do,* not just assume command and wait for some divine guidance to come along and put thoughts in our heads at just the right time.

It is said that genius is one-tenth inspiration and nine-tenths perspiration; and, if you want to apply that to the military profession, maybe it's the answer to why so many of our greatest generals were not high in their studies at West Point.

There can never be any place in Planned Leadership for a phony—for bluffing. Interest cannot be counterfeited: you must be sincerely interested. You cannot simply pamper your mind with the thought you are a professional soldier and a commander by act of Congress and the authority of the President of the United States. No man is ever going to be a leader until his appointment as a commander is ratified in the minds of his men.

51

Be Ready to Do
What You Ask Others to Do

DURING MY FIRST season on the rifle range a young recruit in my platoon taught me a valuable lesson. He was shooting erratically in the "jawbone record" (practice) round, getting some bull's-eyes and 4s, but also enough wild deuces and misses to make it doubtful he would qualify. His corporal told him he was flinching on those bad shots, gave him the hot oil about trigger squeeze — and he got another miss.

So I eased up to the firing line, agreed with the corporal about the flinching, and said I would watch him fire the next shot.

"Lieutenant," he said, "will you fire my rifle, and let me watch your trigger squeeze?"

So I did. After taking the proper prone position for 500 yards slow fire I began a slow squeeze, so that I would not know exactly when the shot would be fired. Then my face turned as red as my hair, because I almost flinched off the firing point, and was lucky to get a wide 3 instead of a miss.

The corporal and the recruit could not resist smiles, but the problem was solved. That trigger had a nasty "creep" in it just before it released the firing pin. Since it was the only rifle he had ever used, the young soldier did not realize this was causing his trouble. So we got the trigger creep fixed, and he qualified easily.

For me the lesson was basic: never ask anyone to do something that, in his position, you would not be willing and able to do. In this case it was to fire *that* rifle.

Soon after taking over one of the three companies I was later privileged to command, I announced my dissatisfaction with the discolored appearance of urinals in the latrine. The platoon sergeant responsible said the urinals were so old it was not possible to clean them to a glistening white. Unconvinced, I told him that scouring powder and enough elbow grease would do the job — and to get them white.

The next day they were still discolored, and the sergeant said they just could not be made white. So I called for a rag and some scouring powder and — with the sergeant and a couple of soldiers as surprised kibitzers, who had never seen a captain clean a barracks urinal before — proceeded to exert pressure and some hard scouring that resulted in a glistening white area the size of my hand. We then continued the inspection, with further reference to the urinal situation, and the next morning they were all nice and white.

Some will tut-tut over a company commander scouring a barracks urinal, but the principle is the same as with the recruit's rifle: you must be willing and able to do what you ask others to do. Of course, as in everything else, judgment and common sense and the special situation are involved. In this case it was my intent, as a new commander, to lift the standard of housekeeping in barracks, and I could sense some quite human resistance to the change — which seemed to evaporate after my latrine demonstration.

In war as in peace, the principle remains fundamental to battle leadership.

The late Maj. Gen. (then Col.) William J. Verbeck commanded the 21st Infantry on Mindanao during the Southern Philippines campaign of World War II. He had been wounded before he joined our division on Leyte, and wounded twice more while commanding the Gimlets — in applying the battle principle that he asked no man to go where he would not go himself.

When one of his battalions was blocked in its movement along a ridge line in Mindanao, Bill ordered a small task force to circle around through the jungle at night and attack the enemy blocking position from the rear at daylight. The little task force got lost, and made its way back without accomplishing its mission.

The next night Bill Verbeck led that task force in person, circling through the dense jungle in the thick darkness — blacker than the inside of a black cat at midnight — to come up behind the enemy position at dawn. As a result the ridge block was quickly broken.

This kind of personal leadership, a readiness to go where he asked his men to go, made William J. Verbeck one of the finest regimental commanders in World War II, loved and respected by his men.

Another gallant leader was Col. Thomas E. ("Jock") Clifford, Jr., commander of the 19th Infantry, who was killed in that same Mindanao operation — the inevitable price that some of our elite up-front battle leaders pay.

History is full of illustrations where great commanders gained the best efforts from their men by demonstrating their willingness to share the hazards and hardships they asked of others.

In the 1942 invasion of Africa, Maj. Gen. George S. Patton, Jr., was observing the unloading of men and supplies at Fedala, where the beach was strafed by planes. Every time enemy aircraft made a run, men would run for cover. This seriously delayed unloading — and the land battle was less than a mile inland, where ammunition and supplies were needed.

Seeing this, General Patton did not issue orders. He simply leaped from his jeep and joined his men, shoulder to shoulder. Why he did this, and with what results, were summarized by General Patton this way:

> By remaining on the beach and personally helping to push off boats and by not taking cover when enemy planes flew over, I believe I had considerable influence in quieting the nerves of troops and making the initial landing a success. I stayed on the beach for 18 hours, and was wet over all of that time. People say that army commanders should not indulge in such practices. My theory is that an army commander does whatever is necessary to accomplish his mission, and that nearly 80 percent of his mission is to arouse morale in his men.

On another occasion, when he commanded the famed Third Army in France, Lieutenant General Patton arrived in his jeep where a truck had got stuck in a ditch. He stood up in the jeep and shouted to men in the truck:

"Get out of that, you blank-blank soandsos, and heave her out!"

The men quickly jumped from the truck. It was an occasion they would never forget — because when they began to push, there was their immaculately uniformed army commander pushing right along with them.

In these and uncounted other instances, this great battle leader cemented between himself and the men he commanded that special rapport — in peace or war — that can be reached in only one way: by establishing in the minds and hearts of his soldiers the sure knowledge that he lived by the same standards he asked of them.

Alexander the Great personifies this fundamental facet of leadership. Almost 2,300 years ago, near the end of his great campaigns and short life (he died at thirty-three) his men refused to mount scaling ladders in a siege. Faced with this, Alexander himself led the way.

He reached the top, cut down defenders, and stood alone. Then in a foolish but magnificently brave gesture, he leaped inside the wall — which nearly cost him his life. Three Macedonians joined him there, then the scaling-ladders broke under the weight of his soldiers rushing to follow their leader, who had obeyed his own order when they did not.

Before his men could smash their way in a postern gate to his rescue, a war arrow pierced his chest above the lungs — a terrible wound from which there is reason to believe he never fully recovered. Here are a few comments:

- When you stand ready to obey your own orders, you give careful thought to what those orders will be, and men in your command instinctively understand this.
- One of the most frequent violations of this basic principle that I saw in nearly thirty-five years of active service was for officers to inspect their soldiers in ranks while they themselves were sloppily dressed.
- Obviously, however, the principle does not apply in many technical skills. For instance, it is not necessary to be able to take shorthand to establish your right to dictate an order, or to know how to operate a sending key in Morse code to demonstrate your leadership before sending a radio message.
- There are also limits to how far commanders should go in leading the way, as the foolhardy gesture of Alexander illustrated when he jumped inside the fortress wall without waiting for others to join him.
- Not everybody can or should display the flamboyance of a Patton. Nor do I recommend as a policy that all

company commanders demonstrate how to clean a barracks urinal. But the idea is there, to be carried out in consonance with your own personality and the existing situation — with judgment and common sense.

52

Commanders Must Earn Loyalty

A TOURIST TURNED off the hard-surfaced highway into the Tennessee mountains, onto a winding, single-lane dirt road. Then he saw a log cabin off the road and noticed the front door had two holes at the bottom, each hole large enough to permit the passage of a cat.

This intrigued the tourist, so he approached on foot toward the ancient, overalled and bearded figure in a rocking chair on the front porch. "My friend," the tourist said, "you have two cat-size holes in the bottom of your front door. Why is one not enough?"

The old mountaineer parted his tobacco-stained whiskers, squirted a jet of tobacco juice over the porch railing which landed near the tourist's feet, and replied, "Waal, I got two cats. And when I say 'scat' I mean *'Scat!'*"

The old fellow had instilled discipline in his cats—but how much loyalty had he inspired?

This raises the question faced by commanders at all levels in military service: both discipline and loyalty are required in a good outfit, so how can their sometimes conflicting requirements be reconciled?

The best case study known to me of this classic problem centers around a change in command of the famous 1st Infantry Division during World War II. This occurred after the Sicily campaign, when Maj. Gen. Terry Allen was replaced. These comments in *A Soldier's Story* by General of the Army Omar N. Bradley are pertinent:

Under Allen the 1st Division had become increasingly temperamental, disdainful of both regulations and senior commands. It thought itself exempt from the needs for discipline by virtue of its months on the line. . . . Allen had become too much of an individualist to subordinate himself without friction in the group undertakings at war. . . . To save Allen both from himself and from his brilliant record, and to save the division from the results of too much heavy success, I decided to separate them.

His successor was Maj. Gen. Clarence R. Huebner, widely known in the Army as a stern disciplinarian. General Huebner was keenly aware of the freewheeling attitude in the division, as well as the high loyalty the "Big Red One" felt toward their departing commander, General Allen.

This was a tough situation for a new commander, but General Huebner met it squarely. On his second day in command, he ordered a spit-and-polish cleanup, then directed a rigid training program that included close order drill.

This program outraged the combat veterans. Why General Huebnew followed this course on assuming command reveals his ideas about how discipline and loyalty are related. Consider these incidents recounted by Arthur L. Chaitt in the *Bridgehead Sentinel* (Spring, 1973, Society of the First Division).

He quotes Maj. Gen. Ben Sternberg, years later:

One memory that stands out in my mind relates to the hard-nosed attitude Huebner exhibited when he took over the division from the fabulous and popular Terry Allen . . . for instance, requiring combat veterans to take basic rifle marksmanship training, practice saluting, close-order drill and the like. And putting the "fear of God" in the chain of command. . . . I asked him later how a gentle guy like him could be such a mean bastard. He replied, "Ben, *remember* when you take over a command, you can start out being an SOB and later become a good guy, *but* you can never start out being a good guy and later become an SOB."

Another way of saying, "First things first — and discipline comes first."

Col. C. M. ("Pop") Eymer, the Division G-4, shared the frustrations of the staff in the initial transition from General Allen to General Huebner. He put it this way:

> Over the next several months while the staff planned for the invasion of France, Gen. Huebner ignored our attitude and patiently imposed his will upon us and eventually won our complete loyalty and affection.
>
> Before leaving Sicily for England I had a talk with him, although I do not recall how the conversation came about. Anyway, I asked why he had not fired all of us because of our attitude toward him when he assumed command. He chuckled with the puckish little squint which was so engaging. "Hell, Pop, I knew you would all come around. I was not about to get rid of the best damn staff in the best damn division in the Army. All I wanted was to earn the same loyalty you gave to Terry Allen."

That is a most perceptive statement on discipline and loyalty. In other words: discipline must be imposed, but loyalty must be earned.

Another point in that simple statement is one I often saw violated. A new commander should not be jealous of the loyalty of his new command toward their previous commander. If he expects instant disloyalty by his new command to his predecessor, on what basis can he hope for their loyalty to him?

How does a commander "earn" loyalty? The first requirement is that he must himself be a competent soldier. But it goes beyond that, for he must be interested in the welfare of those under him, and there are innumerable ways this comes up. Further, how a commander earns this loyalty will vary with situations and individuals. Here are several illustrations mentioned by Arthur L. Chaitt:

One night, during the Battle of the Bulge, General Huebner noticed that his G-3 was heavily fatigued and badly in need of sleep. So the general quietly posted a guard on the G-3's door, with orders that no one but himself could wake him.

In the Hurtgen Forest, Col. T. F. Lancer remembers that General

Huebner would bring coffee each night to the sentry outside his headquarters.

Another revealing sidelight involved General Huebner's orderly, Marvin. Just before the assault landing in Normandy, the Old Man received a bottle of Kentucky whiskey, and said, "We won't need it here, but on the far shore." He then put the bottle in his musette bag and handed it to his orderly, saying, "Marvin, get this to me on the far shore."

As Brig. Gen. John G. Hill related it, "The first thing Marvin did aboard ship was drop the bag on the steel deck and break the bottle. He then took off to find the general's aide, and this conversation followed:

Marvin: "My God, we broke the general's whiskey!"

Aide: "What do you mean, *we* broke the general's whiskey?"

Marvin: "What'll we do? We can't tell the general."

Aide: "Yes, we're going to tell him right now."

Huebner: "Hell, I've no use for such people — transfer him to the 26th Infantry."

Marvin: "No sir, General. You ain't going to fire me."

Huebner: "Why the hell aren't I going to fire you?"

Marvin: "Cause you can't get nobody better!"

Huebner, after recovering the power of speech: "Well, I guess you're right."

So Marvin stayed on. Things like this get around and say things about a commander his men can learn in no other way. It takes human understanding on both sides to cement loyalty.

Another soldier I served under who demanded uncompromising discipline and inspired intense loyalty was my West Point classmate, Maj. Gen. Joseph P. Cleland. After completing jump school he commanded the 504th Airborne Infantry at Fort Bragg, North Carolina.

As Christmas neared, he issued orders that no married man living at home with his family on or near Fort Bragg would be detailed on guard Christmas Eve or Christmas Day. Then on Christmas Eve he inspected sentries on post.

Later that night the jeep driver returned to his regimental commander's home with a message. "Mrs. Cleland," the driver reported, "the colonel said he will not be home until morning."

Then he continued, "You're not going to believe this. The colonel found a man on post whose family is here at Bragg. So he relieved the sentry, took the soldier's rifle to walk post himself, and had me drive the soldier to his home and family."

The stern discipline and hard training that General Cleland demanded were merged with loyalty for such a commander that discipline alone can never achieve. Added comments are:

- When Regimental Commander Cleland inspected the sentries, he exercised his responsibility to insure discipline by checking compliance with his orders; on finding a failure, he took the most direct action to carry out his own order for that soldier to be home with his family on Christmas Eve. And you can bet those in the chain of command who failed to implement his order smelled gunpowder the next day.
- By his action General Cleland dramatized two basic principles: obedience to orders is the essence of discipline, and loyalty is a two-way street.
- In Walter Reed Hospital near the end of his life, Lieutenant General Huebner said in substance, "People are important, things are not — and nothing is more important than the respect of one man for another."

  So now we have this amplified relation: discipline must be imposed, but loyalty must be earned — yet the highest form of discipline exists only when there is mutual loyalty, up and down.

53

The Time Element Can Be Master or Servant

EIGHT MONTHS AFTER Pearl Harbor, time became the over-whelming controlling factor in my professional life — because I was made our division chief of staff. It was not just my time, but the necessity to coordinate the time of others to meet the march of events. However, I never adopted the procedure the grapevine said was used by an Army Air Corps general at Hickam Field.

The story was that a senior colonel came in his office and looked around for a chair to sit in while conducting his business. But there was no chair, and the general said, "You will not need a chair, Colonel — you will not be here that long."

Confederate Lt. Gen. Nathan Bedford Forrest is reported to have explained his outstanding success by saying that he got there first with the most men. Another way of saying he mastered the time factor in his operations.

My division commander, Maj. Gen. Frederick A. Irving, taught me a valuable lesson by his constant attention to the time element. He always came by my office before leaving headquarters to let me know his schedule.

"Red," he would say, "I'm going to visit the three regimental commanders." He then looked at his watch and continued, "It's one-forty now. I'll get to the 21st Infantry around two o'clock and stay about twenty minutes. Arrive at the 19th Infantry around two-forty, and leave about three o'clock. This will put me at the 298th

Infantry by three-thirty, where I'll stay about half an hour. I should be back here around four-forty-five."

This was to let me know where to reach him, but he always figured time and space everywhere he went, *in advance*. And his estimates were never far off. I soon noticed he figured the time element in everything. For example, when he gave me instructions to get a draft prepared he would ask, "When can I see it?"

That kept me figuring the time factor too. Even in minor things, like how long it would take my clerk to type up a handwritten draft. In this way I began to develop a sense of time about the operations of my office. Along with this came a constant awareness of what time it was, and this developed a habit I still follow: before looking at my watch, estimate what time I think it is. This is a procedure every military man should cultivate, to avoid the old problem, "It is later than you think."

The time available for any project or operation is often a straitjacket and, to weave in the work of others, it is essential that a coordinating time schedule be established. When our division arrived on Goodenough Island in the New Guinea area, staging for the Hollandia operation, the major requirement facing me was staffing an operations order for the amphibious landing in Tanahmerah Bay — to be completed by a definite date set by higher headquarters.

This put me in a time straitjacket. A time schedule was required to coordinate preparation of the order — which established a straitjacket within which our staff sections and unit commanders must work. This was doubly important because the work of some staff officers and units must be completed before others could do their part. To check on progress of the work we set up a jungle war room where all drafts would be posted; thus any failure to meet the time schedule would be obvious at once.

Never was the truth of English essayist John Foster's maxim more clearly demonstrated: "Time is the greatest of all tyrants." But, by harnessing time as a coordinator, we had no trouble — only a lot of sweat and overtime work.

As every combat veteran knows, time is the monkey that rides your back in battle, from top planning headquarters to squad-size patrols. So we'll progress to other aspects of time in the military service.

We usually think of time in our professional lives as being measured in minutes, hours, days, weeks or even months; but in one vital professional area it is measured in years. Early in my career I was interested in a detail as instructor at West Point, but delayed asking for it. As a result, when the Department of Drawing, at my instigation, asked for my assignment there, the chief of infantry turned it down.

The time factor had trapped me between two policies. The detail to West Point was for four years, but Army policy required me to attend the Infantry School within three years.

I learn slowly, because I repeated the error some years later. It was then policy, to save travel funds, for officers to attend the Command and General Staff College at the time of normal change of station, and I was due to go when I returned to the States after my second tour in Hawaii. But I requested a year's extension, and got it —then a second extension. Result: when orders were eventually issued to me for the CGSC, the regular course was suspended before my reporting date in order to set up quickie courses to meet projected World War II needs. Finally, two years later, I barely got in under the age limit for one of the quickie courses.

The lesson: never let time sneak up on you and block a key professional assignment, especially if a school is involved.

The ways time can be a booby trap are limitless. As assistant division commander of the 5th Infantry Division in Europe, I monitored the one-hundred-hour field tests of our nine battalions (1954). In one situation battalion commanders were given an order late at night that required them to make a night march and close in an assembly area before daylight. One battalion commander took elaborate precautions to string out his column to avoid bunching up on the road. Result: the time-length of his column was so great it was not physically possible for the end of it to close before daylight.

The higher you go in the rank structure, the more exacting your personal time element. When ordered from the 82d Airborne Division to be deputy commanding general of the Infantry Center, this was my first change of station as a general officer. I knew my plane would be met with some ceremony, so I checked on arrival at the airfield to see that Fort Benning had been notified of my arrival time.

Yes, the commandant of the Infantry School had been notified, but the time was based on a slower plane. This one would get there twenty minutes sooner. Without giving the matter much thought, I told flight operations to make sure Benning was notified that I would arrive sooner than originally planned.

On landing at Benning, I noticed the honor guard scrambling into position hurriedly, and the commandant, my friend Maj. Gen. Guy S. Meloy, arrived several minutes after I did. Which did not make him happy, and he said, "I'm sorry about this change-of-time foul-up, Red, and will find out who is responsible."

"You're looking at him, general," was my reply. You see I had, stupidly, failed to consider the time lag in transmitting the message — including circulating it to all concerned at Benning, whose schedules were based on the original time of arrival.

So I got off on the wrong foot at my new station even before I arrived. The approved solution would have been to tell the pilot the time of take-off did not matter to me, but that he would fly his bird to arrive at Benning on the minute we were scheduled. No sooner, no later.

There are other angles to this many-faceted time factor; such as where it is hard to figure the time element, deciding whether it is better to be ahead of time, or behind time. But I would like to add these comments:

- Every professional soldier should estimate in advance how long it will take to do any task, project or operation for which he is responsible. In this way, time jams can be anticipated and steps taken to avoid them.
- Nothing is more frustrating to loyal, hard-working subordinates than to be given a time limit that is too short — and which they know is unnecessary. So all officers and NCOs should develop a sense of time-empathy: to understand the time element from where their subordinates sit. Which, again, demands accurate time estimates.
- My cyclopedia of useful quotations gives more space to the word "love" than to any other (and I do not knock that priority), but the next largest space devoted to one word is to "time." And with that I have no argument either. The one that fits best here is by the English educator who invented a system of shorthand, Sir Isaac Pitman. He said, "Well arranged time is the surest mark of the well arranged mind."

54

Sleep and the Soldier

For some must watch, and some must sleep
— Hamlet

IN ANY POSSIBLE nuclear war, as in past wars with conventional weapons, loss of sleep by soldiers — especially those in key staff and command positions — can seriously affect the result. Science has produced fantastic new weapons, but it has found no substitute for judgment and other human abilities in the men who use those weapons — and those abilities can be seriously damaged by loss of sleep.

In peace and in war the lack of sleep works like termites in a house: below the surface, gnawing quietly and unseen to produce gradual weakening which can lead to sudden and unexpected collapse. The Walter Reed Army Institute of Research puts it this way: "The daily experience of sleep constitutes one of the major cyclic events in man and ranks with food and water as a major need demanding satisfaction."

In our Army the importance of food and water is constantly emphasized during training, yet the need for sleep by all ranks gets little attention. Apparently this is so because that vital need goes largely unrecognized as the basic cause of many "human error" failures and weaknesses.

This is a curious omission, and the results can be devastating. The careers of some brilliant officers have been irreparably damaged because they were deprived of sleep; battles have been lost by soldiers worn out by loss of sleep; and men have died needlessly when leaders without enough sleep made errors in judgment. In fact, many experts believe an error in judgment by one man, when his mind was dulled by lack of sleep, had a major effect on one of the greatest defeats of World War II. But I am ahead of my story.

What Is Sleep?

Just what sleep is does not appear too important to us as soldiers. What we need to know is this: how much does a man need? What happens if he doesn't get enough? Then we can apply this knowledge to our military activities and operations.

We can safely base our inquiry on this statement by the Walter Reed Army Institute of Research: "The nature of the phenomena of sleep and the defect produced by its deprivation remain matters of controversy."

A distinguished doctor once said, "One sleepless night can raise havoc with our disposition, and with the effectiveness of our work." Any observant and experienced officer or noncommissioned officer can vouch for the truth of that statement. Yet, to recognize the fact does not always solve the problem it creates; the average man will be the first to say when he is thirsty or hungry, but often will not realize he is dangerously short of sleep. Some delicate intangibles are involved in dealing with this, including a feeling about invasion of privacy.

Every combat veteran remembers how exhausted soldiers, kept awake for long periods during battle, collapsed in sleep at the first opportunity — wherever they happened to be. Even civilians on the home front know this from war pictures that showed soldiers sprawled asleep in ditches, trucks — all kinds of places. Not so obvious is the fact that sleep exhaustion usually results from failure to sleep when there was a chance, and the loss in combat effectiveness from this cause is beyond measurement or calculation.

There should be a place on training schedules for instruction in the facts of life concerning sleep and the results from the lack of it, just as we train in the use of drinking water. Knowledge about sleep is an Army-wide need for soldiers of all ranks, and we should stress that it is the duty of each man to get enough.

Effect on Memory

Perhaps the most spectacular demonstration I saw of the damaging effect on a man from lack of sleep took place before World War II.

Not long before Pearl Harbor, all staff and field grade officers of the Hawaiian Department were assembled in a post theater for a briefing by a general officer on one aspect of the defense of Oahu. He got along well until he was halfway through, when he began to stumble and flounder for words. He shuffled his papers and looked at us with a puzzled expression. He then said, "I am sorry, but you will have to excuse me," and left the stage.

As hundreds of officers sat in stunned silence, the department commander rose and said, "We will take a ten-minute break while the general gets his notes straightened out."

The speaker's aide rushed up to check the notes (they were in perfect order) and the talk was resumed. But the general soon got to a sentence he could not finish, so he left it hanging and started to discuss a visual aid — and got stalled on that. It wasn't stage fright; he just looked intensely puzzled.

Finally, he turned to his audience again: "I designed this aid myself, but I can't seem to remember how it goes. You will just have to excuse me." He left the stage again, abandoning the briefing. An amazed audience left the theater in uncomprehending silence.

When the general was hospitalized for observation, it was quickly determined that he was simply suffering from acute fatigue — not enough sleep.

All experiments prove beyond question that loss of sleep heavily affects memory. One authority states: "A startling effect of sleep deprivation was its attack on human memory and perception. Many sleep-deprived subjects were unable to retain information long enough to relate it to the task they were supposed to perform."

Loss Can Be Cumulative

Most of us think of sleep starvation as something that happens after one to several days of heavy sleep loss. But it can inch up on you over weeks and months — even years — and you can be completely unaware of this insidious damage to mind and body. One sleep researcher reports that, if long continued, even a daily shortage of fifteen minutes can build up serious effects.

The result of cumulative sleep loss was brought home to me in painful fashion when, at my request, I was permitted time off from my job as a division chief of staff in the early spring of 1943 to attend a general staff course (a nine-week wartime quickie) at Fort Leavenworth. In the war urgency to get things done, I had been building up (without knowing it) what researchers call a "sleep debt." At Leavenworth I promptly set to work to study everything in sight, still burning my sleep candle at both ends.

The payoff on my sleep debt came quite suddenly one night about ten days after my arrival. As I was reading a manual in studying the next day's assignment and turned a page, my mind went blank. I could not remember what I had just read on the preceding page! I turned back, read it again, turned the page — another blank.

After the fourth or fifth unsuccessful try, I recalled the general who had looked so puzzled when he said, "I can't seem to remember."

That's what happened to me too, but — thanks to the fact that I had seen it happen to him — I understood what was wrong. So I placed the manual aside, went for a hard walk, and then to bed. The start of a pressure-packed course at Leavenworth is an awkward time for the sleep-bill collector to say, "Pay up — *now!*"

Fortunately, by rigidly limiting my study and making a serious business of going to bed, I managed to get through the course — thankful to have learned my lesson in school rather than in combat.

One writer for a national magazine said, "By depriving themselves of needed sleep, many Americans are piling up a regrettable record of irritability and inefficiency; they are taking chances on losing their jobs, their marriages, even their lives. Those 'Sleep Cheats' are not to be confused with insomniacs . . . because Sleep Cheats *can* sleep, but won't." For soldiers this underscores again the importance of teaching about sleep during training, emphasizing sleep as a personal duty and a command responsibility.

Judgment Can Be Impaired

Scientists have clearly established that judgment — a vitally essential element in command and leadership — is severely impaired by loss of sleep. I recall taking part in a large field maneuver of several days duration when, about 1900 hours one evening, the division chief of staff said to the division commander, "Nothing is going to happen for at least five hours, so I recommend that you get some sleep, sir."

The general insisted on staying awake, and nothing happened for seven hours. But when things did break loose, time was a factor, the general's brain was fogged by sleep fatigue, and he made a serious error in judgment which became so evident he was relieved of his command.

A wartime parallel in reverse occurred during the Normandy campaign in France, and was described to me by an eyewitness. At a critical stage in the operation the commander of the 101st Airborne Division (then Maj. Gen. Maxwell D. Taylor, later Army Chief of Staff, and still later chairman of the Joint Chiefs of Staff) called in his second in command after supper and said: "Tomorrow is going to be a big day, and I want to be ready for it. You take over while I go to bed and get some sleep."

He did just that, and my eyewitness says: "It happened as he had predicted. He got a good night's sleep, and the next day when things really popped General Taylor was on top of the action and every decision was right on the nose. It was the most inspiring thing I've ever seen."

One of the serious damaging effects of sleep loss is the high and sometimes almost irrational degree of irritation it causes in dealing with others. In all the publicity about the "slapping incident" in which General Patton was involved after his brilliantly successful invasion of Sicily, it was generally agreed that while his action could not be excused, it had been "provoked." Little was said of the fact that it came after six weeks of furious and violent activity by a combat leader who had driven himself relentlessly. The battle won, he visited his hospitalized men instead of taking the rest he so desperately needed.

I think there is little doubt that an incomparable battle career was nearly terminated prematurely by an incident resulting primarily from *heavy and long-continued loss of sleep.*

One researcher concludes that "disturbances in behavior from lack of sleep closely resemble disorders from certain narcotics, alcohol, and oxygen starvation. . . . Values slip out of focus. We are literally 'not ourselves.' " How and why is this so? Well, it is a lot like being hungry, where the frustration of going without food makes us irritable and aggressive—which is why people on a diet are often ill-tempered. But you can do without food much more easily than without sleep. In fact, animals have lived twenty days without food, yet have died after five sleepless nights.

Sleep Whenever You Can

Of course, not only generals are affected by lack of sleep. When I was with an infantry division in Germany during postwar field exercises—the "100-hour battalion tests"—I walked through the tests behind all nine battalions of our division. Only once did I see a battalion commander take firm steps to see that his command got sleep when the chance came. His battalion scored highest on the tests, while others appeared fatigued in the final stages and performance at all levels deteriorated. Yet they seemed unaware of this, even less aware that it resulted from lack of sleep they could have had by planned daylight sleeping.

One battalion commander not only failed to consider any sleeping plan (though he gave meticulous attention to his feeding plan), but he also needlessly moved his men about in such a way that it was virtually impossible for them to get adequate sleep. The result was quite amazing, for in the later stages of the exercise his whole command was flopping down to sleep at every pause, exhausted—and he made two serious errors in judgment. As a result his unit, which began the exercise as a heads-up-on-the-ball outfit, on the fourth and final day staggered about half out on its feet, putting on such a miserable exhibition that only high grades in the early part of the exercise saved it from an Unsatisfactory rating.

We must note here, however, that in real combat "good grades" in the first part of the battle would not have saved that unit from getting thoroughly shot up, perhaps even destroyed. You fail only once *when the score is written with steel and blood.*

An experimental laboratory found that "with increasing sleep loss the individual takes fewer events into account in arriving at a decision. This indicates deterioration in the ability to make an estimate of the situation which takes account of all possible courses of enemy action." Or, as one research expert expressed it, "They were befuddled in situations requiring them to hold several factors in mind and act on them."

I know a fine decorated and dedicated battalion commander who, during a campaign in the Philippines, went to his regimental commander and requested relief from his command. He said:

"Something has happened to me. I am making poor decisions, have lost confidence in myself, and want to be relieved before I make a serious error that will cost lives of my men."

The colonel told me that battalion commander had driven himself day and night, and was simply suffering from exhaustion — massive loss of sleep. He was taken out of combat and given a chance to catch up. But something had indeed happened in his heart, for he was never the same again, destroyed by his own energy and conscientious determination — and loss of sleep.

During the Leyte campaign I commanded the 34th Infantry Regiment. Several days after landing, while we were still trying to break out of the narrow, confining beachhead, I was called to the phone late one night to hear this message: "This is a warning! Major elements of the Japanese fleet are entering Leyte Gulf, and bombardment of the shore may be expected momentarily."

It is a matter of history (in one of the most controversial major sea battles of all time) that the Japanese naval attack plan had worked to the point where the central striking force (with four battleships, including the great *Yamato*) had penetrated San Bernardino Strait, rounded Samar Island, and by daylight was heading directly toward our crowded beachhead and the thin-skinned invasion fleet. On the bridge of one of the greatest battleships ever built, a small admiral stood on the threshold of immortality as he engaged lighter U.S. forces — until he made one of the most amazing decisions of the war.

With orders to go in at all costs, and facing the chance to strike a devastating blow — the Japanese admiral ordered a retreat!

Not all naval experts agree as to what would have happened, but there seems no doubt the decision was a colossal error of judgment. Many of those who have studied the great battle and the events leading up to it (including myself) are convinced that the apparently inexplicable error of judgment by the Japanese admiral was the direct result of his failure to get enough sleep during the preceding tense days and nights.

Causes of Sleeplessness

From private to general, loss of sleep becomes cumulative, and no man can stand against its effects. Because sleep is such a vital need, here is a summary of useful information about it.

Worry is the greatest enemy of sleep—after you are in bed. But the single biggest reason for not enough sleep is simplicity itself: those who need it do not spend enough time in bed to get it—by their own choice.

People stay up late for various reasons—even just to have a little time of peace and quiet—and, unaware, pay the hidden cost of unnecessary sleep loss. It is ironic, particularly for able, conscientious staff officers, that some men stay awake because they are not satisfied with what they have done during the day. With enough sleep they would have had more efficient and effective days. So it is the old "vicious circle" pattern in action.

Others stay awake because of worries and anxieties, about which one doctor said: "First take care of your sleep. Then most of your worries will take care of themselves."

A curious contradiction sometimes leads hard-working staff officers on, like a seductive Lorelei: experiments at Yale showed there was a *temporary* improvement in speed and accuracy *after* initial sleep loss! You feel hopped up and exhilarated by a kind of tension spur. There are two hidden jokers: the same results required nearly three times the expenditure of energy; and after several nights the trend is reversed, and there is a big letdown in work output.

How Much Do You Need?

To find the amount of sleep you need, note how many hours elapse from the time you go to bed until you wake, refreshed, without an alarm clock. (Average need for most people is generally accepted as eight hours.)

Also remember that the amount needed will vary not only with individuals, but with what they do. The more physically tired you get, the more sleep you need.

Sleeping pills are dangerous—and are especially undesirable for soldiers who, in an emergency, could be awakened while still in a drugged condition. Besides, regular use of such pills can make you more irritable and difficult to work with.

Lack of sleep lowers the attention span in tasks that require constant alertness, such as on sentry duty or scanning a radarscope.

After you have reached the threshold of sleep exhaustion, your determination to stay awake is not in itself enough to keep you awake.

You can make up lost sleep. While it does not have to be hour for hour, neither can a large loss of sleep be made up in one night or several nights.

If you can't go to sleep it is important to know that merely lying in bed is almost as helpful as sleep, especially so because you are getting more sleep than you think.

When anxiety, exhaustion, and compulsion are added to pure sleep loss, it follows logically that a person will break down more quickly under strain—and that many cases of so-called battle fatigue are little more than victims of cumulative loss of sleep.

In general, loss of sleep causes these direct harmful results: it dulls the memory, sometimes spectacularly so; it can seriously affect judgment; it produces added tension and irritation; it blurs perception and mental acuteness; it reduces accuracy and speed of performance; it impairs physical and mental health.

Finally, it creeps up silently. Look out for it!

Here are some pertinent summary comments:

- Whether or not you get enough sleep is not accident, but the result of effort on your part and the determination to have it. However, it does not generate the same inborn desire like the need for food and water. Therein lies its danger!
- Having looked at lessons of the past resulting from loss of sleep in wars with conventional weapons, it is important to realize that danger from sleep deprivation will be even greater in a nuclear war. Few will think of sleep then.
- In such a war time will be foreshortened, and pressures increased beyond all past experience, yet the mental and physical need for sleep will remain the same. Further, not only should the facts of life about sleep be

included in our training schedules, but they should be integrated into our civil defense program as an essential element to ensure sound decisions by leaders at all levels, and as a measure to avert panic by people under strain everywhere.

- We now come to this final conclusion: Knowledge about the vital importance of sleeping habits is needed in military and civilian life, as a duty, as a command responsibility, and as a matter of stern self-discipline.

55

Sense of Duty: Cornerstone of Military Careers

TO JUSTIFY THE fundamental importance of duty to a soldier seems a bit like trying to prove that love is an important element of marriage. But I'll try. By way of examining duty in more depth, we'll look at what some thinkers and sages have said.

Cicero: "There is not a moment without a sense of duty."

That is a truism for soldiers today, whose duty is not merely to attend to assigned responsibilities but also to determine things to do without waiting for orders. If there is an hour in your duty-day with no task to do, you have failed in your duty to be a self-starter.

John Wolfgang von Goethe: "Duty is carrying on promptly and faithfully the affairs now before you."

This goes a step farther and requires that tasks be done "promptly and faithfully"—which is what we call efficiently. A passive, passable job does not meet the full requirements of duty.

One day in 1929 my company in the 31st Infantry in Manila was at bayonet practice under my supervision. I stood by in my nice tailor-made starched khaki uniform while the sergeant instructor illustrated "parry and long thrust"—making them two separate motions.

When my oral instructions failed to get across the idea that the parry should lead directly into the thrust without pause, I yanked off my tie, unbuttoned my collar and proceeded to demonstrate. At this point my gentlemanly old regimental commander (in his sixties) arrived on horseback, accompanied by his adjutant.

The adjutant rode over to me.

"Lieutenant Newman," he said, "the regimental commander directs you fasten your collar and put on your tie."

This illustrates a sometimes puzzling point: people often vary in their concept of what the primary demands of duty are.

Frederick William Faber: "Exactness in little things is a wonderful source of cheerfulness."

Well-shined shoes, clean weapons, swept floors — all the little chores of military life — these things well done lead to a happy outfit. Without this group sense of duty the fine spirit of well-being among trained soldiers is lost.

When we fired the Browning automatic rifle for record in Company F, 19th Infantry (1940), we had only one stoppage — a misfired round. Sergeant Bosco, our senior duty sergeant, meticulously checked three minor things: that all gas-cylinder tubes (the size of the end of your finger) were clean and free from powder fouling; use of the chamber brush after each firing; tested magazines during preliminary firing, and taped on them the number of the guns in which they "worked."

We had a cheerful and pleasant range season, but the company next to us — who had no Sergeant Bosco to check minor things — was not happy, because they had to deal with the frustrating experience of many stoppages. In battle, neglect of such minor things could be the difference between life and death.

Charles Kingsley: "Every duty that is bidden to wait comes back with seven fresh duties at its back."

A case in point is neglect of maintenance in motor vehicles — as when the duty to check the oil is bidden to wait, the resulting damage means more work. This is true in countless ways; where one little spot of rust forms today, if bidden to wait, there will be others tomorrow.

Samuel E. Brydges: "Duty by habit is to pleasure tuned."

Nothing could be more true. The more often you meet your responsibilities with a high sense of duty, the more you know about them and the less effort to get them done. The higher the standards you maintain in your duties, the more they become a professional pleasure to carry out.

William Shakespeare (As You Like It): "Old man . . . thou art not the fashion of these times, where none will sweat but for promotion."

To do duty only in the hope of reward takes away the pride of accomplishment. Maybe I am old, out of fashion with the times, but it does seem that "what's in it for me?" and "let Joe do it" have more followers than in my day. Conscientious objectors, draft-card burners, inordinate pay raises proposed for recruits as a substitute for the draft — and a growing list of other things — are symptoms of a cancerous wasting away of our national sense of duty. When the length of haircuts looms larger than a sense of duty, when "let me do my thing" takes precedence over discipline, this old man is indeed out of fashion with the times.

From these generalized observations we now come to war and fighting — the ultimate test of a soldier's sense of duty.

Lord Horatio Nelson of Trafalgar: "England expects every man to do his duty."

The great admiral, in one of the most decisive battles of history, sent that message by flag signal to his fleet. It is one of the most magnificently clear and meaningful statements ever issued by a commander. He did not doubt every officer and sailor would understand his message: that each man would do his job, come shot, shell, and havoc.

John H. Moore: "Perish discretion when it interferes with duty."

Another wonderfully simple statement; another way of saying that, come hell and high water, duty comes first.

John Foster: "It is wonderful what strength and boldness of purpose and energy will come from feeling that we are in the way of duty."

When faced with danger and the need for boldness in battle, just ask yourself, "Is this my duty?" If the answer is yes, then there comes with it new strength, for to falter then would be from more than lack of courage; it would be failure to meet the call of duty. The lead scout, when called on to walk down the road as a living target, is doing his duty; and that knowledge gives him the will to look death in the face with each step.

John Hay: "He weren't no saint — but at jedgment/I'd run my chance with Jim/'Longside of some pious gentlemen/That wouldn't shook hands with him./He seen his duty, a dead-sure thing — /And went for it thar and then;/And Christ ain't a-going to be too hard/ On a man that died for his men."

Many a soldier has died for his friends and buddies: "seen his duty, a dead-sure thing — and went for it thar and then." Like

"Rodger Young, fought and died for the men he marched among."
Pvt. Rodger Young, in the 148th Infantry on New Georgia Island
during World War II in the Pacific, found himself in a battle position to save others in his platoon. Since he was the only one who
could see the machine gun that pinned his platoon down, he called to
them that he would cover their retirement. He was twice wounded
before he was finally killed in answering his call to duty as he saw it.

Finally, we come to the quotation at the end of Robert S. Allen's
fine article "Patton's Secret" (ARMY, June 1971): "Death is as light
as a feather." Jan Valtin gives it this way in his book, *Children of
Yesterday:* "Duty is weightier than a mountain, while death is
lighter than a feather" (from a Japanese Imperial Rescript).

There will always be times when death is preferable to failure of
duty in battle. As I look back now, though I did not think of it that
way then, it was a sense of duty — more than any other one thing —
that sustained me in combat.

Three comments seem pertinent:

- A soldier can have no greater professional asset than a
  high sense of duty. This applies with equal force to
  menial administrative tasks as well as to major military responsibilities.
- While our military schools should emphasize this, and
  superiors should inculcate it in their subordinates, the
  basic responsibility for a keen sense of duty lies within
  the person himself.
- It is hard to maintain a high sense of duty in peacetime
  when there is no immediate emergency. But a sense of
  duty, nurtured and cherished during years of peace, is
  the cornerstone of military careers, and will provide the
  inner strength to meet the searing test of combat.

56
Power of Words

FACETS OF LEADERSHIP and techniques of command often require written words for a commander to reach out to and influence his men during crises.

In late 1943 and early 1944, I was chief of staff of the 24th Infantry Division in the wilds of Australia, where we trained for an undisclosed operation in New Guinea. One day an officer courier arrived in my office tent from headquarters, Southwest Pacific Theater, and handed me a paper parcel the size of a large book with a covering letter of instructions.

I was required to sign for the parcel, and read the letter in the presence of the courier. The letter directed me to:

Inform the division commander of the contents of the package, and no one else.

Ensure that one copy of the papers in the parcel be posted on the bulletin board of every company, battery and detachment of our division at 11:00 A.M. on a specified date — and that no one, except myself and the division commander, see or know of what was in the parcel until he read it on the bulletin board.

The same notice would be published at the same time in all other units throughout the theater. Unfortunately, I have been unable to find a copy in my files, but I have an indelible memory of its nature, purpose, and the results. In substance — double-spaced and centrally located on a single mimeographed page — it read like this:

Headquarters, Southwest Pacific Theater

Soldiers of the Southwest Pacific:

Through your superb fighting qualities, we have won impressive victories over our enemies.

As military men I know you will understand it is imperative we exploit our successes by driving on in relentless attack before the enemy can regroup. Therefore, in order to have enough men to follow up our hard won successes, and thus avoid unnecessary casualties and suffering later, I have issued orders that the Rotation Policy be discontinued until further notice.

> (signed) Douglas MacArthur
> General, United States Army
> Commander in Chief

Our division had been stationed in Hawaii at the time of the Pearl Harbor attack in 1941, and we had thousands of men who, after years overseas, were due for rotation home under the established point system of that policy. Thus this was a devastating blow to them and could be expected to cause widespread unrest.

But that did not happen. The notice went up on every bulletin board at 11:00 A.M. on the date specified. As a result, when men formed up for chow at noon everybody knew it, also who made the decision and why. The basic reaction was simply disappointment, because:

The order was *personally signed* by General MacArthur, and its wording made clear it was a personal message — from him, as soldier to soldier, to each one of them.

Also, they realized he knew what such a reversal of policy meant to them, and showed his confidence in them as military men that they would understand this was the proper course to follow, hard as it might be.

No distorted rumors preceded the appearance of his order; thus bitter discussion and resentment toward unidentified higher authority were avoided. No one had ever before seen General MacArthur's personal signature, much less on an order that, in effect, bypassed every echelon of command to go from him to individual men in ranks, explaining directly to them why the decision was made, and that he had made it.

Unstated, but implicit in the wording and method of distribution — including that personal signature — was respect for his "Soldiers of the Southwest Pacific," and his understanding of the terrible disappointment this decision would be for thousands of them. Equally important was the fact there was no long harangue, merely his confidence that they would understand his explanation and know he had made the hard decision only after consideration of what it meant to them.

This was leadership by a military genius, revealing the human touch of General MacArthur that is so little known. As a result there was no loss of morale, only soldierly acceptance of a fact of war. And the brilliantly conceived "bypassing" Hollandia amphibious operation followed; this, literally, broke the back of Japanese strength in New Guinea and saved uncounted American lives, as he had predicted.

Another great battle leader of World War II, on the other side of the world, faced a violently different situation. During the Battle of the Bulge in France, December 1944, the Third Army was driving its vital counterattack into the side of the bulge. The weather was bitterly cold, and heavy rains robbed our soldiers of air support in addition to making roads a muddy quagmire of an obstacle to the speed necessary for their counterattack to succeed.

In this critical situation, Lt. Gen. George S. Patton, Jr., had the same leadership instinct to reach out to his men, as had General MacArthur. His method was radically and imaginatively different, yet the same in principle. This has been publicized, but is not covered in detail in the fine definitive biography by Ladislas Farago, *Patton: Ordeal and Triumph*. While the famous "Prayer" is given, both the method of publication and the Christmas greeting are omitted. So these seem worth detailing here.

General Patton directed his engineer to print thousands of cards, and distribute one to each man in Third Army. On one side of each card was this greeting:

HEADQUARTERS
Third United States Army

To each officer and soldier in the Third United States Army I wish a Merry Christmas. I have full confidence in your courage, devotion to duty, and skill in battle. We

march in our might to complete victory. May God's bless-
ing rest upon each of you on this Christmas Day.

G. S. Patton, Jr.
Lieutenant General
Commanding, Third United States Army

On the other side of the card was the following prayer, which he
had instructed his chaplain to write:

Prayer

Almighty and most merciful Father we humbly beseech
Thee, of Thy great goodness, to restrain these immoder-
ate rains with which we have to contend. Grant us fair
weather for battle. Graciously hearken to us as soldiers
who call upon Thee that armed with Thy power, we may
advance from victory to victory, crush the oppression
and wickedness of our enemies, and establish Thy justice
among men and nations. AMEN

Though the physical means used by Generals MacArthur and
Patton were vastly different, yet each message fitted the special
crises to get across the same message: "I am thinking of you, and
know how tough this situation is for each of you. But I have confidence in you, as soldiers, to meet this great challenge we face together."

It must be emphasized, however, that compelling words from a
commander to his men apply at all levels — from corporals to generals. Of all the messages from a commander known to me, none sur-
passes this one by an Australian machine-gun section leader during
the German Army's offensive in March 1918:

Special Orders To No. 1 Section 13/3/18

1. This position will be held, and the section will remain
   here until relieved.
2. The enemy cannot be allowed to interfere with this
   programme.
3. If this section cannot remain here alive, it will remain
   here dead, but in any case it will remain here.

4. Should any man, through shell shock or other cause, attempt to surrender, he will remain here dead.
5. Should all guns be blown out, the section will use Mills grenades, and other novelties.
6. Finally, the position, as stated, will be held.

> F. F. Bethune, Lt.
> O/C No. 1 Section

Comments are:

- The above order is on record in the *Official History Of Australia in the War of 1914-18*. Fortunately, the section did not have to fight to the last man, and Lieutenant Bethune himself survived the war. But that in no way dims the battle leadership and iron determination revealed in his order—a wonderful illustration of a commander reaching out to his men with words.
- Messages from a leader to meet critical situations — in peace and war — should be limited to as few as possible, be short and to the point, and fit the situation.
- One I like to remember is the story of how the American eight-oared shell won an Olympic championship in 1928, with gold medals for each member of the crew. After a desperate stretch race, in the final yards they found a last surge of strength they did not know they had when the lightweight coxswain screamed through his megaphone, "Are you big bloody bastards going to quit right here in the middle of the water?"

57

A Brotherhood that Binds the Brave

SEVERAL YEARS AFTER World War II, the 24th Infantry Division held its annual reunion in Baltimore. This was sponsored by our division association, organized primarily by veterans in civilian life. I attended as former G-2 (Intelligence), also as former chief of staff, and as a regimental commander — with memories of fine soldiers of all ranks.

The first familiar face in the hotel lobby was that of Tom, our G-1 (Personnel), who had returned to his law practice. He held a special place in my memory, for Tom made compassionate allowances for my paperwork quirks as chief of staff. Like the time in New Guinea jungles, after fighting was over at Hollandia, when our division was issued two cans of beer per man.

It had been months since we had anything to drink except chlorinated water, and coffee at mealtimes. Now, thousands of soldiers were relaxed and happy in a way that defies description: with two cans of warm beer, and no way to chill it. My two cans were in a sock, tethered in the running water of a nearby creek, when Tom walked into my tent, papers in one hand, can of beer in the other.

"Chief," he said, placing the beer on my folding field table, "as G-1, I have declared an extra dividend for you. If you have not earned it before, you will now," and he dropped a handful of paper trouble on the table. That's the only time a staff officer ever handed me an unpalatable paper, along with a beer chaser to make it go down easier. You don't forget such empathy.

It's a long jump from wartime New Guinea to hotel lobby, especially when you change a jungle suit for the sharp-looking pinstripe gray Tom was wearing. But as we shook hands it all seemed only yesterday.

"Come on, Colonel," he said with smiling urgency, "you can register later. We heard you were coming, and some of the boys are waiting in the bar to buy you a drink."

When ten of us were seated around a wide coffee table, each armed with a glass, I noticed they looked expectantly toward Tom. He had been a quiet leader on our staff, the intangible value under stress of his strong character and never-failing good humor exerting a relaxing and steadying influence. Those around the table were from division headquarters, including a signal officer, the commanding general's former aide, and other staff officers of assorted ranks from various staff sections — all back in civilian life except the aide.

"Colonel," Tom said, "there's a story you ought to hear," and his eyes glinted through his rimless glasses with their familiar laughing light.

After the war (Tom began), somebody asked one of your former staff officers what he planned to do.

"Get a job under a redheaded man," he replied.

When asked why, your former staff officer said, "So that the first time he gives me any guff I can tell him into what shape to compress his job and where to store it."

All eyes glanced at my rooftop, which a sportswriter once described as "a particularly violent crop of red hair."

Tom continued: Then your former staff officer was told, "OK, that sounds logical, so what will you do next."

"Get a job under another redheaded man, so that when he hands me any stuff I can tell him, too, in detail, what to do with his job." He then added, "I'll keep that up until I'm even — then get a job to keep, under a man not redheaded."

There was a belly laugh around the table, and they looked at a former staff officer named Walter, seated opposite me. I recalled that he had more than normal difficulty with my quirks as chief of staff, and now sat silently smoking his pipe. He met my eyes with a level, bland look, and slowly shifted his pipe from one side of his mouth to the other — which said more eloquently than words that he still felt that way.

Some years and several reunions later I arrived to register for one in Chicago. Among the first familiar faces was the pipe-smoking former staff officer.

"I'm glad to see you, Walter," I said.

As we shook hands he removed the black briar from his mouth. There was a reflective look in his eyes — perhaps even a little puzzled wonder — when, with the quiet dignity of the college professor he is, Walter said, "Well, General, I never thought the day would come — but I'm glad to see you, too!"

The renewal of wartime acquaintances through the 24th Infantry Division reunions — and forming new friendships — has been and continues to be one of the most rewarding experiences of my life. Two years ago a car drove into the front yard of our retirement home, and three of my best friends got out: Ed, CG, and Bill — men I would never have really known had we not cemented wartime bonds at reunions. One had been a soldier in my company when I was a captain shortly before World War II, another was a warrant officer in the judge advocate section when I was division chief of staff, the third a decorated sergeant in my regiment on Leyte — all now successful in business.

We sat in my Florida room, drinks in hand, looking out over the water, and kicked the gong around from Hawaii to Australia, through New Guinea, and all over the Philippines. Then we went down to the local inn for a barbecued shrimp lunch and to continue "remember whens."

Don't get the idea, however, that our reunions are stag assemblies, laid on a bottle foundation. Far from it: they are family affairs. Many wives and other relatives attend, including quite a few youngsters. Several wives have told me they look forward to yearly reunions, because it helps them understand the part wartime service played in their husbands' lives and they can share his special friendships.

The highlight of our reunions is the Saturday night banquet, a sit-down and guest-speaker dinner affair. We begin with memorial services for our honored dead, the honor roll of names placed front and center on a table flanked by candles. A military color guard brings in our national flag, which lends to the ceremony an indescribable grandeur and reason for being. Then our chaplain reads the tribute to our fallen comrades, while we stand, silent heads bowed — each with his own burning memories of names on that honor roll.

For me, there is always a kaleidoscopic series of memory pictures: the sprawled, motionless figure of 1st Lt. Howell Barrow, gallant commander of Company I, 34th Infantry, where he fell leading the assault at Red Beach on Leyte; that silent line of still forms on the ground at Pawing the next morning; and many others.

The memorial tribute emphasizes comradeship of men in uniform who shared dedication, hardships and stark dangers of war, "a special friendship, like no other in the world." Those who have not renewed and expanded such friendships, by attending wartime unit reunions, have deprived themselves of one of the most worthwhile experiences soldiers can share—from privates to four-star generals; Regular Army, National Guard or Army Reserve; active duty or retired; and veteran civilians.

That "special friendship" was something I witnessed for years before facing battle myself. When veteran soldiers met—regardless of rank or status—they shared something that left me an outsider. Their eyes would brighten—yet sometimes look far away in sadness, too—while names, dates, places and battle situations so real to them left me groping to understand. Poets and writers have tried to capture the idea in words, like the phrase, "the Brotherhood that binds the brave of all the earth."

For me, however, it was best said at Plattsburg Barracks in 1938 when I commanded a company there. On this afternoon a small major came to see my first sergeant. They had been in the same company in World War I—the major a lieutenant, my first sergeant a soldier—and wore the same battle ribbons and decorations, including the Silver Star and Purple Heart.

After two hours in the orderly room with our first sergeant the small major came back into my office.

"Please forgive me, Captain," he said, "for taking so much of your first sergeant's time. But he and I fought, bled, and got scared together!"

58

A Reunion:
Red Beach Plus 30

ON 14 OCTOBER 1974, I boarded a plane in Tampa for Chicago-Anchorage-Tokyo-Manila, thence to Tacloban on Leyte in the central Philippine Islands. Mission: to participate in ceremonies on 20 October at the new Philippine National Memorial of World War II near Palo on Leyte. The occasion: the thirtieth anniversary of D day on Red Beach when Gen. Douglas MacArthur landed in my regimental sector of our 24th Infantry Division area to keep his famous "I shall return" promise to liberate the Philippines.

But two hours out of Anchorage, Alaska—where our plane would refuel—the fates that govern what happens to young soldiers in war and old soldiers on the way to reunions, caught up with me. Suddenly, there was trouble in breathing, my face beaded with sweat, and the nice, efficient stewardess quickly produced an oxygen tank and mask.

This was an old enemy, a type of ticker trouble that had been controlled by medication. But here it called for a decision; to go on, or disembark at Anchorage and return home. That is why, after an overnight rest in Anchorage, I write this on the plane headed home —with the hope my baggage will find its way back from Tokyo.

My thoughts are with friends now en route to join me at the bar in the Manila Hotel. But I will not be there to accompany them to Tacloban on Leyte, or go with them to Palo, Jaro and elsewhere on memory's trail of where, and what happened there thirty years ago. So I sit here and remember.

From the violence of war it is the people that come back in techni-

302

color pictures. Some succeeded magnificently, like the gallant commander of Company I, 1st Lt. Howell E. Barrow, who fell on Red Beach as he led his company in the assault. A few failed and the broken bodies of so many who did not fail were, often, names I never knew. But among them all one name comes back again and again, and unforgettable is the word for him.

Soon after I assumed command of the 34th Infantry in New Guinea, the adjutant came in with a problem. We were preparing for the amphibious assault on Leyte, so men in the guardhouse were returned to us. The adjutant's problem was that the company commander of Pvt. Harold Moon did not want him back.

"All right," I said. "At the company commanders' meeting after lunch see if another company wants him. If not, his own company must keep him."

Later I learned that the commander of Company G had said, "I'll take him. He sounds like a man looking for trouble and where we are going there will be all the trouble he can handle."

That first night on Red Beach at Leyte the Japanese counterattacked our beachhead on the far side of the swamp, at Pawing. So at first light I got hold of an Alligator — that wonderful hybrid of an amphibious tank and deep-bed truck, with a 50-caliber machine gun mounted topside. This was ideal transportation to get across the swamp and see what the situation was there after all that shooting in the night.

But first I arranged for an air strike by Navy planes. Then, standing deep in the Alligator as we crossed the swamp, I witnessed planes diving on visually located remnants of the Japanese attackers — bombing, rocketing and strafing with .50-caliber guns.

On our left flank, Japanese bodies literally carpeted the roadway and along the shoulders of a raised road in front of the position held by Company G. The attacking Japanese had approached uncautiously down the road before splitting into attack formations, and our alert battalion commander correctly decided the nebulous moving mass in the darkness could only be enemy.

So machine guns mowed them down. But the fanatical enemy continued to attack in the darkness and all but overran Company G before daylight, although at terrible cost to themselves.

The air attack after daylight put the finishing touches on the Japanese, for the remaining enemy were hidden in high grass, invisible to ground observation but sitting ducks from above.

As this great jetliner plows through the air over Canada, taking me home, that scene flashes and reflashes through my mind. And the name of Pvt. Harold Moon, that unforgettable soldier, is remembered with respect, awe, and admiration.

When I arrived in Pawing that day and saw the tremendous havoc our fire had visited on the attacking enemy, I did not think of Private Moon. The brief jubilation among officers and men over the successful air strike was soon replaced by a somber quiet. The reason was plain to see: about twenty-five of our own dead were lined up neatly where all could see them.

This was no time, however, for us to stand and grieve for lost buddies whose names I did not know but whom others knew so well. It was a time for action: to attack and gain the high ground to our front before enemy survivors could organize that ground for defense. We would exploit the opportunity brave men had paid with their lives to give us — and save other lives.

So I turned to the battalion executive officer, indicated the silent row on the ground, and said, "Get them out of here, to the rear, immediately."

"Colonel," he replied, "we have no transportation."

"Use the Alligator I came in; I am not going back."

"Sir," he replied, looking at the line of dead but thinking only of floor space in the Alligator, "the Alligator is not enough."

"They are dead, aren't they?" I said. "Take them back. *Now!*" And I turned toward the battalion commander to ensure an attack for the high ground was launched at once.

At that moment thirty years ago I did not recognize Pvt. Harold Moon among the dead (for I had never seen him), or know of his tremendous battle performance that would bring him our nation's highest accolade, the Congressional Medal of Honor.

But now I know and remember.

Six months after that day on Leyte, following recuperation from a taste of Japanese steel myself, I rejoined our division in the Southern Philippines. There I read the magnificent citation for the posthumous award of the Medal of Honor to Private Moon. Other details are in our unofficial history, *Children of Yesterday.*

Nearly two hundred dead Japanese were within one hundred yards of Pvt. Harold Moon's foxhole. In a signed affidavit S.Sgt. Verdun C. Myers said, "By 0545 Private Moon was running out of ammunition. His position had been the focal point of the enemy attack for over four hours and the Japanese had worked men around on all sides of him.

"At dawn an entire platoon of the enemy rushed the position in a desperate bayonet assault. Private Moon remained sitting down, steadied his tommy gun between his knees — and calling to the Japanese to come and get him — emptied the entire magazine into them, killing eighteen before they overwhelmed and killed him."

As other men in nearby positions were killed or wounded (the record shows) Private Moon, although wounded and alone (because the other two men in his three-man position had been killed), not only held fast but inspired all within hearing as he carried on a running battle of oral insults with the enemy across the raised road, especially with an English-speaking officer whom he eventually killed. For more details of his incredible battle actions you will have to read the record.

As my plane drones on its way, there is a changing montage of memories. As always, Pvt. Harold Moon is there. And always, too, there is the unanswerable question: Where was he in the Alligator — in the bottom layer? In the top layer, when he and others with him should have gone back in state, with a guard of honor and a band of clashing cymbals and proud trumpets?

While Pvt. Harold Moon and those with him would understand and want it that way under the circumstances, still I cannot forget — and never want to forget.

Some comments are:

- Every combat veteran has memories of the realities of battle, and there is no limit to the variations. This is one of the things that forges a special bond that others who "were not there" can never comprehend.
- In peace and in war, in every rank at all levels, the one great principle that overrides all others is: Do what you think is right, no matter what — and you will seldom be wrong. The problem then is reduced to what you decide is right, not what you want to do.
- An officer is not worthy of the rank he holds unless he honors and respects his subordinates, especially sol-

diers in ranks. Without them he is an empty, futile figurehead — and nowhere is this more true than in command in battle.

- No one can understand, except another combat soldier, the depth of my disappointment in turning back from my pilgrimage, for that is what it was. Now I will never stand on the same ground again to pay my respect and homage to Pvt. Harold Moon, Lt. Howell Barrow and others who made the success of our regiment possible.

But, like all who have exercised authority in battle — from corporals to generals — I'll continue to pay them homage in my heart until I hear that Last Bugle Call.

Epilogue

On returning from Iceland (in May 1952) my next assignment was command of the 505th Airborne Infantry, 82d Airborne Division at Fort Bragg, North Carolina. This was my third regimental command, a professional privilege and honor whose memories I cherish.

In early July a telegram from the Pentagon stated that the President of the United States had submitted my name to the Senate for confirmation in the rank of brigadier general. Some days later a phone call directed me to report to the division commander.

On my arrival in his office I found my wife Dorothy already there, with my friend and former classmate at West Point, Maj. Gen. Charles D. W. Canham. Each of them pinned a star on opposite sides of my collar—custom-made sterling silver stars that Chuck Canham himself had worn as a brigadier general.

I then walked down the hall to my new office as Assistant Division Commander, 82d Airborne Division. Life in uniform would never be quite the same again. My next collection of memories, and my thoughts in the premises, is being assembled under the title What Are Generals Made Of?

PHOTO SECTION

My "zombie" picture as 2nd lieutenant, 31st Infantry in Manila, P.I., 1929–30. (Chap. 7)

Author as a cadet at West Point. (Chap. 2)

In Hawaiian Division Military Police Company, 1934–35.

"Best Damned Company in the Army"

Your first command (like your first kiss) can never be duplicated, and so it was for me as company commander, Company G, 26th Infantry at Plattsburg Barracks, New York (1936–39). (Chaps. 12, 24)

It was the good fortune of a military lifetime to serve with the sergeants pictured above, from whom I learned lessons beyond value. Seated, left to right: Sgts. Andrew Zak and John Smith, 1st Sgt. James S. "Big Jim" Redding, Sgts. William Dickerson and Jesse Stinson; standing, left to right: Sgts. Martin Osatzow, Harvey Delaney, Andre Jessie, Stanley Gancaz.

The six World War I veterans averaged 20 years' service and wore 3 Distinguished Service Crosses, 4 Silver Stars, 4 Purple Hearts, 1 Croix de Guerre with Palm, and 30 battle stars.

The lucky company commander of Company G, 26th Infantry, 1st Infantry Division, 1936–39. (Chaps. 12, 14)

The author as chief of staff, 24th Infantry Division, in his jungle office on Goodenough Island (New Guinea), planning for the Hollandia invasion (1944) of central New Guinea. (Chap. 46)

Maj. Gen. Aubrey S. Newman (Ret.).

Pets and soldiers the world over have an affinity for each other. (Chap. 6) An anonymous soldier and friend on a bleak foreign station.

One view of Supply Sgt. Andre Jessie's supply room. (Chap. 10)

On right, *Lt. Kennard S. Vandergrift (nee T. Sgt. Promoted after Pearl Harbor) stands in front of the office we shared before the war; another of those great Old Army NCOs, so many of whom were commissioned during World War II.*

Facing page: On right, *that wonderful "Old Soldier," 1st Sgt. Doc Dougherty, Company M, 27th Infantry, Hawaiian Division, Schofield Barracks, Hawaii.* (Chaps. 35, 37)

At farewell review for regimental commander of the 19th Infantry, Schofield Barracks, Hawaii (1941), Col. Charles H. Bonesteel with his staff. The new S-2, and neophyte staff officer, stands on the left (junior) end of the staff line. (Chaps. 19, 22)

Airborne. "The law of gravity does not salute." I came late to the paratroopers (1949), in the 11th Airborne Division as division chief of staff; then regimental commander, 511th Airborne Infantry. (Chaps. 35, 38, 39)

October 16, 1944, aboard U.S.S. Fayette *at sea. Presentation of American and Philippine flags to men who are to take them ashore with assault troops. American flag to Silas Thomas (34th Infantry); Philippine flag to Ponncinso Dacones, P.I. Affairs, U.S. Army.*

Gen. Douglas MacArthur talks to President Sergio Osmena of the Philippines near the water's edge on Red Beach near Palo, Leyte (October 20, 1944) as he waits for equipment to be set up for his "I have returned" broadcast to the Philippine people. It was here I reported to him earlier that day—astonished that a high commander of his rank would follow the assault so closely, as the beach was still under sporadic fire. (Chap. 57)

319

Maj. Gen. Frederick A. Irving, a decorated veteran of World War I, leads the 24th Infantry Division in World War II from Hawaii to Australia, through New Guinea, and into the Philippines — clearing the way for General MacArthur's famous "return" at Red Beach on Leyte. (Chaps. 46, 57)

Those who have "fought, bled, and got scared together" share "a special friendship like no other" that "lasts beyond the grave." Here is a small group in a gathering years after the Leyte landing; friends with memories of their battle days in many varied assignments, but all returned to civilian life after the war. (Chap. 57) Seated, left to right: Sanderson, Ciangi, Williams, Muldoon, Wilson; standing, left to right: Stevenson, Harris, Ross, Kawa, Henry, O'Donnell.

"Be ready to do what you ask others to do" was exemplified by Col. (later Maj. Gen.) William J. Verbeck, whose decorations included 3 Silver Stars for gallantry, 2 Bronze Stars (v) for heroism, and 3 Purple Hearts for battle wounds. (Chap. 51)

Lt. Col. (later Lt. Gen.) Clarence R. Heubner, one of our truly great combat leaders. He rose from the ranks to a heavily decorated regimental commander in World War I, then commanded the 1st Infantry Division with distinction in World War II, and retired as a three-star Army commander. (Chap. 52)

Maj. Gen. Joseph P. Cleland, another truly great leader and commander, was promoted to brigadier general on the battlefield in World War II and commanded with exceptional ability a division in Korea. Wide Airborne service, retiring as commanding general, XVIII Airborne Corps. (Chap. 52)

Squeaky, the mountain lion mascot of the 511th Airborne Infantry at Fort Campbell (1950), became one of my problems as commander when he grew from a cub to what you see here. (Chap. 6)